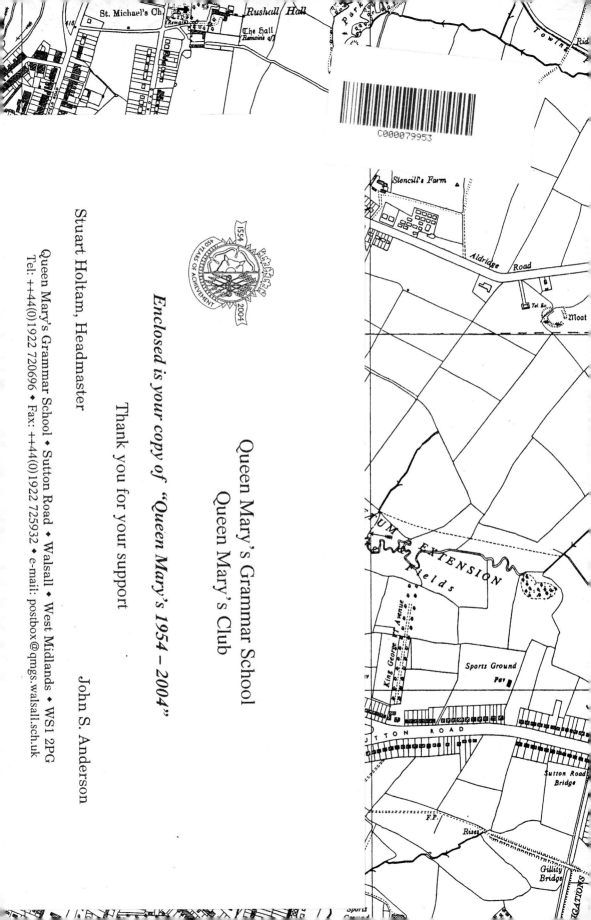

C000079953

Queen Mary's Grammar School
Queen Mary's Club

Enclosed is your copy of "Queen Mary's 1954 – 2004"

Thank you for your support

Stuart Holtam, Headmaster

John S. Anderson

Queen Mary's Grammar School ◆ Sutton Road ◆ Walsall ◆ West Midlands ◆ WS1 2PG
Tel: ++44(0)1922 720696 ◆ Fax: ++44(0)1922 725932 ◆ e-mail: postbox@qmgs.walsall.sch.uk

1554 · 450 YEARS OF ACHIEVEMENT · 2004

Queen Mary's
1954–2004

Queen Mary's
1954–2004

THE RECENT HISTORY OF THE FREE
GRAMMAR SCHOOL OF WALSALL

by
John S Anderson MBE MA
former Second Master

Design
David Cockayne

Queen Mary's Club
WALSALL

First published in 2004 by
Queen Mary's Club
Sutton Road
Walsall
WS1 2PG

© John S Anderson 2004

John S Anderson has asserted his right under the
Copyright, Designs and Patents Act 1988
to be identified as the author of this work

ISBN 0-9547426-0-5

All rights reserved.
No part of this publication may be reproduced
or transmitted in any form or by any means,
electronic or mechanical, including photocopy,
recording or any other information storage
and retrieval system, without prior permission
in writing from the publisher.

Printed by the Welshpool Printing Group
Severn Farm Enterprise Park
Welshpool, Powys

CONTENTS

MEMORIES AND REFLECTIONS

APPENDICES

ACKNOWLEGEMENTS

I wish to record my thanks to contributors. Past governors helped enormously, especially David Jeffries. I had great help in the early stages from Messrs Bill Cheesewright, Bob Christie, and Bill Stephens. Sadly, several contributors have died: Sam Darby, Godfrey Caddick, Phil Bull and Phil Evans. I used notes on Farchynys by the late Ken Yates. I have Phillip Holmes to thank for his considerable contribution to Chapter 3, "The Fifties". I am grateful also to Andrew Parrott, Stanley Hewitt, Ian Bednall, Roger Pinson, Geoffrey Paxton, Beverley Wragg, Richard Cooper, Ian Davison, Brian Archer, Graham Chesterman, Tony Wiggin, Roger Metcalf, David Pennington, Philip Sturrock, Keith Howard, Janet Martin, Mark Purcell, Mike Redfern, Melvin Woodhouse, David Etherington, Ian Cooksey, Jude Daniel, and Sheba Sergeant and her sisters. Adam Draper, David Vodden, Sallie Magnante, Lawrence Woodhouse, Tim Swain, Steve Law, Graham Stokes, Seamus Moran have all provided valuable artistic and other assistance. Stephen Gregory, John Taylor, David Brown, Trevor Homer and many other Old Boys, staff and pupils of the school have given their valuable help.

Above all my thanks to David Cockayne who has taken responsibility for the design and illustration of this book and with whom I have worked for the past year. His devotion to the book has been outstanding.

Gill Columbine and the office staff have given their assistance, as has Chris Ward in the school library and archives. Advice from Marina Oliver, author of the recent history of Queen Mary's High School, has been very useful to an inexperienced author.

My very grateful thanks also to my wife Margaret Anderson (née Hayden) who has given her total encouragement and support, together with advice throughout based to such a degree on her own understanding of the school throughout the last thirty years.

May I thank the Headmaster, Stuart Holtam, for his encouragement throughout, and the Queen Mary's Club for their support and backing for this project.

FOREWORD BY THE HEADMASTER

I am very pleased John Anderson agreed to my suggestion that, following his retirement as Second Master, and in anticipation of the celebration of the 450th Anniversary of the foundation of the School, he should publish an account of the last fifty years of the School's history.

He worked at the School for most of this time and has an intimate knowledge and understanding of events and the people involved in them. His book has been carefully researched and is a mixture of anecdote, analysis and comment that will delight his readers, especially those who were also members of the school community during this period. It is a fitting continuation of David Fink's account of the School's first 400 years, and will help readers to understand how QM survived, against all the odds, as a selective school, and has evolved into the school it is today.

A disadvantage of being both the author of the book and a participant in the story is that John has been characteristically modest about his own contributions to the success of the School. In his roles as Head of History, Second Master, Commanding Officer of the Combined Cadet Force and, since his retirement, a Foundation Governor, he has made an immense contribution to the life and work of the school over the last 38 years. The award of an MBE in recognition of his work for the CCF alone indicates the strength of his commitment to the School and the quality of his work. I therefore take this opportunity to thank him for all he has done for the School, not least in the preparation and writing of this splendid book: I am sure that many others would wish to echo my gratitude.

Stuart Holtam
Headmaster

March 2004

FROM CHAIRMAN OF GOVERNORS
HIS HONOUR JUDGE PETER J STRETTON

It is a privilege to contribute a brief preface to this excellent book. In bringing the history of QM up to the present, it admirably illustrates the values of the school, and the outstanding contribution that it has made and continues to make to education in and around Walsall.

Parts of the book tell of the struggles that have been needed to maintain the character of the school. We must be vigilant to ensure that the essence and values of the school are preserved.

Peter Stretton

FROM THE MAYOR OF WALSALL
COUNCILLOR ARTHUR BENTLEY

I welcome the publication of the history of the last 50 years of Queen Mary's Grammar School. During that period the school has maintained its tradition of excellence in education, and I have always been proud that Walsall should have such a high class school.

It is vital that its character and its tradition of high achievement continue to be retained in the town. As Mayor of Walsall I am extremely pleased to be asked to write this short preface to the book, which will help to remind the people of the status Queen Mary's School has brought to their town.

Arthur Bentley
Mayor of Walsall

INTRODUCTION
by the Author

Queen Mary's Grammar School 1554–1954 was published to coincide with the Quatercentenary. David Fink's work is hugely impressive as a study in the development of an ancient school from its medieval origins to the fine Grammar School which stood until the 1950s in Lichfield Street, Walsall, with its daughter Girls' High School beside it.

In his opening paragraphs David Fink states the central truth at the heart of the school's history. The Queen Mary's Foundation is an ancient Corporation with liberties which have been and still are respected by the state, even in times when our form of education may not always be favoured by the state. The Foundation has an independence which must be treasured above all else while ours remains a free society.

Much of what is taught in our schools today is laid down by government in a way that could not have been foreseen in 1954. The freedom of the Foundation, and the Headmaster with his colleagues in particular, to determine the curriculum has been circumscribed. Today the Governors nevertheless retain their authority to appoint the staff and control the policies and practices of the school, and this they must never yield.

As David Fink has said, the lands of the chantries of medieval Walsall gave the school its endowment which is still its birthright. The ideals of a liberal education are inherited from past generations and world-wide cultures, and, maintaining our freedoms, we hand these on.

* *

Since 1954 Queen Mary's has changed yet remains the same. This book records fifty years of enormous change including the move to a new site at Mayfield, the move to a centralised curriculum in education, the expansion of higher education and its impact on secondary schooling, and social, cultural and economic changes which have had a great impact on the school and its pupils. Nevertheless the essential content of what is taught, the standards of behaviour and attitude, the structure and philosophy of the school – these have not changed. The same uniform is worn, the same games are played, much of the pattern of day to day schooling is unaltered.

Queen Mary's is an academic school, but it does not and has never crammed its pupils for exam results. It has always been intensely proud of its extra-curricular activities. A glance through this volume will convince anyone of this. Boys have always had a range of voluntary activities from which to choose, from Games, through Cadets, Scouts and the Duke of Edinburgh Scheme, to Drama, Music, and a myriad of societies of all kinds. More recently there have been increased numbers of inter school competitions, regional and national. Above all, the school *has* remained high in the League Tables, proud of its Oxbridge successes, and determined to develop best practice to *educate* its pupils.

There is something special about QM. It generates intense loyalty. Its Queen Mary's Club dinners remain the best attended of those we know. What other school of comparable size has to keep the numbers at the annual dinner down to 200, because of the limit on its accommodation? What other such dinner has such a wide range of ages, with so many young ex-pupils present as well as those of all other generations? Staff who have moved on return for plays, concerts and retirement parties, long after they have left Walsall. Families become attached to the school through the QMA and remark on the friendliness of QM.

There can be no school which has seen such an increase in the number of those from a range of ethnic minorities, especially having origins in the Indian sub-continent, which has made them part of the school so happily. Even within the school there has long been an adult relationship of mutual respect and fellowship between staff and senior pupils. In writing this book I have sensed all these feelings, feelings I remember well from my years on the staff, among all those who have helped me so willingly from whichever generation.

Queen Mary's is a Grammar School which draws from all sections of the community, from the poorest to the well-to-do. It takes able boys from all backgrounds and offers a route to university and beyond. It is not a one class all ability school, but an academic school for all classes of boy. For those who believe in giving opportunities to all, it remains a school of great unifying value in a society where rich and poor remain divided.

* *

Throughout this book "Mayfield" is used as a word to describe the whole school site. It does not refer to the Preparatory School as it usually does in today's parlance.

Research for this book has involved the use of Governors' Minutes, Minutes of the Queen Mary's Association, and Welsh Centre committees, use of David Fink's *History*, use of the invaluable records contained in the *Marians* of the last fifty years, and a multitude of school records and photographs. All has also been made possible with the recollections of governors, staff, past and present pupils, and my own recollections. I have not credited sources with references in the book, but throughout I have tried to be as accurate as possible. Naturally some readers will have recollections which conflict with those I have used. There will be errors that have crept into the manuscript, despite our efforts. My apologies for such mistakes. I have tried to paint a picture of an evolving institution, and I hope I have succeeded to some degree, despite any mistakes that readers may find.

Floreat Reginae Schola Mariae

1

THE SETTING: WALSALL SINCE 1954

In 1954 Walsall was an industrial town on the edge of the Black Country. It was a County Borough in Staffordshire with its own Mayor, Aldermen and Council. Its boundaries were limited to include Walsall, Bloxwich and their immediate suburbs and estates. Its industries included leather, brass, some other metal trades: mostly small family-owned firms. There were still coal mines around the edge of the town to the north, and at Hamstead to the south.

A visitor to Walsall could arrive by (steam) train from Wolverhampton, from Dudley, from Derby, from Birmingham, from Cannock or from Lichfield. Coming out of the station through its circular polished ticket hall and under the glass entrance canopy into Park Street, the visitor would notice the blue corporation buses and trolleybuses. Sainsbury's was then in Park Street, a deep shop with light grey tiled floor and mahogany counters on either side, an old-fashioned grocers', like the Home and Colonial in Bradford Street. Turning right down Park Street, the main shopping street, he would soon reach The Bridge, a very busy traffic crossroads, where he could look up Digbeth and from not far up could gain an uninterrupted view of St Matthew's Church

beyond the Market. There, on The Bridge, would be Patterson's the first-floor restaurant and tea room on one side, the George Hotel opposite with Burton's Tailors alongside, together with Shuffrey's ironmongers and Vardy's tobacconists on the corner of Bradford Street.

In Bridge Street there was Taylors', the music shop with its terracotta musical instruments on its exterior. Next door to Taylors' was The Clover Milk Bar, serving frothy coffee in glass cups and saucers, the place to meet girls from the High School, and frequently put out of bounds by Hamilton in the fifties. Further on, between Lichfield Street and Upper Bridge Street, was the multi-department Co-op, next to the Walsall Mutual Building Society and opposite the Council House, with the finest kitchen and home wares department for miles around.

Opposite top
Park Street entrance to Walsall railway station, dismantled in 1978 – on the site occupied by the school from 1811–c.1850

Middle
Blue corporation trolley bus at the bus station 1968

Lower
The Bridge from Bradford Street, c.1954

Terracotta musical instruments on front of Taylors' Music Shop in Lower Bridge Street

French Renaissance-style roof to Walsall's Building Society

*The Council House tower of
1902 – 5 with its imperial
crown*

The major landmark of central Walsall for a century has been the stunning Edwardian tower of the Town Hall with its crown on top, and then ahead the unchanging view of Lichfield Street.

The junction of Littleton Street, Lichfield Street and the Broadway hill was marked by traffic lights. The branch of Holliers, the bakers, near the Royal Oak pub, provided sticky buns for sale in school at break. Already plans were being drawn up for by-pass routes which might result in the widening of Lichfield Street in the area of the school. Most boys came to school by bus, by cycle or on foot. Several boys arrived each day by train from Great Wyrley, Cannock or Hednesford and then walked up from the station.

In 1954 Queen Mary's drew from the Junior and Elementary schools of the old Borough, and a proportion of pupils was selected from Staffordshire, mainly from the Cannock area. In the years since 1954 there have been major changes to the character and physical structure of Walsall. In 1966, the Urban Districts of Willenhall and Darlaston were added to Walsall. In 1974 the 'Metropolitan Borough' was placed in the new West Midlands County, and no longer in Staffordshire. Walsall absorbed Aldridge–Brownhills Urban District, parts of Wednesbury, Pheasey, and the Streetly area of Sutton Coldfield. This enlarged Borough changed the intake of QM, so that more boys came from the newer and more prosperous areas including Aldridge and Streetly. With the establishment of Comprehensive education throughout the county, Staffordshire ceased to send County entrants.

More recently boys have been able to apply to the school from any address irrespective of boundaries. This is discussed later. It has led to an increase in numbers from Birmingham (the Sutton Coldfield area), from Sandwell (the West Bromwich and Great Barr areas), and from Wolverhampton, while a small number again apply from

Left
*Pedestrian crossing by The Stork
Hotel c.1954*

Right
*Traffic at the Arboretum junction,
c.1958*

Staffordshire (Cannock and Lichfield). The entry remains 96 (three forms of 32 boys), so the pressure has reduced numbers from the old Walsall borough area. It must be said that as Comprehensive schools became established in the 1970s, so loyalty to those schools developed. Many Junior schools ceased to encourage their pupils to apply to Queen Mary's, and this fact has helped to bring about a change in the pattern of feeder schools. For example, it has meant that fewer boys come from Bloxwich and very few boys now apply from Willenhall and Darlaston.

The visitor to Walsall now arriving by car via the M6 motorway finds a town very different from that of 1954. Much of the old industrial heart of the town has disappeared, though the leather trade remains in a reduced form. Mining has long ceased. New industrial and retail parks have been built, and there is still an air of modest prosperity.

Corporation blue buses and trolleybuses have long gone, replaced by the West Midlands Travel bus. Trains which, for years, only ran to and from Birmingham, now also travel on reopened routes to Wolverhampton and beyond, and to Stafford via Cannock and Rugeley. Walsall station has lost its presence, and has to be sought out within a shopping mall. Much of the centre of Walsall is pedestrianised, with traffic encircling the town centre and none crossing The Bridge. The market remains, lively and thriving as ever, but the view of St Matthew's was destroyed by an unpopular bridge development across the High Street, The Overstrand, completed in 1970.

Most of the old shops have gone, replaced by branches of the retail chains in the two main shopping centres: Old Square and the Saddlers Centre. Sainsbury's Supermarket is at the top of the High Street. As a result, Park Street and Bridge Street are sad shadows of the past. A fine new Bus Station has been built in the centre of St Paul's Street. The New Art Gallery lifts the surrounds of Townend. From the past, Boots and WH Smith's remain in Park Street; Poxon's Butchers is still at the end of the alley by the Bus Station; the main Banks are where they were fifty years ago; and Sister Dora still looks down on The Bridge. The War Memorial stands proudly, and the school CCF is the largest unit to take part in the Town Parade, led by the Mayor, which marches there each Remembrance Sunday. St

Sister Dora statue, with Midland Bank behind. Bronze statue of 1957 which replaced the earlier marble one from 1887. The marble statue is now in the Council House

The County Court House

Paul's Church, built as the school chapel by the Governors in 1826, and rebuilt since, has been divided into an upstairs church, and a shopping and conference area known as The Crossing. The school stained glass windows remain, but for Speech Day and Carol Services the school now uses St Matthew's Church. For those who climb the hill, St Matthew's stands on its own, a determined and active spiritual beacon. The original Queen Mary's school building, until it was demolished in the 1850s, was situated to the south of the church where the cars are parked, not far from the lych-gate, and by the gardens created there in the late 1950s.

Speech Day Prizegiving is still held in the Town Hall, and the Council House, Library and the remainder of Lichfield Street are remarkably unaltered. The huge roundabout which dominates the approach to the High School and the Arboretum gives way to the continuation of Lichfield street. The Arboretum is unchanged, while

The Arboretum Lodge

the Butts is an area which has been conserved and restored with new housing in-filling the gaps between the old; WT Hill & Son, family butchers since 1888, remains.

Further out from the centre, new private housing from the 1960s has covered the farmland around Park Hall and Sutton Road, the area well known to the cross-country runners of the 1950s. Similarly all the land between Barr Beacon and Sutton Park has been built up with the Hundred Acre estate and adjoining housing. In the area beyond the

Delves, the Yew Tree council estate has been built, one among many after World War II. Beyond Sargent's Hill the open land between Walsall and Great Barr has been largely filled and is cut through by the M6 motorway, though the hamlet around St Margaret's Church remains miraculously rural.

  Such are some of the changes in the area around the school. Boys do not cycle to school, and the old cycle racks have long gone. Most boys come by bus, or are driven to school by car. Very few live within walking distance nowadays. Queen Mary's now serves Walsall and a wide region around. In recent years boys have come to the school from Tettenhall, from Wheaton Aston, from Wylde Green! In teaching a class of Year 7 boys it can no longer be assumed that the majority have any knowledge of the town of Walsall, nor can many of them picture the centre of the town. The school is no longer anchored in its town by the close links and sentiment of the past. This is a major change in the last fifty years.

*Queen Mary's Grammar School
1968*

2

QUEEN MARY'S 1554 TO 1954

The Founders and our Royal Benefactor

Queen Mary's Grammar School was founded in 1554. Two leading townsmen, George and Nicholas Hawe, spent weeks in London and succeeded in bringing before the Privy Council of Queen Mary Tudor their petition to found a school in Walsall. Many towns at that time were setting up schools to teach reading, writing and the classics to a generation for whom education had become fashionable.

Opposite top
Queen Mary I 1553–1558,
by Antonio Moro 1554

Educating boys had been the prerogative of the priest in villages and towns of medieval England. The recent Reformation had led to the abolition of chantries which were chapels within churches where prayers were said for the souls of the dead. Funds which had been given in wills for this purpose had recently been expropriated by the Crown, and local people were keen to find new charitable uses for this money. The young Protestant King Edward VI had died in 1553, and had been succeeded by his Roman Catholic sister Queen Mary. The Letters Patent brought home by the Hawe brothers in 1554, benefiting from the policies of Edward VI rather than the new Catholic Queen Mary, allowed rents from fields around Walsall – amounting to £10 per annum – to be used to maintain a new school. This would be housed in an old town guild-hall with yard and cottage, which was then lying empty in one of the narrow lanes that faced the old parish church on the hill in the centre of Walsall. QM was, in this way, a protestant school which happened to be founded in Catholic Queen Mary's brief reign! The Hawe brothers were our Founders, Queen Mary our royal patron and benefactor. A Headmaster was appointed along with his assistant or usher and there were probably up to 60 boys eventually, and it was known as a 'free Grammar School'.

House of Joan Hawe in Cherrycroft, Lower Hall Lane, Walsall. Probably the house mentioned in George Hawe's will as belonging to his mother

The presumed early school building on Church Hill

The Early School on Church Hill

In the hall the master would teach from a dais at one end, while the usher would teach his class from a dais at the other end. Boys arrived at about 9 years of age, and left when they were about 14 or 15. School lasted

The Letters Patent 1554, a photograph of which hangs in the school entrance hall

from 7 o'clock until 11, and from 1 until 5 or 6 in the evening. There were breaks for breakfast 'and necessities' at 9, and again at 3. Latin was the basis of study (using Lily's *Grammar*), until the 5th form when Greek and Rhetoric were added. The school still possesses the 15th-century volume of Virgil with teaching notes, presented by one Petypher, appointed headmaster in 1556, 'the use whereof he willeth the schoolmaster for the time being always to have', and this, along with the original charter or Letters Patent of 1554, remains the school's oldest possession. It is possible that Petypher may have been appointed headmaster without ever taking up the post (see Appendix 1: *Master Petypher's Virgil, by Mark Purcell*).

In the 17th century three pupils may be mentioned. Phineas Fowke of Little Wyrley Hall, physician, theologian and classical scholar and local squire of great wealth; Lord Chancellor Somers, defender of liberties, patron of Locke and Newton, and John Hough, president of Magdalen College Oxford, and bishop successively of Oxford, Lichfield and Worcester who defended his college's liberties against James II.

The school in Park Street

The school declined in the eighteenth century, but in 1797 the governors obtained an Act of Parliament to divide the school into a classical or grammar school, and an English or commercial school. The grammar school was moved in 1811 to a house in Park Street where it expanded, while the commercial school continued at the old school by St Matthew's Church. The Commercial school emphasised writing and arithmetic and taught book-keeping for the benefit of the sons of local shopkeepers and merchants. A description of life at Park Street is given in David Fink's book.

The New School at Lichfield Street

In 1850 the two parts of the school came together in the fine buildings newly designed and opened in Lichfield Street, on land purchased from Lord Hatherton. The Park Street school was demolished to allow the building of the South Staffordshire Railway and Walsall station, while the original school by the church was pulled down also in 1852 or 1853, and the land there may have been exchanged for the land and two houses next to the new school in Lichfield Street. Briefly, in the changeover, the school may have been housed in the Grandstand building of the Walsall racecourse, which was on the meadow subsequently used for the

The Racecourse building

railway sidings, beyond Bradford Street. By 1854 there were 50 boys in the grammar school and 84 in the commercial section. In the new Lichfield Street buildings the commercial boys were kept apart from the grammars by its design, including a solid wall under the cloisters. Boys fought each other out of school 'and many times the commercial school had been victorious and carried their captives to the assembly room and locked them there'.

In 1826 the governors had built the St Paul's Chapel in Darwall Street for the school and, in the nineteenth century, headmasters were ministers of the chapel also. In 1875 St Paul's became a parish church, when the Rev Alexander Irvine, headmaster, ceased to be curate, and the direct connection with the school was lost. However the pulpit was presented by the old boys of the school when the present church was built in 1893, and a stained glass window which includes scenes from the school was presented in 1900 in memory of TA Hill, Chairman of the Governors in the 1890s. In 1893 the Governors founded the fee-paying Queen Mary's High School for Girls using land behind the school facing Upper Forster Street. In the same year the first physics and chemistry laboratories were built along with a gymnasium. It was in this year also that the Commercial School was finally fused with the Grammar School. In May 1900, during the Boer War, a cadet corps was founded as a cadet company of the South Staffordshire Regiment.

EN Marshall

In 1904 a new block of buildings, the 'Art Block', was opened with armoury, art room, dining room and classrooms. The foundation stone had been laid by Sir Oliver Lodge, principal of Birmingham University. Above all, under the headmasterships of JA Aldis and H Bompas Smith, the school became a place of 'enlightenment and good sense' and old 'regimes of terror' passed away.

EN Marshall

Born in 1865, Edward Norman Marshall was educated at St John's, Cambridge. He had been a housemaster at Loretto and then headmaster of Kingston-on-Thames Grammar School before he moved to Walsall. Appointed in 1906, Marshall was the first of three great headmasters of the 20th century, and during his headmastership the school increased from 204 in 1906 to 514 when he died in harness in 1926. He increased enormously the number of scholarships and prizes offered. He began a genuine sixth form, introduced a house system, and expanded and strengthened the Queen Mary's Club which had been founded in 1874.

The new headmaster introduced the present school badge instead of the Queen Mary's personal badge, and, later, after the first war, Marshall himself, presumably, knowing the works of the Latin author Martial, found the present motto of the school: *Quas dederis solas semper habebis opes:* 'Alone the wealth thou givest shalt thou hold', or 'What you give will be your only permanent riches' (See Appendix 2: *Marshall's Martial by SL Darby*). Early in his headmastership the school became officially 'Queen Mary's Grammar School' though it has always been known colloquially as QMS or just QM. In 1908 he introduced the present School Song, and a new green school cap with 'QMS' in yellow. By 1926 he had replaced this cap with the segmented red, yellow and green cap which was later modified but essentially was to last until caps were abolished in the 1970s. In 1909 the house system was introduced by Marshall with School, Dellow's, Frith's and Powis's houses. Each had a housemaster and 2 prefects. In 1924 the four houses became 6 and were renamed: Petypher's, Somers's, Hough's, Docker's, Gnosill's and Thrustan's.

When George V succeeded to the throne, the new Queen Mary agreed, on the headmaster's petition, to give a History Prize for the school, and a book was presented every year from 1911 until her death in 1953. Boys at Queen Mary's are now surrounded by paintings as they walk the corridors. This practice was first introduced by Marshall from about 1911. Pictures for form rooms were gifts from masters and others over the years but were lost when the school moved to Mayfield. Pictures on the corridor walls were reintroduced in the late 1990s. The Honours Boards, renovated and moved to Mayfield in about 1990, had been put up in big school in 1913. The shields, now in the library, had also been added around the ceiling of big school.

In 1913 the first nine and a half acres of Mayfield were purchased for £850. Grants in 1920 enabled advanced courses in Natural Sciences to be set up and by 1926 sixth forms were established for Natural Sciences, Classics and Modern Subjects. In 1918, the school having doubled in size since 1906, the house and gardens of Moss Close was leased for £200 a year as a junior boys' department. In 1921 and 1924 the rest of the Mayfield estate was bought for playing fields, and the house was made a kindergarten for boys and girls, and a preparatory school for girls. A wooden pavilion had been built. In 1925 architects were commissioned to design the first section of a new school for the boys at Mayfield on part of the playing fields, but the financial troubles of 1926/7 prevented any government aid so that the project was shelved, eventually only being pursued in the 1950s.

Visit of HRH The Prince of Wales 1923

The Great War 1914–1918 was the most traumatic period of Marshall's Headmastership. An enormous proportion of the boys who left school in that generation went to war, and the War Memorial is a tribute and silent statement of the vast numbers from a relatively small school who died in the war. Walsall families were torn apart by the grief of their loss. The War Memorial board was unveiled in 1920 by Brigadier-General Campbell, VC of the South Staffordshire Regiment. In the War the school sent help to Serbia amounting to £4000, while regular cultivation of the old school fields in Leigh Road produced 36 tons of potatoes a year by 1918.

In 1923 the Prince of Wales visited and inspected the school, with scouts and cadets lining the road. Marshall became a member of the public school Headmasters' Conference, and the school looked forward to a new future in new buildings. Marshall was still full of plans for his school. Then in 1926, without warning, he died of double pneumonia during the summer holidays. It was a terrible blow and the school and all Walsall mourned him. Known as 'Mush' by generations of Queen Mary's boys, Marshall was a dominant but humble man with a natural dignity and directness of speech. In his time Queen Mary's became the school we know today.

HM Butler

HM Butler

Following the brief reign of ASC Barnard, HM Butler arrived in 1931 from Hexham Grammar School. Bringing fresh ambition to QM, he immediately set about planning a major new building as numbers of pupils began to increase. The result was the 'George' Building, the new science building opposite the Art Block, named after King George V. The building was opened in 1933 by Sir Raymond Beasley, professor of History at Birmingham University. Even then the Chairman of Governors, TA Smith, believed they should have been opening a new school at Mayfield rather than an extra building at Lichfield Street. However at that time the Board of Governors' policy was to rebuild the Girls' School first, at the strong instigation of the then Headmistress, Miss Stafford.

During the 1930s the school staff changed considerably, with the appointment of new masters including SH Chadburn in 1937 and DPJ Fink in 1940, who were to teach at QM until the 1970s. The house system had a revival and competition in all areas of school life was strong. Rugby football was introduced in 1932. A new school pavilion had been built at Mayfield in 1930 to replace the green wooden structure which had burnt down.

World War II had a serious impact on the life of the school. Saturday morning school was abandoned. Several younger masters were called up and were replaced in many cases by ladies on the staff. School uniform was lost for most of the war. Incendiary bombs fell in the school yard, and trenches were dug across the playing fields which were also partially used for growing crops in the 'Dig for Victory' campaign. The OTC became the Junior Training Corps (JTC), and the 1599 QMS (Walsall) Flight of the ATC was established in 1944, commanded by F/O JC Barnsley, an Old Boy. These became joined in the Combined Cadet Force (CCF) in 1949. Throughout the war period every effort had been made by Mr Butler to see that normality was maintained.

In 1944 the Education Act set up new procedures for Direct Grant Schools. The Queen Mary's Foundation was not sufficiently strong financially and failed to qualify, and therefore adopted Voluntary Aided status. All fee-paying ceased, as subsequently did the education at Moss Close of boys under 11. Butler retired in 1951 after an extraordinary era in the life of the school. The structure of the school and its governance were by 1951 more or less as they are today, as Butler handed to AN Hamilton, his successor, a fine school on the eve of its 400th anniversary.

This chapter is a brief survey of 400 years. For the full study of the early History of the school, please see David Fink's masterly volume 'Queen Mary's Grammar School 1554–1954' published by the Queen Mary's Club as part of the Quatercentenary celebrations.

WALSALL GRAMMAR SCHOOL,

FOUNDED BY QUEEN MARY, A.D. 1554.

3

THE FIFTIES

I am indebted to Phillip Holmes (1951–59) and Roger Pinson (1949–56) for providing much of the material for this chapter. The period is before my own arrival in Walsall, and their memories pervade this description of the school in this decade.

The work of masters who went on to teach in the later sixties and beyond is more fully considered in Chapter 11.

The period from 1951 to 1959 were years of great change at Queen Mary's. The summer of 1951 saw the end of HM Butler's long Headship, and the school was to have three Headmasters during the decade. The boys who joined the school in 1951 were interviewed by HMB during June and July, but in September Mr AN Hamilton was in post as Headmaster, having joined Queen Mary's from Repton School. These boys who arrived in 1951 spent their sixth form careers under the eye of SL Darby.

New boys who walked up Lichfield Street in 1955, past the main school and up towards the Butts, turned into the grounds of Moss Close in which house they spent the first two years of their Queen Mary's life. These same boys, in their upper sixth, seven years later, cycled or walked to Mayfield, into the new buildings of Queen Mary's as the first phase opened with the new Science Block in 1961.

Opposite top
View of school c. 1960

Opposite lower
Moss Close

AN Hamilton

Hamilton was a very personable man – many boys had a better relationship with him than with HMB. Boys had been in awe of Butler: he frightened them to death! But there had been a warmth and sincerity about him. He was one of the great older men of that time. Before 1951, being at school was like living in an old house. Then Mr Hamilton came. Butler's was such a hard act to follow. A previous generation talked about Marshall this and that. Butler men were the same! Boys believed that many of the staff didn't like Hamilton. But the new Head had an informal warmth that one didn't associate with Headmasters. Boys of course had no idea whether he was a good Head, but many liked Hamilton. There was a greater sense of freedom for older boys, and he had a sense of humour. He was the inspiration behind the quatercentenary gates which were to set off the appearance of the school.

AN Hamilton

HA Hawkins

Moss Close

The new First Years were welcomed to Moss Close – in those days a physical entity – by the stern Mr WE Terry (appointed in 1915) known affectionately, of course, as 'Wet' and his deputy Mr HA 'Porky' Hawkins MC, JP (appointed in 1922). Mr Terry taught physics and Mr Hawkins, who had been awarded his Military Cross in the Great War, taught mathematics. Moss Close was a large, Victorian-Gothic house with an impressive entrance above which was Mr Terry's study and from its window he could observe the boys lining up on the tarmac drive. The window had a curtain pole over which Mr Terry had hung his canes. These were not visible in the room but were very obvious from outside the building. Twice each day boys, lined up outside, could observe these implements of Mr Terry's wrath and, occasionally, you would see his hand reach up and take down a cane which meant someone was about to receive a punishment. Although it seemed that his sole purpose was to terrify new boys, he showed his humanity in many ways, not least on the day of the death of King George VI in 1952 when he visited each form to inform the boys that His Majesty had died. He found it difficult to hold back the tears. After 40 years service, WE Terry retired in July 1955. Harold A Hawkins was master in charge of Moss Close for its last years until 1961, and then in charge of the first two years of the school, still known as 'Moss Close', but at Lichfield Street, until he retired in 1963.

Boys entered the premises of Moss Close through a wide gate on the corner of Mellish Road and Buchanan Road (now Buchanan Avenue). In those days, Moss Close boys wore shorts. On the left was a shrubbery in which, on the first day of the September term, lurked Second Years ready to remove the shiny new caps from the new boys and dirty them. They would attempt then to catch a few to 'bump' them as an initiation rite. Most escaped with a slightly grubby cap – for which they were grateful. Beyond the shrubbery was the play area which at the beginning of the term had some grass on it, at least around the edges near the trees which still today line the old boundary wall along Mellish road. The area was lined with trees on three sides, the open side being that facing the house itself.

To the left of the house, looking from Mellish Road, were the stables which were used by the school Scouts, 13th Walsall, and there was a sunken path leading on to Mellish Road. Today you can see where the pedestrian gate was set into the wall. This path was the scene of many games of British Bulldog, the aim of which was to get from the main playing area across the tarmac pathway to the opposite bank without being caught – usually somewhat violently. Another favourite game was tip cat: a stick 6" to 8" long, sharpened to a point at both ends (the cat), was struck with a longer stick causing it to fly up. It was then struck with the larger stick with the intention of making it vanish into the distance. With hindsight it was a very dangerous game which was banned with great frequency. In 1951, to coincide with the General Election, a mock election was held by the first year boys. The Conservatives gained a massive victory much to the chagrin of the Labour candidate Barrie Blower (now MBE and past Chairman of Walsall Hospitals Trust) and Mr Hawkins, who was at that time a Labour County Councillor for Staffordshire.

To the right was a path which led to the back of the house and which also branched off towards Buchanan Road and then led down to the Dell which was Out Of Bounds during the normal school day. At the back of the house was a conservatory large enough to hold a class of boys and where the rudiments of Rugby Union Football were taught – chiefly what a try was and that it scored 3(!) points. Also, outside the house was a HORSA (Hutted Operation Raising School Age) building which was the domain of the formidable (to First Years) Mr GA (Sam) Crudace APTI. The building was a very basic gymnasium where 'Sam' introduced boys to Swedish drill and basic gymnastics usually with fierce threats as to what might befall any individual who did not follow his orders. You would either break something (probably your neck) or he would have to 'stick you son'. Although he so often threatened to use a cane he was never known actually to have caned any boy in all his years at the school. 'Sam' Crudace was loved by every generation of boys and was a very kind man for, in spite of his threats, should any boy suffer even the most trifling injury, out would come the bottle of Dettol

The drive into Moss Close

and the words of comfort. GA Crudace also reigned over the Dell which was a sunken area behind the house and had been part of the limestone workings in a chain from the two large pits in the Arboretum across Mellish Road and to the Park Lime pits at Daw End. The Dell was used as an open air, small bore, rifle range by the CCF and as Mr Crudace was RSM to the CCF he was also the range marshal. Careful negotiations between the Scouts and Mr Crudace had to be carried out when the former wished to use the area for their activities. (*I have included a further section on George Crudace with an assessment of him in Chapter 15, The CCF.*)

There was one other HORSA building on the site and this was at the top of the drive. The smell of powdered potatoes and sago pudding could be savoured half way down Lichfield Street and, if the wind was in the right direction, at the Main School! Yes, this was the school meals kitchen and dining room and food rationing was still in force until 1954. Moss Close residents dined at the first sitting and the Main School pupils had to walk up from Lichfield Street for the second sitting. Entrance was by dinner ticket only and these were purchased on Monday mornings from Mr Crudace. It is fascinating to note that in 2004 dinner tickets remain the method used, and they are still purchased on Monday mornings. Whatever the weather, boys had to queue outside the Canteen until let in by the Prefect on duty. Seating was on long forms at long tables although the staff had chairs and a tablecloth!

Masters in the mid-Fifties

Most of the staff at Moss Close taught there permanently and did not go to main school. On the other hand masters from Lichfield street journeyed up to Moss Close. Stalwarts of Moss Close were Mr CJS 'Charlie' Ward, JWL 'Daddy' Symes, Russell H Green and RET 'Toffee' Everton. All were great characters who, it must be said, at least bordered on the eccentric!

JWL Symes

'Charlie' Ward was Group Scoutmaster, wore strange shoes with heavy rubber soles, had (to the boys) a 'posh' Oxford accent and, when roused to a contrived and theatrical anger, would leap up on the boys' desk tops and march up and down showing his disgust at whatever minor disciplinary or academic breach had caused him to react in the first place. The result was a series of imprints of the strangely patterned shoes on one's desk. As a form teacher he was admirable and in the days before the phrase pastoral care was coined, he did it. He taught history and sometimes English. He left the school in 1953.

'Daddy' Symes looked remarkably like Richard Hearn in his role of 'Mr Pastry' and seemed old but never aged. His most despairing comment was 'Oh, death! Where is thy sting!' He too could feign being cross, appalled, disgusted, but he was an avuncular character and was always solicitous when any of his charges were in difficulties of any kind.

Russell HC Green was a larger than life character. A brilliant professional musician in his own right, he taught music with huge enthusiasm, panache and gusto! His performance on the Town Hall organ on Speech Day always caused the earth to shudder as he opened all the stops for the school song, with a great extemporised fanfare echoing across the hall at the words 'trumpet forth her fame'. Expecting the fanfare the school tended to shout the word 'fame' but there was no competition with the power of Mr Green's playing. One of his great gifts was to persuade even the most timid boy that he could sing and could even sing solo in St Paul's Church on Speech Day. A breaking voice was no excuse – you became a tenor immediately. Russell Green's enthusiasm for music was infectious and it was a great loss to the school when he left in 1958 for New York and later to live in Canada. He was greatly supported by Eric Boothroyd, who was a very respected master, a real gentleman, and a most talented musician.

Bob 'Toffee' Everton taught English. His greatest love, however, was the theatre and he produced the annual Shakespeare play. His particular method of dealing with recalcitrant pupils was to grab the boy's hair just in front of the ear and twist it, forcing the unfortunate victim to his feet. He took over the Scouts in 1953, with David Fink remaining as Assistant Scoutmaster.

French was taught by three very different teachers: WJ 'Froggy' Taylor a fierce disciplinarian prone to using a slipper; BW Muncey a quiet, rather inoffensive type; and PJS 'Big Pat' Whitmore who at over six feet tall was a threatening sight to the 1951 new boys with whom he had joined the school. He had a habit of leaning back in his chair and lifting the teacher's desk from the floor with his knees. He also enjoyed warming himself by the fire in the form room of 2S. Big Pat had a very old, small car known as 'Emma' (after its registration letters EMA). This vehicle was on one occasion carried from the Lichfield Street playground down the steps by some Sixth Formers and left in the cloisters, before the street wall was broken through and the new gates were erected in 1954 and, therefore, the only way to get it out was to take it back up the steps! Big Pat left the school in 1954 and became an HMI and author of books on the teaching of modern languages. His place as second in Modern Languages and as an officer in the CCF was taken by PM Alexander, a first class linguist, and the first teacher to come to school on a motor cycle.

Latin was taught mainly by the other 1951 'new boy', who was to remain for almost forty years, JA Dickson. The relatively new subject of Geography which only came in to the school's curriculum in 1949

F Phillips

with the appointment of BJ Edwards, was also taught by the ebullient WA 'Bill' Emerson. John Dickson was also Officer Commanding the RAF section as a Flight Lieutenant (and qualified pilot) while Bill, a parachute instructor, was his second in command. While at Oxford, Bill had played as a goalkeeper for Pegasus and was renowned for being able to kick a rugby ball the length of a pitch. He was a popular teacher who had a passion for the works of John Buchan.

Once each week Moss Close boys were time-tabled for Manual Instruction at Main School under the hawk-like attention of Mr Frank Phillips. Manual Instruction (MI) was in fact woodwork. The room was on the ground floor of the Sixth Form or 'George' Block to the left as you entered the building and it and its owner had rules which had to be observed strictly. The format of the lesson was to watch Mr Phillips demonstrate a task, then to go and do it. The first 'job', after learning how to use a plane, a saw and a chisel, was to draw, then make *a spade scraper*. This was a piece of wood about 6" x 3" with one end sharpened and the sides chamfered. It could be made into *a pencil sharpener* by sticking on a piece of glass paper! Next, having learned to make a housing joint, the scraper/sharpener became *a watch stand* by fixing a piece of wood into the back of it and inserting a small screw on the front. By the end of

the first year, the most advanced wood workers had made a cruet stand. Nevertheless, boys did learn how to handle tools properly and safely, and most became used to the smell of fish glue which bubbled away through every lesson. Appointed in 1927, Frank Phillips retired in 1971.

Big School

The weekly trip to Lichfield Street meant attending Assembly in Big School. Assembly was prefaced by the presence in Big School of the Prefects and School Captain. In 1951 the School Captain was Ken Ives (later an actor and producer who famously starred in the BBC production of *Last of the Mohicans*) and with his height, physical presence and strong voice, he was a young man who impressed his juniors. At his 'Dry up!', Big School was silent for the entrance of the Headmaster and staff. On Thursdays Assembly was always taken by the Second Master, the revered

WA 'Wab' Burn MC TD, also a Great War veteran. To the boys this was the best assembly of the week as it always followed the same pattern and included the singing (loudly) 'Lift up your hearts' and the repetition of the school motto '*Quas dederis solas semper habebis opes*'. The most memorable Assembly of the year was on Remembrance Day in November. The names of those Old Boys who had lost their lives in two World Wars were read out, the CCF buglers played the Last Post and Reveille in the cloisters with the poignant sounds rising as if through the very floor boards into the silent assembly in Big School. After a lapse of some years, a simpler annual Remembrance service in the present School Hall was resumed in 1998.

WA Burn

Main School

These visits to Main School, the annual Speech Day in Walsall Town Hall and the Speech Day Service in St Paul's Church served to take out some of the anxiety about moving from the security of Moss Close to Main School. The Town Hall was used for the Prize Giving part of Speech Day in order to accommodate parents of the boys receiving prizes, the hall was full, including the balcony and there is a handwritten note in Phillip Holmes' programme for 1957 that the 'Beak's' (Headmaster, S L Darby) speech lasted 25 minutes and that he had won the bet on its length.

The Prefects and The Headmaster (1954–55)

Standing: HJ Wootton; GB Thomas; DGW Edwards; NJ Ellis; A Wood; E Williams.

Seated: ME Brownjohn; M Fuller (Capt. of School); The Headmaster; GH Matthews (Vice-Capt.); PP Smith.

Becoming a third year was a milestone in a boy's school life. Although he still had to wear his brightly coloured, ringed, cap he could finally discard his short grey trousers for 'longs'. Although, sharply tapered 'drain-pipes' (it was the Teddy Boy period) were not allowed, a boy might ask Brian Salt's mum to taper his standard trousers for 7/6 (37 1/2p), and risk being sent home! Being at Main School also meant that one could purchase buns and doughnuts at morning break – sold in the wash room in the cloisters by the ubiquitous 'Sam' Crudace. This was also the time for the free milk at break – in the third-of-a-pint bottles in the stairwell in the art building off the playground. There might be punishment by those legendary beings the *prefects*, who did not operate at Moss Close, by being given a 'drill'. This required attendance at the Gymnasium after school to endure additional Physical Training supervised by Mr Crudace and the duty Prefects. There was also, for a short time, a Saturday morning detention which was administered by staff. These punishments could be given for fairly minor offences such as walking to or from school without wearing a cap, or for arriving late at school. Boys could be reported for not giving their seat to a lady on the bus. David Groom (QM1950–55) remembers playing rugby with the empty milk bottles in the cloisters, surely a punishable offence!

Those who remember the main school refer to 5R form room with a window which looked down into the gym. Masters found difficulty with the form's concentration when the girls were there. It was joint gym, but the girls had separate lessons and entered by their own door. Boys would wonder what was beyond that door! One old boy remembers his girl friend whom he met under the stairs near the gym. Sometimes he didn't go into prayers, and he used to wave to her as she passed by.

Sport

Wednesday afternoons were reserved for senior sport which in the winter was rugby. Rugger was the world of 'Stub', Dick Hopkins. Of that, more later, in Chapter 13. But, when the weather was too bad to allow play on the field, there was cross country. The course for this was from Mayfield, up Prince's Avenue and along Broadway North to the pathway that divides the Arboretum from the Extension. Along the path to Buchanan Road, across what is now Cameron Road (then part of Calder Fields), through the gully next to the house where Judge Harold Tucker lived, and on to Mellish Road. Then turn right towards

1st XV Rugby (1954–55)

Standing: DG Stretton, CP Fulford, GB Thomas, FW Thomas, AT Gray, RL Hughes, DG Reid, D Hinds

Seated: WT Morris, M Fuller, DGW Edwards, GH Matthews (Capt.), PP Smith, R Riggs, E Williams

1st XI Cricket (1955)

*Standing: CP Fulford, F Farmer,
I Ross, JA Owen, GM Evans,
J Messenger, DW Goldfinch,
ME Brownjohn (Scorer)*

*Seated: LW Thorley, M Fuller,
HJ Wootton (Capt.),
BGW Rogers, PP Smith*

Aldridge and continue along Aldridge Road to Longwood Lane. Run (or by now, walk) to the end of Longwood Lane to Sutton Road. Here the Fifth and Sixth Form turned left, up Three Crowns Hill then along Skip Lane across the fields (Park Hall Estate was as yet a planners' dream) over the canal bridge near Wood End Road and emerging on Broadway (where the United Reformed Church now is), across the road and back up to the pavilion. Third and Fourth Years turned right and ran the length of Sutton Road, back to the pavilion. The Moss Close cross country began at the top of Leigh Road and proceeded past Rushall Church, across to Daw End, back past Park Lime Pits and back out at the top of Mellish Road, finishing at Moss Close.

In the summer it was cricket with some after-school athletics in preparation for Sports Day. There were more cricket wickets laid out than there are today as there was much more space at Mayfield. No one had yet built a school on it. It is therefore worth pointing out that you walked from Lichfield Street to Mayfield in your lunch break for games in the afternoon. Also, you walked from Lichfield Street to Moss Close (and back) for lunch and, if you were in the CCF, you marched, wearing your World War II heavy serge uniform, buttoned to the neck (till the late sixties), to Mayfield and back every Friday afternoon in the summer term in preparation for the General's Inspection (yes it usually was a real general like Sir Oliver Leese and, of course, in 1954 a Field Marshal). Although boys were allowed to cycle to school, they were not allowed to cycle between sites.

The Corps

To return to the General's Inspection of the CCF each summer term. The last two Friday periods and beyond were dedicated to the 'Corps'. Drill was conducted in the yard by cadet NCOs and this included drill

practice for the House Drill Competition although, on occasions, the RSM of the South Staffordshire Regiment would arrive to add some professional polish. House teams were a mix of Army and RAF sections personnel. In preparation for the General's Inspection, RSM Crudace took the practices himself. Early practices involved marching round the yard with 'Sam' calling the pace. He would then call on one of the drummers to mark the beat and it was

4th June 1954 – Major General Sir Guy de Courcy Glover inspects the CCF

known for him to take over the drum if the cadet wasn't beating loud enough. On more than one occasion the drum head (calf skin at that time) was put through. Exit Sergeant Major. When it was deemed that the contingent was not going to embarrass the officers they were marched to Mayfield to practise drilling on grass, where the actual inspection would take place. The drum and bugle band led the procession: Army Section, RAF Section, Basic Section: up Arboretum Hill past Crabtree's factory, along Prince's Avenue and so to the field. The contingent was then lined up on the lower, Broadway, side of the running track, with the band and RSM Crudace in the centre of the oblong round which they had to march. Each cadet carried a Lee Enfield Rifle and arms drill was practised, including a snappy 'General Salute, Present Arms'. On one memorable occasion the powerful, Geordie voice of Sam Crudace, during the silence and stillness of the whole

Quatercentenary Decorations

Corps standing at attention, cried out, 'that boy in khaki, you moved!!'

The Quatercentenary 1954

In Quatercentenary Year, 1954, the Headmaster invited Field Marshal the Earl Alexander of Tunis, KG, KCB, DSO, MC, ADC, to visit the school to open the new gates in Lichfield Street and to Inspect the Corps in the afternoon at Mayfield. Probably every boy in the school was expecting him at least to be in uniform and carrying his Marshal's baton. In the event the great man, who until 1952 had been Governor General of Canada and now was Minister of Defence in the Conservative

Government, came in a civilian suit. It was a sunny day, hot and humid. The band with whiter than white webbing and white gloves stood in front of the cloisters. The Headmaster, Earl Alexander, the School Captain and Vice Captain with School Governors stood at the gates on which was emblazoned the new round school badge (boys preferred the old shield-shaped badge!) and the rest of the school formed a fairly orderly crowd in Lichfield Street itself, the traffic having been diverted along Upper Forster Street. The part that sticks in the memories of most witnesses is that the band were obviously wilting under the heat and the weight of drums and winter style uniforms. One was sick, but the show went on. The contingent paraded in the afternoon (the band performed well) and the Field Marshal professed himself pleased with the turnout. They had marched up and down, 'and trained like hell'! Major Phil Bull was pleased, and even Sam Crudace was pleased. It was a great occasion.

Further to celebrate the Quatercentenary, a Founder's Day Supper was organised at the Town Hall. After the feast there was entertainment from three Old Boys: Harry Lamb (QM 1919–25), the well-known baritone, sang some light opera songs and was joined by not a few Old Boys to whose heads the fruit squashes appeared to have gone! He was

Top left
Civic reception

right
TJ Fox, Captain of School, making
the speech of welcome

Lower left
Major Bull greeting Field
Marshall Alexander in the
presence of the Headmaster

right
Staff entering the school by the
Quatercentenary Gates

E Dennis Smith, Imperial Headquarters Commissioner (QM 1922–29) inspecting the Group at the Quatercentenary Parade. Group Scoutmaster RET Everton to the right of the Commissioner, and DPJ Fink on near side of Headmaster

followed by N L Gellion (QM 1920–36), who performed magic; and finally the local orchestra leader Graham Rockett (QM 1938–44) who played the violin including his trademark *Flight of the Bumblebee*. The musicians were accompanied by David Fink on piano and Russell Green on the Town Hall Organ. As usual, Russell, and his choir of 600 rowdy boys, had the noisiest finale with the school song.

After many years as Second Master, WA Burn, 'Wab', retired in December 1954. Appointed to the staff in 1921, he had been Second Master since 1932.

AN Hamilton left the school to be Head of a Grammar School in Dorchester in July 1955. On departing he is said to have made a few derogatory remarks about Walsall and alluded to his children suffering from catarrh because of the smoky atmosphere! As a new Headmaster had not yet been appointed, a 'book' was opened by boys in years 4 and 5 as to which of the senior staff would become acting Head. All bets were off when it was announced that the new Second Master, the young Oxford historian and author of the new school History, David PJ Fink, was to be acting (temporary) head. With his catch phrase in Assembly of 'Quite Quiet' spoken in his gentle tones, David Fink proved an admirable choice.

SL Darby

Arriving in January 1956, SL Darby was a man with a mission. He acknowledged that the school needed new buildings. New staff had joined the school and there was a need to encourage more boys to stay on for two years in the Sixth Form. In addition to the old form divisions within a year – 'remove' for the most able (e.g. 2R) and 'shell' for the least able (e.g. 2S) – a new form was introduced which would take its O levels in four years instead of five. So, for example, in 1957 this form, although of Third Year age, was in the Fourth Year. This was the 'transitus', or, later, the 'alpha' form. However, the rigid streaming system was very divisive.

SL Darby inherited a strong academic staff, who gave such an abundance of their time to the boys in their care in all manner of extra-curricular activities – Games, CCF, Scouts and the very many clubs and societies. Darby must have been delighted to see so many Oxbridge graduates. He once remarked to an Old Boy who was about to embark on a teaching career that he was sure the young man would be a good teacher but never good enough to teach at Queen Mary's as he (Darby) wanted only to employ Oxbridge graduates, or possibly those from the next tier – Durham and London! Yet in FB (Fluffy) Shaw who had a Master's degree from the red brick University of Birmingham and a *Licencié ès Lettres* from Grenoble University, he had a linguist and teacher of remarkable ability, though it is said he had a wonderful Midlands French accent.

Growth of the Sixth Form

Until to September 1956, the Sixth Form had been divided into Humanities and Science, Upper and Lower with a small Art Sixth under Mr E Kedwards for those interested in Fine Art, Crafts and

School programmes commemorating the Quatercentenary

Architecture. A radical change was made that September and a new-style Sixth Form was born. With the former Humanities and Science sixth forms the curriculum had been simple: of a 40 period week, 24 periods (8 per subject) were given to A level study plus 1 period for PE, 3 for games and 2 for CCF/Scouts leaving 10 periods for Private Study, some of which was supervised but most of it not. SLD knew that much of this time was wasted, and a new format was introduced. The old divisions went and VI Classics, VI History, VI Modern Languages, VI Geography, VI Science, VI Art, VI Mathematics and VI Medical (natural sciences) took their place. Mr Wiggin (QM 1944–51), a Biologist, had arrived in 1957 and boys wishing to take natural sciences no longer, to their dismay, had to 'cross the line' and go to the High School to study Botany and Zoology, as Tony Wiggin had had to do himself. This had

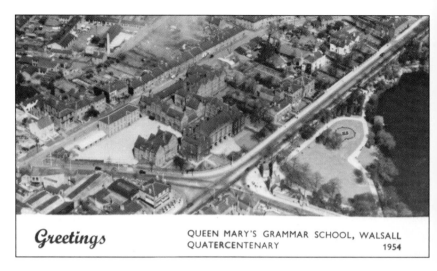

Greetings

QUEEN MARY'S GRAMMAR SCHOOL, WALSALL
QUATERCENTENARY   1954

Postcard published by the school

been a reciprocal arrangement with the High School as girls had come
to the Grammar School throughout the Fifties to study Spanish which
had been the second modern foreign language, taken up only in the
Sixth Form and taken to A level in two years – GCE in the lower sixth
and A level in the upper sixth. Mr Muncey had taught Spanish since
1951 but left the school in 1957 to be replaced by Harry J Lapworth
(*aka* 'Black Harry' because of the furious way he could dictate notes
for a treble period and set vast quantities of homework – his only serious
rival being Brian Edwards with his VI Geography). His other language
was German and with Paul Alexander (French and German) he began
to introduce German lower down the school.

New Staff

One of the academic successes of the 1950s was the rise of a highly
successful Mathematics department, led by EG (Eggie) Law, a
Birmingham graduate. A contemporary recalls that Eggie Law
'transformed my view of Maths'. He was a brilliant teacher and many
owed so much to him, though it is said that Dick Hopkins was probably
the best Maths teacher in the school for lower sets. ('Now, who's the
expert, then?') They both enabled boys who were not natural
mathematicians to understand the logic of the work they were doing.
EG Law represented a new generation of masters who helped the school
to raise its standards higher than before, and the sixth form grew. In
the year 1954–55 there were 70 boys in the Sixth Form; in 1958–9,
the last year of the decade, there were 138 and VI Science was divided
into two groups under SH Chadburn and Fred G Nash, while VI
Mathematics had 25 boys under EG Law.

Also from Birmingham had come Brian Edwards, senior Geography master, who overcame his physical disabilities, treating them as though they did not exist, and who in turn was an inspiration to so many boys. Brian was another first-class teacher and, although he drove his pupils as hard as he drove himself, was always highly respected. Later he became Second Deputy Head, and he retired in 1989, to become for some years a Foundation Governor.

Many remember a fine science master DR Allcott who had come to QM in 1949. An officer in the Army section and a terror in training on the rugby field, he too was an inspiring teacher and a superb role model. 'Jersey Joe' (after the boxer Jersey Joe Walcott) led by example and by persuasion. He could persuade a boy to achieve things the boy believed he couldn't do. He left for a post in another school, and while on holiday was drowned attempting to save a boy who was in difficulties in the water.

So the fifties ended with a new Headmaster, plans for new buildings, and many new staff, replacing an elderly pre-war generation: a school with tradition and ambition.

The Old and the New

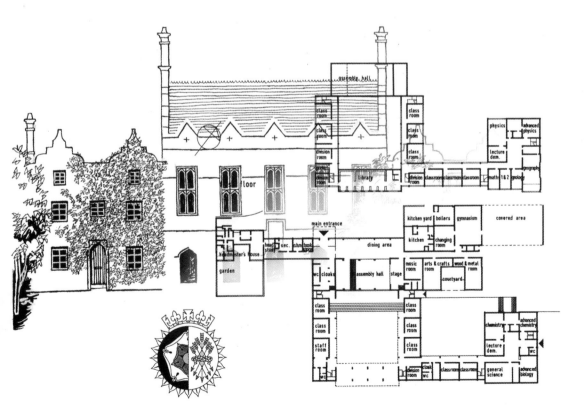

The four Headmasters

4

HEADMASTERS

AN Hamilton

When the school celebrated its quatercentenary, AN Hamilton was Headmaster. In 1951 he had succeeded HM Butler who had been Head for 20 years and had seen enormous developments in the school before and after the Second World War. His was a difficult act to follow.

Hamilton had been educated at Kelly College, Tavistock and Exeter College, Oxford. He had taught previously at Clifton College, Bristol and then had been Headmaster at Strathallan School. He held a senior post at Repton from which he moved in 1951 to Queen Mary's. He was both a scholarly man, and a games player in both hockey and cricket. His introduction to the school was made easier by the decision of WA Burn not to retire but to remain as Second Master while the new Head settled in. Hamilton was much appreciated by many of the boys in the school, especially the seniors. He seems to have had warmth and sincerity. He was approachable and he had a sense of humour.

The school's 400th anniversary was being planned for 1954. There were to be major celebrations. It was Hamilton who suggested that there should be a permanent memorial to the 400 years of the school's life by setting up wrought-iron gates which could be transported to a new site in the future. An appeal was launched for the gates, which were designed by Jack Ballinger (QM 1922–28), and other costs of the celebrations, and Mrs Hamilton and Mrs Burn formed a committee of staff wives to run stalls for a hugely successful fête in the summer of 1953 as a contribution towards this appeal.

The quatercentenary was a great success as the previous chapter testifies. Apart from the gates, a lasting contribution which AN Hamilton made to the life of the school was the Consolidated Fund, now known as the Central Fund. The school's funding from the Walsall Education Committee covered salaries and all the running expenses of the school, but the wide range of extra-curricular activities, especially games, could not be fully funded from this source. Therefore Hamilton set up the Consolidated Fund to be supported by every parent at 7s 6d (37½ p) per term, and this fund would support games, music, drama, and the Scouts. Much modified, the fund continues to the present day. It has been invaluable in maintaining the quality of extra activities

which play such a major part in the life of the school. It has especially helped in running Farchynys.

Hamilton's reign was brief. Sadly his family had never settled down well in Walsall, and he moved in the summer of 1955 to take up another appointment as Headmaster of Dorchester Grammar School in Dorset. It is said that he had wrought-iron school gates constructed for Dorchester Grammar School. He performed his role quietly and firmly, but it was his successor who made the greatest impact on the post-war school. Tony Hamilton died in 1991.

Samuel Leonard Darby

After a term when the second master, David Fink, made a most effective acting Head, Sam Darby and his family arrived in January 1956 from Bromsgrove School, where he had been a Housemaster. Educated at Wolver-hampton Grammar School, he was a classical scholar at New College, Oxford. In 1936 he was appointed to teach classics at Winchester College. In WW2 he served in the Intelligence Corps, and married his wife Betty. At the end of the war he was appointed to Bromsgrove where he gained a reputation for making boys work hard.

Here was a powerful intellect and a man of tremendous determination. At Queen Mary's he was to lead the Governors in making the decisions which enabled the school to be rebuilt on the playing fields site at Mayfield on the Sutton Road. This involved the sale of Moss Close and the creation of an enthusiastic (and later, professionally run) appeal so that the funds could be raised. Details may be found in the next chapter.

Sam Darby's achievements form the heart of this book. Not only did he lead the rebuilding of the school, but he then inspired the purchase of the Welsh Centre at Farchynys; he defended the school against the threat to its existence as a Grammar School; he founded and developed the support of parents in the Queen Mary's Association, and he developed the pastoral and academic quality of the school with a generation of new staff he appointed. All this is detailed in other chapters.

Opposite
Portrait of SL Darby by HF Blewitt
1979

He was a demanding and often intimidating man. Boys and staff were in awe of him until they became very senior. Many boys could not relate at all to this aloof Headmaster. However, he cared deeply for his school, and by a policy of divide and rule, he always ensured that he retained authority over boys and masters. Very sensitive to personal problems, he showed his feelings clearly to those who were ill or in personal difficulty. His wife, independently minded, but a strong

The carpet of crocuses

support to him, ran the school Tuck Shop for years, and from its profits she provided outdoor benches and the carpet of crocuses which still provides such spring beauty under the trees in front of the school. The first crocuses and three benches were bought in 1963, while the building work on Phase 2 at Mayfield was still in progress.

Quizzical and shrewd in manner, SLD kept what is often called a tight ship. Woe betide those whose marks or reports appeared late! Yet senior staff could find him looking for suggestion and support, while very senior boys could also be surprised by his willingness to listen to them and their ideas. These brief interludes did not alter their general wariness of him. From assistant masters attending the Duty

Master's briefing to first year boys having their first encounter with him, there was total respect for his calm authority but also fear of 'that sang-froid manner from which his erudite wit and sarcasm could dart out at the unsuspecting'. He was a superb teacher. He sometimes taught Oxbridge candidates to write general essays. When he moved into classical philosophy, he is remembered for his animation and sparkling eyes, as he showed enjoyment in his real academic love. He was of the last generation of those who routinely quoted classical proverbs and allusions in his normal conversation, expecting his listener to be equally conversant! After retirement, Mr and Mrs Darby lived in Wimbledon. He devoted much time to the life of Westminster Abbey where he was a steward. He died in 2002.

Keith G Howard

SLD was succeeded in 1979 by Keith Howard who came from years of teaching Modern Languages at Bristol Grammar School by way of a brief spell as Deputy Head at St Mary Redcliffe and Temple School, Bristol. He had an upbringing in the Wirral. In his 17 years as Head, he enjoyed that period of time after the long-haired and rebellious 70s which Sam Darby had had to endure, when conformity reigned again in the Margaret Thatcher generation. His arrival coincided with the aftermath of the Iranian revolution, so that his natural strictness of manner led him to be nicknamed the 'Ayatollah' at once.

KG Howard by HF Blewitt 1995

The Howard years were also largely the final years of autonomy in the running of the Grammar School. He arrived when caning was still totally acceptable as a punishment, and the curriculum was the business of the Head and his Heads of Department, and he retired when the National Curriculum and externally dictated policies were turning Headmasters into administrators, to a large extent at the behest of central government.

Keith Howard was a schoolmaster first and foremost, married to Elsbeth, a Dutch lady of great charm. Keith suited well the traditions and academic rigour of the school. He believed in hard work and the virtue of traditional sport. He believed that Farchynys should not have a television or be in any way less spartan than he found it. If, from his study, he spied a boy walking down the drive in a multicoloured outer jacket, he would dive through to the Entrance Hall and berate the boy fiercely on his arrival. While Sam Darby was an Oxford man (from New College), Keith was a Cambridge Modern Linguist (French and Russian) from Christ's. He loved music; he sang for the Lichfield Cathedral Chamber Choir as well as the school choir, and he was devoted to sport, especially to rugby. He had played rugby in his younger days, and he would explain how many of his bones he had broken while playing the game.

The 1980s was a decade when extra-curricular activities were at their height, and this is recognised in a note at the end of Chapter 16. Members of staff were experienced and of an age to give their considerable energies to running drama, music, sport, scouts, chess, the CCF – without the drag of the educational bureaucracy which later intruded into the system. The Headmaster was the man for this age. He was dedicated to the kind of Grammar School which the time allowed to flourish. The school was fortunate to have Keith Howard in that era.

He was Headmaster when the funding of the school was at its tightest, and his own rather puritanical ethic suited the times. He was Headmaster when central government began to overturn the traditional autonomy of school and local education authority, and he became a past master at retaining his authority and ignoring all but the most insistent demands of centralising power. In his last two years he did enjoy the benefits for the school of Grant Maintained status, a short-lived attempt to allow proven schools to bypass the local authority and receive central funding. From 1993 this enabled a start to be made with much needed capital development. New computers could be acquired, labs refurbished (the first two before 1995), lockers replaced, and outside areas improved. Chapters 5 & 9 spell out the major changes during the Howard years. In academic life and sport they were great years. Keith and Elsbeth Howard retired to Leominster in 1995.

In *Some Thoughts on Education* (1995), Keith Howard said that education in the future will depend on all of us, because education is about adapting to life in all its aspects, and we all depend on each other, and will do so increasingly. In the end, education is about the development of our faculties and abilities: in everyone there is some good, some talent, so that we can lead a life – our only life – which is as full and rewarding as possible. And if that is a life of service, what should be one of the main purposes of education will have been achieved.

Stuart G Holtam

In 1995 Stuart Holtam was appointed Head. An internal appointment, having been appointed to QM from Manchester University in 1972 to teach Geography, he then became Head of Geography, and then Second Deputy Head in 1989. He had, therefore, little to learn about the workings of the school he now led. His task, as a Head of a younger generation, was to meet the challenge of Headship in the 1990s, accepting some of the new philosophies of secondary education. His is the world of externally set strategies, curricula and targets. Yet he has also a strong sense of the school he has known for 30 years and its academic quality, which he is as equally determined to maintain as his predecessors.

SG Holtam

Having been briefly more economically independent as a Grant Maintained school, Queen Mary's reverted to Voluntary Aided status in 1998, keeping much the same control over its finances. From 1993 onwards, more capital had been available. It was Stuart Holtam's vision to start a Development Campaign; to use the new policies of government and turn them to the school's advantage through applying successfully for Language College status; to work to enable staff to enjoy upgraded facilities, and to apply successfully for funding for a much needed Sports Hall. He has shown himself ready to grasp all the benefits of his time.

In all this Stuart Holtam's mild manner and determination are well mixed. To him his colleagues could now be 'teachers' rather than 'masters', and senior staff could form a Senior Management Team. He has no hang-ups about new language. The school still is a highly selective boys' Grammar School, and has to aim to be at the top of the League Tables to continue to attract good pupils and good staff. He is of a new generation of quiet, more informal Heads whose example and steady manner can set the tone every bit as well as his more awe-inspiring predecessors. Standards continued to be maintained and pupils suspended for major bad behaviour. The firm drugs policy of Keith Howard has been maintained to the letter. Above all, like Keith Howard before him, Stuart Holtam is a workaholic! The modern Head has to be, if he attends the committee meetings of the Queen Mary's Association, staff, governors' and other meetings, concerts and all sorts of school performances all through the week, and if, sometimes, he stands on the touchline on a Saturday. Living on the premises has some advantages. Stuart has the fullest support from his wife Margaret, vital when so deeply involved in school life.

Queen Mary's Club Annual Dinner 28 September 1979

Guest   K G Howard Esq MA

5

BUILDINGS

There is an excellent account of the Lichfield Street buildings, their development and use, especially since the Grammar School moved to Mayfield, with photographs, drawings and maps, in Chapter 4 of Marina Oliver's history of QMHS, A Century of Achievement, *published in 1997. Chapter 9 similarly covers Mayfield Preparatory School. The full story of the Lichfield Street school is of course in David Fink's* Queen Mary's Grammar School. *There is a very good set of reminiscences of life at Lichfield Street and Moss Close in the* Marian *of July 1964. This chapter covers the period to 1995. Developments since that date are fully described in chapter 10.*

Opposite
Aerial view of the school in the setting of the town

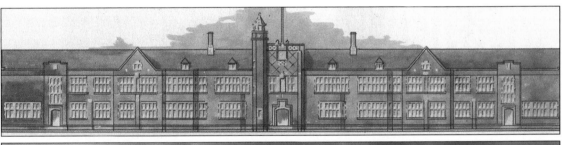

New Buildings for the Grammar School

By 1954, the school buildings in Lichfield Street were exceedingly cramped. The Grammar School and the Girls' school occupied a joint set of buildings (carefully separated though they were!), and, given the industrial life of Walsall before the 1970s, the site was much dirtier and noisier than nowadays. The playing fields at Mayfield were a mile away, while the Junior school was in an old building, though much loved, a house beyond the Arboretum called Moss Close, described in Chapter 3.

Rear elevation from the 1925 plans for new school buildings

Present buildings with the swimming pool on the right, and the new Language College wing on the extreme left

After a century at Lichfield Street, the major contribution of Headmaster SL Darby to Queen Mary's was to be the creation of new buildings for the Grammar School at Mayfield. There had been many schemes for rebuilding. In the late 1920s there were proposals and designs for a new Boys' school, to be built at Mayfield. Two proposals for a design were made in 1925 by the architects Jeffries and Shipley. To Headmaster EN Marshall's great sadness funds were not available from the Board of Education, and the project was postponed and then dropped. Then, under the influence of Miss Stafford, Headmistress 1923–46, the Governors approved designs for a new Girls' school, and an architect was appointed in 1937. The school for 350 girls was to be built at Mayfield at a cost of £35,000. There was land to build a school for the boys later. Miss Stafford said subsequently that 'every detail' of the new school had been planned. The Second World War intervened and that planned school was never built.

A special meeting of the Governors of the schools was held on 20th March 1956, during Mr Darby's first term. As well as the future policy on school building, the restoration of the school to the Direct Grant List was considered. The Chairman, Judge Harold Tucker, advised the meeting that in the event of the schools being restored to the Direct Grant List the governors would receive an annual capitation allowance for each pupil, but would not then receive a capital grant from the Ministry toward the cost of new building. Under the existing Voluntary Aided status they would receive approximately 50% of the cost. Mr Darby then dealt with the position of the Grammar School. Even if the governors were to spend £20,000 on the Lichfield Street site, it would not be possible for the Grammar School to meet the many urgent requirements of the school which he outlined. If left on the site, in 30 years the school would sink in reputation and standing. He urged the governors to build a new three-stream Grammar School. Miss M Carter (the Headmistress) said she agreed with much that had been said, but that the arguments could equally be used for building a new Girls' school. There was a very full discussion, and then Mr JA Robson proposed that the Minute of 30th July 1937 as to the building of a High School for Girls be rescinded, and that the Governors adopt the policy of building a new three-stream Grammar School for boys. Mrs Howard Keay, Vice-Chairman, moved an amendment to proceed with the plan to build a new Girls' school. The amendment was defeated by 14 votes to 2. Mr Robson's proposition was then put to the meeting and carried unanimously. For the Queen Mary's schools, this was an historic meeting. It prepared the way for the Grammar School's move, but it was desperately disappointing for the Girls' school.

Subsequent clarification of the Direct Grant regulations revealed that there was then no prospect of the Direct Grant List being reopened anyway.

At Speech Day in October 1956, the first Speech Day of the new Headmaster SL Darby, Judge Tucker, Chairman of Governors, outlined the proposals for new boys' Grammar School buildings at Mayfield. 'The Governors,' he said, 'are prepared to build a new school as soon as that becomes possible.' He added that they hoped the Local Education Authority would include the proposals in a development programme for an early date, and that the Authority will also be

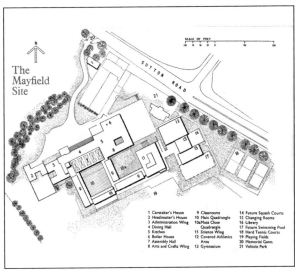

successful in obtaining the sanction of the Ministry of Education in due course. The new Head referred to the proposals as welcome and courageous. By 1958 planning was possible, and designs of the new buildings were prepared with detailed suggestions from senior staff.

Left
Cover of the 1959 Appeal Brochure

Right
Ground plan of the proposed new buildings, planned tennis courts on extreme right

The Buildings Appeal

By October 1959 Judge Tucker could announce that, after government grants had been taken into account, an Appeal would be launched for the school to raise £75,000 - a seemingly vast sum in those days. An ambitious appeal brochure was issued.

The first instalment was approved for the 1959/60 LEA building programme. Already the site was being prepared, and the first phase, the new Science Block, was to be ready for occupation by September 1960. In SLD's words: 'This is one of the landmarks in the school's history, and the builders are already on the job.'

An appeal Committee was set up, restricted to those who could attend and work between very frequent meetings. It was seen to be sad that two great enthusiasts, Messrs Butler and Burn, the previous Head and Second Master, were now too far away to assist on the local committee, though Mr Butler's devotion to the Appeal was such that Sam Darby later said that 'he is as closely identified with Queen Mary's now in retirement, as ever he was in 20 years of active Headmastership.' In three months to Christmas 1959, the enthusiastic committee raised as much as £25,000 from local industry, Old Boys and parents, a lot of money when the starting salary of a graduate schoolmaster in 1956 was under £600 a year. In his letter to the Queen Mary's Club at the time, the Headmaster said that he had had the pleasure of meeting many industrialists in the district who had an abiding interest in Queen Mary's, and valued the part it had played in local life for centuries. It had been the source of great pride to know that the school was served and supported by such devotion and respect. Parents and Old Boys had been wonderfully generous. Proceeds of school fêtes were raising over £2000, and parents were committed to regular termly contributions to the Appeal.

One of Mr Darby's concerns at this stage was that 'we must not have "utility" buildings because we are not a "utility" school.' The buildings must fulfil efficiently their practical function, but also 'call forth by their atmosphere those remembrances of the past which we sum up by the word "tradition".' Yet the times were not good for the design and construction of large public buildings, and despite all that was hoped at the time, the school that was built was a '1960s school'. It was to be dominated by large areas of glass with flat roofs. Though the library and hall were to have much to commend them, it was not to be the quality building foreseen in the pre-war plans of the 1920s, or the Girls' School buildings planned in 1937. It was sadly not to be a set of buildings to last.

Headmaster's house

Phase One

One of the early issues had been the provision of a house for the Headmaster. At this time it was highly unusual for a day school like Queen Mary's to build a new Headmaster's house on the school site, but for Mr Darby, probably with his background at Winchester and Bromsgrove, it was a fundamental matter of principle. About £7000 was set aside for such a house, and for a time the Governors did persuade Mr and Mrs Darby to look at existing houses in the Birmingham Road area. There was sharp division among the governors on the cost and style of house that might be built. Ultimately a design was agreed, so that the Headmaster's House would be part of the new school.

Another concern was the position of the school entrance on Sutton Road. The route of the drive affected a main High School hockey pitch and, rather than restrict the girls' school pitches, consideration was given to a road entry through the gardens of 48 and 50 Sutton Road. The owners were unwilling to sell, and the levels were unsuitable.

After debate the position was agreed, with a caretaker's house to be built beside the gate. At this stage Mr Darby also hoped that, in the new buildings, there would be facilities for the Queen Mary's Club – a hope that would take till the year 2000 to be realised. The cost of the first phase amounted to about £100,000, of which the Governors were responsible for half.

By 1959, as Phase One was being built, the governors were already considering the enlargement of the High School to a three-form entry school. Led by Miss Carter, the governors considered using Moss Close to help the High School in the interim while Phase Two of the Mayfield buildings was going up. Miss Carter wrote a detailed memorandum to the governors in November 1959. Eventually the enlargement took place using temporary premises in Upper Forster Street. For the next few years the re-building of the Girls' school was an insistent cause. Miss Carter and her successor Miss Godwin maintained pressure on the Governors. Mayfield itself, Gorway and land in Rushall were all considered. Redevelopment of Lichfield Street and the construction of a by-pass might have forced the issue, but this road development was not to be. When Miss Godwin departed in 1967, the re-building of the High School was clearly not to take place. This was a bitter disappointment. Since then, however, the High School has done wonders with existing and with new buildings on the Lichfield Street site.

It was April 1961 when all sixth form scientists, geographers, and mathematicians, together with 80 fifth-formers, left Lichfield Street to form the nucleus of the new Queen Mary's at Mayfield. The First and second forms of the school left Moss Close to take their places at Lichfield Street. Moss Close, after 30 years of bustle and life, fell silent. A bus service at morning break, taxis during the day for staff, and much walking, ensured that boys and staff could maintain a unified timetable. Amid the building works Phase One, the Science Block, was

Architect's drawings of the new buildings

open. Staff were appointed to run the Mayfield section of the school, and their staff common room was that which became the Prefects' Room, and is now the Resources Centre. Mr Howard Chadburn, Senior

Science Master, was master-in-charge at Mayfield, along with FG Nash (chemistry), AJA Wiggin (biology), and BJ Edwards (geography). The

staff picture appears in Chapter 11. Brian Edwards had wisely insisted that geography should be considered a science, provided with a lab. sized room with prep room attached, and a second room for geology. He had been very instrumental in planning the science block. Sam

Darby paid warm tribute to these heads of department who had in term and holiday moved old equipment and installed new, so that teaching could begin after Easter.

Phase Two

In October 1962 the turf was lifted for the second phase of building, though building work did not begin until early 1963. It is clear that the

quality of the Hall and Library were two of the major areas where the Governors did not want the school to appear merely utilitarian.

The architects were Robert Matthew, Johnson-Marshall & Partners of Welwyn, and the general contractor and builders were J & F Wootton Ltd of Bloxwich. Maurice Lee ARIBA, the lead architect, wrote:

> Dominating our ideas for the new school was the importance of the senior forms culminating in a very large sixth. It was an early decision that the senior school accommodation would surround a central quadrangle forming the focus of the school, while the junior forms would occupy a separate wing in a transitional position leading towards the senior school.

The natural position was at the top of the site with a fine background of established trees and a commanding view southwards across the playing fields towards Barr Beacon. The main quadrangle retains this view. The dining hall and assembly hall are at the upper level flanked by two-storey wings of senior classrooms. On the fourth side the Library is placed at first floor level above an arcade which opens out to a terrace above the playing fields.

The library is a special feature. At first floor level it can be approached from the junior wing to the east and from the senior form rooms to the west. There is a long gallery lit from a clerestory, with views down into the quadrangle, which has special study desks for sixth formers and two seminar rooms. The sixth form accommodation consists mainly of common rooms and division rooms.

The junior wing provides a link to the science block which is particularly well equipped. Physics and Chemistry each have main and advanced labs, preparation rooms and a lecture demonstration room. In addition there are general science, biology, and geology labs, a geography room and two mathematics rooms.

The crafts and music rooms form another complex to the east of the assembly hall, together with a large engineering lab with drawing office. The physical education centre has both gym and a large covered area. Beyond the changing room is the site for the addition of a swimming bath and squash courts.

One might be surprised at this idealised description 40 years on! Undoubtedly the use of the site and the concept of the library on stilts with a great view to the south was a success. The overall plan has never been challenged. The contrast between the quality of the Library and the merely utilitarian dining hall is explained by that fact that the local authority funded the dining hall without embellishment. The Queen Mary's Club upgraded the furnishing of the Library as a major project.

The architect makes nothing of the assembly hall in his description, which is interesting. Since completion in December 1964, the striking copper roof, soon toned to blue-green, with its tower, has made the hall the most photographed feature of the school. From within, the hall with gallery has been a great success, though sadly its acoustics are appalling! The rich timber, its high roof, its ability still to hold the whole school: it is a most attractive and memorable feature. Now, housing the honours boards, it has become that centre of tradition that SL Darby hoped would be found at Mayfield. Given the overall quality of the new buildings, the hall and the library are the outstanding areas.

In 1960 it had been announced that Phase Two would be fitted in the 1962–63 building programme. By 19th September 1961, at the governors' meeting, the details of Phase Two were agreed. This entailed improving the facilities in the Hall and Library, and the decision to plan for a swimming pool, but not to include it, for reasons of expense, in this phase. Not only would the cost of the Canteen and Kitchens fall outside the Governors' costs, but it was expected that the Army would pay towards the cost of the CCF accommodation (which they did). Ancillary buildings for the ground staff would be provided at the bottom of the field. The rifle range proposal was dropped, and the CCF informed that the range at Gordon House would be suitable for their use. (20 years later and after much pressure, and with aid from the TA, a new range was provided!) Finally governors agreed to build a caretaker's house and, in the future, a small cricket pavilion.

In 1962 came the death of a most experienced and senior governor, Frank Cooper, who had for some years been Chairman of the Property and Finance committee.

View of new buildings under construction (from swimming pool appeal brochure)

Queen Mary's Grammar School WALSALL

Sadly, in mid-1963, as building work on the second phase began, Judge Tucker, governor since 1939, and chairman for 8 years since 1955, suddenly died. There was deep regret that neither man saw the buildings finished. The completion date was by this time December 1964, and it was hoped that the final move of the whole school into the new buildings would take place at Half Term in February 1965.

A New Appeal

The Ministry grant for Voluntary Aided schools had been increased to 75%. The cost of this second phase would be £180,000. In the end the agreed tender was for £204,000 including costs not falling on the Ministry or Governors. The Governors' 50% share of the first phase had been £50,000. However the governors'

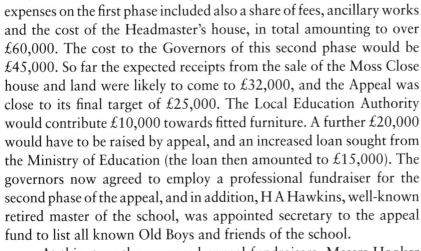

The school under construction

expenses on the first phase included also a share of fees, ancillary works and the cost of the Headmaster's house, in total amounting to over £60,000. The cost to the Governors of this second phase would be £45,000. So far the expected receipts from the sale of the Moss Close house and land were likely to come to £32,000, and the Appeal was close to its final target of £25,000. The Local Education Authority would contribute £10,000 towards fitted furniture. A further £20,000 would have to be raised by appeal, and an increased loan sought from the Ministry of Education (the loan then amounted to £15,000). The governors now agreed to employ a professional fundraiser for the second phase of the appeal, and in addition, H A Hawkins, well-known retired master of the school, was appointed secretary to the appeal fund to list all known Old Boys and friends of the school.

At this stage the proposed appeal fundraisers, Messrs Hooker Craigmyle & Co, were pressing that arrangements be published for an official opening of the buildings. They wanted new appeal literature with a programme of future developments for the grammar school, the swimming bath proposal in particular, in addition to details of the present building programme. This was agreed, and a second appeal was launched in 1965 for £45,000 to include the swimming bath. Arrangements were then put in hand to invite Princess Mary, the

Princess Royal, to open the new buildings in July 1966. Minor matters now concerned the Governors as the school was fully installed in the new buildings. Mr Stan Davies was appointed caretaker and, with his wife, moved into the new caretaker's house. The quatercentenary gates were moved from Lichfield Street to adorn the entrance in Sutton Road,

All complete!

The Headmaster and Philip Sturrock, Captain of School, admire the plaque and badge unveiled by the Dean of Westminster

and new gates placed in Lichfield Street. The architects were called in to improve the soundproofing in the administration block and the LEA made a special grant of £2000 for books for the new Library. In the summer of 1965, after the move, the Governors were invited to an open air performance of *Troilus and Cressida* in the new quadrangle.

Reunited at Mayfield

On 1st March 1965 the whole school was united in the new buildings as the second phase was completed. 'Cyclists are to arrive by 8.45; the ex-Lichfield Street contingent assemble on the Parade Ground at 9.00 to be taken through their entrances to pegs and form bases; at 9.15 the whole school to assemble in the Quadrangle; at 9.45, Forms to Form Masters. Then practice assembly in the Hall and drill on how to get to the canteen. 10.40 Break; 11.00 Normal Periods!!' These were DPJF's final instructions, after many suggested plans from senior staff. In the event, when the whole school met in the new quadrangle there was a sudden and heavy snowfall. The forms were dispersed to new classrooms very rapidly. Lichfield Street days were over.

The sudden death of the Princess Royal, who had accepted the invitation to the school, upset all plans. After many attempts to find a royal substitute, the Very Revd Dr ES Abbott, the Dean of Westminster, accepted the invitation, and the Opening of the Mayfield Buildings took place on 25th May 1966. It was a fine celebration of the work of the Headmaster, SL Darby, the Governors, Old Boys, parents and many friends of the school. It was a glorious day, and the hall and dining area were filled with school, parents and

THE OPENING OF THE NEW BUILDINGS AT MAYFIELD

Philip Sturrock was Captain of School in the year of the Opening of the new Mayfield Buildings. He is a publisher, of Macmillan, then Cassells, and now the Continuum Publishing Company of London and New York which he owns.

The opening of the new school on the 25th May 1966 had a particular sense of completion for me personally. In the life of the school it was the ending of one chapter and the beginning of another. For me, it was the completion of an educational journey. When I joined Queen Mary's in 1959 I went to Moss Close in my first year. Thence to the old school, and, only for the last year and a bit to the new school on Sutton Road. I'd been part of three locations.

Mayfield may have lacked the history and traditions of the other sites, but it was exciting to be one of its first occupants. Of course, the science sixth had been there at the frontier longer than we historians, linguists or classicists, but when the new Library and Hall opened, and all the school came together in one building, there was great excitement.

I remember particularly the light. So much glass, so open, so fresh. Blue blazers, white shirts, red, green and yellow ties and caps, and 600 boys on one site. Light, colour, noise and a sense of achievement. It wasn't our achievement. The governors, local council, Old Boys, parents – all I think cajoled by Sam Darby to realise this new vision. But we were its inheritors, and we had to make it work.

I remember putting together exhibitions on each corridor to show how we had used the new facilities, or would do. And on the day of the opening, we had to open the side doors to the Hall to get everyone in to celebrate this moment of our history. It always falls to the Captain of School to make a speech on these occasions. In all the excitement I had lost my voice the day before. Fortunately it came back when I had to greet Dean Abbott, but that frisson of expectation stayed with me for the whole of my last year at School when we explored all the possibilities of the new buildings.

PJ Sturrock

guests. The School Badge and plaque were unveiled by Dr Abbott in a ceremony with the Chairman of Governors, Mrs Howard Keay, the Headmaster, and Phillip Sturrock, Captain of School. A marquee was erected on the field for teas, Mr Fink put on a major historical exhibition in the Library, and there was justified pride in the design and quality of the new school.

Apart from the sixth form Division or D rooms, the classrooms

The Swimming Pool

of the school were planned so that the Middle school form rooms were arranged round the main Quadrangle, while the Lower school, 'Moss Close', had a set of rooms in the connecting wing between the main Quadrangle and the Science Block. Outside their rooms at ground level, was an open grass area and pathway, which belonged to the Lower school. In the early days there were strict rules for walking in the corridors, and senior boys, other than prefects, were excluded from the Moss Close area.

The Swimming Pool and Squash Courts

The swimming pool was soon built and, later, the squash courts and the small cricket pavilion. The swimming pool was really the last part of Phase Two, and it was opened in May 1970, by Mr AD Munrow Director of Physical Education, Birmingham University. The

Governors' appeal was to cover the cost of the swimming pool, but the squash courts were to be self-financed and a Squash Club was set up to attract members from outside as well as within the school community. The aim was to repay the cost in five years. The courts were built, together with women's changing room accommodation, and were opened by the chairman of governors, Mr FD Jeffries, in October 1971.

The New Cricket Pavilion

At the same time a new, but small, cricket pavilion was opened. The main changing rooms were to be used for cricket so that the pavilion was to be a base for matches, with kitchen facilities for teas, and a scoreboard. In early 1973 £40 was granted by the Queen Mary's Association for catering equipment for cricket teas in the new pavilion. The basement area under the new pavilion was used for storing Duke of Edinburgh hiking equipment until the 1990s when the Scout Hut became available. More recently, in 2000, the Queen Mary's Club, with support from the school, enlarged this cricket pavilion to double up as a QMC clubroom, and this excellent development is outlined in Chapter 18.

Top
The library

Middle
Main quadrangle

Lower
Moss Close quadrangle

Since 1965

How does the school differ physically now from what it was when newly built in 1965?

There has been remarkably little building since 1965. As has been said, the voluntary aided selective sector of education has been totally out of favour, so that no capital funding for development was available at all until after 1990.

The first noticeable change is that there is a car park between the parade ground and the gardens of the Sutton Road houses where there were rows of fully used cycle sheds. The covered play area and the kitchen yard were, until recently, open to all: these have now been put behind steel fencing, and are locked out of school hours. The old pavilion was allowed to decay between the early sixties and 1970, though it did have its roof clock. Only the sailing club used it. For the thirty years since, it has been fully used by the CCF and once again it has been smartened with new steps in front of it. The least successful design of the 1960s was the carrel gallery above the library. Boys were to prove insufficiently virtuous as students to use this space as SLD intended. Much of the philosophy of the sixth form assumed an average quality of sixthformer which rarely dominated. The carrels were misused and ultimately taken out. Two modern seminar rooms, one with an electronic whiteboard, have recently filled the space most successfully. The D or Division rooms in the sixth form corridor proved too small and have been merged or changed their use. Too few interview rooms for Yearmasters (now Year Tutors), and too few storage rooms, were built into the design. So rooms have been found and doors added under stairs,

and the prefects and captain of school soon lost their separate and prestigious rooms for staff purposes. These rooms became the Resources Centre in the 1970s, being enlarged further in 2000. The Canteen or Dining Area, very plain from the beginning was, in the 1980s, with energetic encouragement from Elsbeth Howard, very much upgraded with curtains, and, much more recently, has been provided with a modern and attractive serving area. Many new building developments since 1995 are described later, in Chapter 10.

For very many years after the Mayfield buildings were opened, the governors owed a great deal to the careful work of GH (Gordon) Foster, MBE, RIBA (QM 1942– 48), architect, who regularly inspected the buildings and advised the governors on its maintenance. His local work outside QM gained him awards also: his restoration of Walsall Guildhall and the Walsall home and museum of Jerome K Jerome.

The Eighties

During the harshest time of financial restriction in the early 1980s, one piece of self-help must be told. By this time the two semi-detached houses on Sutton Road between the school entrances had become derelict. In use for a while as staff flats, major work had to be done, or the properties demolished. With funding from the Governors and from Central Fund, Mr Howard, with rigorous determination, devised a scheme for converting one of the houses and the ground floor of the other into sixth form accommodation. Plumbing and electrical work were contracted out. Then materials were provided free by parents and old boys, and the work was done by a Community Task Force of lads convicted of offences, who were on Community Service, and they were led by a skilled craftsman, Mr Jeff Parkes. They did renewal of timbers and floors, bricklaying and plastering, and interior decorating. When the job was done, history and economics were given rooms in the Houses, and as Head of Sixth Form, Mr Bob Fletcher had an office there. Though the rooms were small and the facilities fairly basic, it was a successful and inexpensive conversion which provided much needed rooms. The passageway past the Fête Hut and cycle sheds was improved, and at the bottom of the gardens of the Houses a new Scout Hut was placed, provided from insurance after a fierce fire destroyed the old Hut at the bottom of the field. The grassed gardens area was kept pleasantly tidy. Later on when the Sixth Form Common Room was taken over as the first full-scale Computer Room for the school, a conservatory was added to the back of the ground floor of the Houses, the whole ground floor becoming the replacement Sixth Form Common Room, with economics still taught above. In the financial climate, no more could have been done.

1983 saw the construction of the CCF Indoor 25-metre Rifle Range, to which the governors and the Ministry of Defence (through the Territorial Army or TAVRA) contributed. It came into use early in 1984. A range had been part of the original scheme in 1958, but had been set aside because of cost. Wing Cdr John Dickson, who commanded the CCF then, was very enthusiastic over cadet shooting which he ran personally, and the range was the culmination of years of persistence on his part.

The grammar school had been politically under threat or completely out of favour for much of the time since the buildings were opened in 1966. No capital funding had been available. Larger and older school buildings in the country needed what funds were available and many new schools had been built. As has been said, the Mayfield buildings were sadly of the 1960s and in the long term, not durable. By the time the school became Grant Maintained, the 1960s buildings were looking drab, and the structure was showing its age. Wood was rotting and very many windows had to be replaced, the electrics needed urgent attention, the boilers were ending their life, and much had to be done to the concrete, slabbed and tarmac surrounds. From the Head's house to the leaking roof of the covered play area there were long lists of works to be done. As a Voluntary Aided school buildings maintenance was then entirely the responsibility of the Walsall Education Authority, and with low key maintenance they had done as much as they could. The school owed a great deal to the care of the officers of the LEA in this period. However, when Keith Howard retired in 1995, the school *felt* much as it had done in 1979 when he arrived. As much had been done as possible to care for the buildings and the site. Much of the extra funding available during the Darby and Howard years came through the QMA and termly parental donations into the 'Consolidated' (later Central) Fund. What began as seven shillings and sixpence a term, became a fund which raised £5000 a term. By the 1980s, to this was added the £15,000 a year raised by the QMA. Very many

THE MARIAN

The Marian

Despite the new buildings, much of Mayfield remains unaltered

small projects were funded through the use of Central Fund, into which pot all these funds went, and over the years Farchynys was maintained as well, and, for most of the time, every three years a new minibus bought by part exchange.

As a result of government funding in 1991, a scheme called the Technical and Vocational Education Initiative (TVEI) was introduced and after much hesitation the school became associated with it. Many of its vocational aspects did not apply to QM, but some funding was made available with which early BBC computers were acquired. Following this, Central Fund money was added and the first small computer room was set up in S5. John Farrington took the lead in developing the technology, teaching staff and boys, and writing much of the early software himself. The entry, albeit slowly, of QM into the computer age is fully examined in Chapter 10.

Grant Maintained Status

In 1990 a new scheme of school government was introduced, as funds were devolved to the school, and in 1993 Queen Mary's became a Grant Maintained School. This system lasted only 5 years, but it provided welcome independence from the Local Education Authority, and, by more generous grants direct to the school, it enabled major capital refurbishment to begin under the aegis of the school's own Board of Governors, now reformed to include more staff and teacher representatives. Early GM funding under Keith Howard, enabled the school office to be upgraded and administrative computer systems installed (the SIMS package) with extra office staff for the increased workload that devolved funding produced, including an administrator (Mrs Gill Columbine) and a finance clerk. The first major refurbishment of science labs took place in S4 and S7.

The development campaign, and eased government financing in the period of the Grant Maintained school and since, have greatly helped the school to catch up after a serious period of capital stagnation. Since the return to Voluntary Aided status the freedoms for the school to develop itself have been largely retained and there has been more generous funding though with complex conditions. As explained at the head of this chapter, the developments since 1995 are described in Chapter 10. This building and refurbishment has enabled the school to teach its pupils more effectively, but a radical proposal produced by the government in 2003 to demolish and rebuild schools nationally, and in Walsall in particular, may lead to a remarkable development for Queen Mary's. Within the next ten years the Mayfield and Lichfield Street buildings may be completely replaced as part of a government initiative. Little is known yet of the details of this scheme

6

THE WELSH CENTRE

At an Oxford conference in early 1962, Kurt Hahn, then Headmaster of Gordonstoun, spoke of the benefits for a school with a Centre near the mountains and the sea.

The Search and Purchase

Inspired by this, Sam Darby, with parents and old boys, began the search for a Centre in Snowdonia. The intention was reported to the Governors' meeting by Mr Jack Aspinall in May 1962. They had information about many buildings, and they inspected a Presbyterian Chapel at Rhyd, a Church in Wales vicarage, and an abandoned Primary School. Mr Harold Taylor (parent and Bloxwich builder) spent most of his holiday in July 1962 looking for something suitable. The Rhyd chapel had possibilities and plans were drawn up by Mr Bob Christie, governor and architect, for its conversion. Later Phil Bull said that he remembered a Forestry Commission farmhouse, rather small but in fair condition, and a rambling vicarage in Bethesda, riddled with woodworm and a full attic with many Churchillian bowler hats! Then the Coach House at Farchynys came up for sale. On the Mawddach estuary, it was away from the bustle of central Snowdonia. It was right for size and price, and it was near a main road.

The Hall next to it had been built between 1870 and 1876 by Thomas Oliver, a cotton mill owner from Bollington in Cheshire. Prior to that only the 200-year-old cottage known as Farchynys Fach existed in the vicinity. From 1897 onwards the Oliver family used the Hall and estate regularly as a summer residence, and for Christmas and New Year parties. The family would travel by train from Macclesfield to

Opposite
Farchynys dominated by Cadair Idris

The Coach House

Penmaenpool, and would complete the journey by horse-drawn coach which had been driven from Bollington to Penmaenpool by their coachman, with overnight stops at Chester and Corwen. While at the Hall the Oliver family would enjoy walks in the gardens and on the hillside where level terraced paths were cut out, with steps. At the highest point was a gazebo. They would play tennis on the court, the foundation of which survives, and would go boating, fishing and shooting. Mrs Sylvia Reid, widow of Old Marian, WEL (Haggis) Reid is great-granddaughter of Thomas Oliver, and she just remembers life at Farchynys Hall before the Second World War. The Oliver family sold the estate in 1937, and it was bought by a Mrs Morley who in turn sold the house in 1957 to a Mr Frank Cocksey of Barmouth. The Coach House then belonged to a Mrs Herbert from the Wirral, who had partially converted it for holiday use. Mr Jack Aspinall, Governor and future Chairman of Governors, knew the Hall was also for sale, and he bought it in 1963, with the land on the headland that went with it.

There were two initial concerns about the purchase of the Coach House. One was the tenuous water supply, fresh water gathered into a tank on Y Figra opposite, and piped via a feeder tank on the hillside above the coach house. This supply was for the Hall as well as the coach house. The other issue was the access to the headland. Originally it was thought there was a public footpath round the headland, but then it was clear that access to the paths was subject to the goodwill of the owner of the Hall.

As we shall see later, the water supply was to remain poor until a full connection was made to the mains supply. The purchase of 10 acres between the coach house and the estuary was to provide access to the beach and headland over school land. Given the later decision that the school land excludes the 'gazebo', it is interesting that in the letter to Mr Cocksey's solicitors on 22nd February 1963, it is stated that 'the land to be acquired includes the Fort, being a prominence which commands magnificent views...' The 10 acres has been valuable, but full access to the headland area (the boathouse end) is still not generally available, and is at present subject to permission being granted by Mrs Fisher, the present owner.

The Coach House was bought for the school for £1675, together with 10 acres of land at £50 per acre. Mr Cocksey allowed £200 of this price, so the school paid £300 for the land. By the spring of 1963 funds were available – the original donors being Messrs J Aspinall, Norman and Ted Franks, R Wiggin, Douglas Gilbert, LE Podmore,

A Stephens, Frank Stretton, Harold Taylor, RB White, Henry Wilkins, and Frank Wootton. Each of these gentlemen offered £200 for an unlimited period.

Conversion, Preparations and Opening 1963

Mr R Christie, parent and architect, planned the conversion, and, with Mr Harold Taylor, travelled backwards and forwards through the winter, supervising the work. The old kitchen and lavatory were ripped out and a bigger kitchen built with a larder; a store room under the staircase was converted into the boys' showers and toilets; the coach room was divided by a wooden partition to become the staff lounge and entrance hall or warden's office; the wide coach doorway was replaced with a wood and glass screen and the present staff doorway; large picture windows were inserted into the tack room, which became the day room, and into the new staff lounge; a new stairway was built up to the staff bedrooms; a staff toilet was built where the passageway to the Cadair Idris Room is now, and the hayloft became the boys' dormitory with an external fire escape built from a door in the end wall of the dormitory.

The coach house soon after its opening in 1963. Note the wooden fire escape from the boys' dormitory

An outbuilding was added to house the central heating boiler, a central heating system was installed, and connections were made to the mains gas and electricity supplies. All the work was completed between June and October 1963 at a cost of £2,172.

Then came all the furniture: cooker and fridge, pots and pans, bedding and so on. Some were bought, some were given – often by the CCF or the school kitchens – and it was convenient that the school was then moving from Lichfield Street to Mayfield which allowed the day room tables and wooden chairs to come from Lichfield Street to have a new life at Farchynys. These tables and chairs remain in use to this day. Phil Bull, then the new Warden, remembered a remarkable warehouse in Bloxwich which specialised in supplying the likes of big saucepans to shipping companies. Amazingly, some items from 1963 remain in use in the kitchen in 2004: heavy frying pans, milk jugs and at least one sugar bowl. Parents provided second-hand furniture for the staff room, and the whole operation was encouraged by the fund-raising of the QMA. The Headmaster, Mr Darby, recalled that he watched the lorry ready to depart on 23rd November 1963, to install all the equipment.

So, on Friday 29th November 1963 the first weekend party set off in a Commer 14-seater minibus, a diesel-powered contractor's vehicle with inward-facing wooden seats. By the first meeting of the Welsh Centre Management Committee on 25th February 1964 seven parties had been to the coach house, a total of 94 boys and 9 staff. The property was handed over to four Trustees, members of the Queen Mary's Club, so that its ownership would remain independent. From the beginning the QMC has been closely involved in Farchynys, and has always paid the annual Rates/Council Tax bill and has appointed a member to the Welsh Centre committee. In these ways the Club continues to show its commitment to the Welsh Centre.

Since the late 1960s one person has consistently worked for Farchynys. Mrs Mae Clark from the Old Smithy in Bontddu has been caretaker and cleaner. For very many years she was supported by her husband Desmond until his relatively early death. For at least 25 years she delivered milk as part of her village milk round. The school has been much indebted to her for her work and interest.

Celebration of the opening of Farchynys 1963.
The Headmaster, parents and well-wishers.

Centre standing: SL Darby. On bench: Mrs Taylor, Mrs Kath Evans, Mrs Keay (Chairman of Governors), Mrs Cheesewright and Mrs Stockley.

To right of SL Darby's head: KJ Stockley, PW Evans and J (Bill) Cheesewright.

Above Mrs Stockley are Mrs Stan Davies, Mrs Dawn Carter and Mrs Ken Wilson. On the extreme right is Mr Stan Davies, school caretaker.

A fine local man who maintained interest in the school's Welsh Centre in the early days was W (Bill) Tillman of Bod Owen, beyond Caerdeon, an outstanding world-class climber, explorer, sailor and author, who disappeared tragically with his yacht and crew on a south Atlantic voyage in 1977.

Developments since 1963: The Coach House

Subsequently some important developments have taken place. In 1971 the canopy, bench and wooden screen were added outside the main door. In 1973 a more ambitious project was to add the first floor workroom (now the Cadair Idris Room) which involved a bridge over the driveway. This scheme was designed by Mrs Judy Lindon-Morris, architect to the Welsh Centre Management Committee. The design involved provision of a new staff bathroom as well as the commodious and excellently equipped workroom, all at a cost of £8,421.

As mentioned above, all the houses on the Farchynys estate had been supplied with water since the 1870s from a reservoir built on Y Figra, the hill opposite the hall and coach house. For the Hall and coach house this water was piped to a secondary feeder tank on the hill behind the coach house. As early as 1974 visits had to be cancelled in the summer because of the water shortage. This problem got progressively worse, as it was originally feared that it might. In the 1976 drought year the First Year weeks were cancelled. Then the long-standing problem of the local water supply was partly resolved with a temporary or unofficial connection to mains water in the middle of the field below the coach house. The full connection to the mains supply did not occur till 1980.

In 1979 the kitchen was remodelled with the removal of the pantry and provision of new cupboards and work surfaces. In 1982 the old wooden fire escape was replaced with a new steel structure on the driveway side of the building. This was designed by Mr John Barratt, who had taken over as consultant architect from Mrs Lindon-Morris, and who for some years gave invaluable advice to the Welsh Centre Committee. Over three years from 1988 the Walsall College of Art carried through major external and internal decoration which was bright, lively and colourful. The work was carried out as training for its students. The boys' showers were renovated including new tiling and sanitary ware. The main features of the 1963 conversion have proved to be totally sound for the school's purposes. Since 1990, apart from a considerable amount of maintenance and work on the estate, little has been needed, apart from extra tarmac round the site. Over

The opening of the workroom extension, 26th April 1974.

Nearest to the camera from left: Mrs Julienne (Judy) Lindon-Morris ARIBA, Architect for the extension, secretary of the Welsh Centre management committee, and of the QMA Amenities Committee which organised the new parents' annual visits to Farchynys; Ralph White, Welsh Centre treasurer; SL Darby; Mr Pugh of Dolgellau, builder; Mr Jack Aspinall, vice chairman of Governors.

Centre back is Mr R (Bob) Christie FRIBA, architect for the original conversion of Farchynys in 1963. Behind Ralph White and side to camera is PA Bull, Farchynys warden.

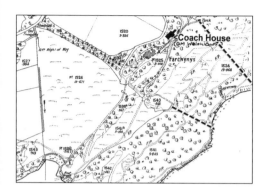

The Farchynys site, the broken lines show the approximate boundaries. The boat house is in the lower left corner.

top
The headland near the boathouse

lower
Boys at the boathouse

the years the Coach House has been maintained by a mixture of local contractors and friends and parents of the school. Decorating parties have worked for several years in July after the end of term. The day room floor has recently been resurfaced after 40 years' wear, and other works done with money from the bequest of Raymond Wilcox (QM 1927–32). The dormitory ceiling is to be insulated to protect the roof and keep the building warmer.

Regeneration of the Headland

The school was fortunate that the Hall had been bought by one of its governors, Mr Jack Aspinall. Fears over access to the headland were therefore largely hidden while he generously allowed boys to roam over the headland and to the boathouse whenever they liked. Then in 1979 Mr Aspinall sold the Hall and the estate to Mr Alan Goadby who ran it as a hotel, until he sold it to Mr Alan Fisher in 1982. With these sales the school lost the privilege to roam the headland at will, but of course the paths over the school's own land remained. The boundaries of the school land were fenced in the 1990s. However Mr and Mrs Fisher proved excellent neighbours and the school was represented at Mr Fisher's funeral which sadly followed a long illness in 1988. When Mrs Ruth Fisher sold the Hall and Gardens in 1990, she had a new house, Farchynys Fedw, built within what had been the walled vegetable garden, and she retained ownership of the headland part of the estate. She has remained a friend of the school, and she has always given permission for her land to be used on any occasion when she is asked. The treasure hunts, wide games and night exercises of earlier years are therefore still features of weekends at Farchynys.

From 1987 and during the 1990s, led by Stuart Holtam, then warden, much effort was made with grant money available to clear the heavily overgrown rhododendron from the school's land between the coach house and the estuary. The Forestry Commission had cleared their land next to the school's. Parties laboured, contractors were brought in, and regrowth was consistently sprayed so that a new carpet of undergrowth could develop

MR JACK ASPINALL (QM 1919–1924)
PAST CHAIRMAN OF GOVERNORS

Walsall born and bred, Jack Aspinall attended QM from 1919 – 1924. He served in the Royal Navy in WW2, and saw action in Iceland and the Mediterranean. He married in 1946, and had two sons. His life's work was within the family firm, Walsall Lithographic Company, and he worked his way from bottom to top, succeeding his father as Governing Director and then Chairman. He was for many years a national figure in the printing industry. His firm became well known for their printing contract for British postage stamps, and postage stamps worldwide. He was a very keen cyclist and swimmer.

Appointed a Governor in 1959, he served on the Property and Finance committee, eventually as its chairman, the Buildings sub-committee (during the building at Mayfield), and the Squash Courts, and Appeal committees. During the long and difficult negotiations over the future of the Foundation, he set an example by his untiring hard work, and his contribution to maintaining morale. From 1978 to 1984 he was Chairman of the Board of Governors. He had a particular interest in Farchynys, and he bought the Hall and estate when the school acquired the Coach House. He had sound common sense and business acumen combined with strength of purpose and warm humanity. A loyal and devoted Marian.

From The Marian, *by the late PW Evans*

to replace the deadly effect of the rhododendron which had spread like a weed.

All the work on the house and grounds, and the provision of the minibus, has been the remit of the Welsh Centre Management Committee with the warden, a governor, QMC and staff representatives, under the chairmanship of the Headmaster. Mrs Judy Lindon-Morris was the first secretary of the Welsh Centre Committee, and held that post from 1964 until 1979 when Mr Ken Yates took over and remained secretary until his retirement. Bob Preese, Head of Biology is now secretary, and he combines this with his responsibility for care of the Farchynys grounds: all ten acres of it. One of the longest serving members of the committee has been Mr Roger Pinson.

Following redecoration the Coach House was made ready for the 25th anniversary celebration in 1988. A considerable number of friends attended including Mr and Mrs Darby and many ex-colleagues who had taken parties in years past. A plaque was unveiled in the day room, and Mr Darby planted commemorative oak trees on the hillside now cleared of rhododendron. More recently, in 1997, 500 oak trees have been planted to accelerate the natural regeneration of the woodland. As Stuart Holtam said in his 1998 Headmaster's Report, 'the grounds are once again beginning to look more Welsh than Himalayan'.

Farchynys Open Days

Every year since it was opened in 1963, new boys and their parents have been introduced to Farchynys with an Open Day, held each October. Several coaches are booked for the 200 plus visitors, and the warden and a party of senior boys go on the Friday to prepare. Parents are asked not to take cars because of the restricted parking. On the Saturday the Amenities committee (now the Lower School Events committee) goes in force to prepare tea and cakes for the invasion. Parties of visitors are conducted round the headland and the Coach House, and are provided with tea. It is a wonderful introduction to Farchynys for all QM families and the QMA, from its inception, has hosted the event.

The Minibuses

Since the first minibus all its successors have had forward-facing upholstered seats! Their power and equipment has vastly improved over the years, so that the hill at Dinas Mawddwy (Bwlch Oerddrws) is no longer the driving challenge that it was, when occasionally boys had to get out and walk! Until the mid-nineties the luggage was stowed on the minibus roof rack with a large canvas cover and heavy cords. Then to follow safety requirements, a trailer was bought which certainly improved the speed of loading as well as the safety of the vehicle. In the early days the QMA tried to replace the minibus annually. But this was shown not to be necessary, and until recently, using Central Fund money, the minibus was replaced every two years. Now, the robust purpose-built minibuses are adjudged tougher than their earlier predecessors and they are made to last longer! The stop at Welshpool has always been a feature of the journeys to and from school. The route taken has always been a standard one but, over the years, the roads have improved and now the M54 and new Shrewsbury by-pass have cut the travelling time. Only David Fink insisted on travelling via Llangollen and Bala, partly because he preferred the road, and partly for the narrow-gauge railways which were nearer that route.

The Pattern of a Weekend

Weekend visits at first cost 25/-. This went up to £1.15.0d (£1.75) in 1970 with the food element per head in 1973 going up to 80 pence, and now (2004) the cost is £30. The cost has always included transport and food, with a proportion going towards regular maintenance costs. If necessary boys have been helped if family circumstances require. The cost of running Farchynys has been met by these charges plus about £3000 per year from Central Fund (in 1972 the school put in £800). As has been mentioned already, the Old Boys (QMC) has always paid the rates or Council Tax.

The pattern of the weekend visit has hardly changed. Leaving about 2 pm on Friday with the party having Friday afternoon off school; taking prefects; having the cooking and washing up rotas; running the activities according to the type of visit; clearing up at the end with departure after an early lunch on Sunday. The inability of boys to get to sleep on Friday night, and the somnolent minibus journey back on Sunday afternoon have been consistent features over the years! Table tennis has gone in and out of fashion, but many have been the games played in the dayroom in the past with saucepan lids for bats. As mentioned above, wide games on the headland have been a feature of many weekends, while boys enjoyed finding the bat caves among the rocks. Barmouth beach and the dry ski slope near Trawsfynydd have also been consistent recreational attractions. Menus for weekends have varied, some being ambitious and others decidedly not! Staff have cooked, boys on rotas have helped, and days have begun with porridge and a cooked breakfast on many weekends, while the Saturday evening meals over the years have included lasagne or spag bol, or even roast chicken and all the trimmings.

Farchynys Visits over the Years

Through the years there have been geography, geology and biology parties using the Farchynys area for their A level fieldwork. Over the years Brian Edwards, Stuart Holtam and Steve Law have led very many geography and geology weekends, while Ken Yates was the leading figure in devising biology field courses. These departments in the school have been the main academic ones to use Farchynys for examination work. For years their A level option papers were chosen with the natural opportunities of Farchynys fieldwork in mind.

There have been many serious walking weekends in Snowdonia and the Cambrian mountains. In the past, 5th year walking parties went up after their O levels or GCSEs. Stuart Holtam and Steve Law

have taken parties to climb the Welsh 3000 ft peaks over three days. The senior CCF walking expeditions have taken on some high routes with success.

The CCF has been a consistent user over the years, as is also described in Chapter 15. Every Easter an Adventurous Training party has spent 6 days based at Farchynys, sections walking and camping in the Rhinogs to the north, and in the hills south of the estuary. Wing Cdr John Dickson was a great Farchynys enthusiast, and he devised adventurous training schemes. He personally met the farmers every year when planning his scheme, a tradition which the author continued while he was commanding officer. Through these visits friendships developed with many local farmers in the Bontddu and Llanfachreth areas, especially the Jones family at Fridd-bryn-côch near Ganllwyd. Indeed the young Dickson family made adventure films of their holidays there. Other staff similarly enjoyed the centre in the summer holidays with their young families, having given up term-time weekends to take school parties. In recent years Steve Law, warden and CCF Army Section officer, has maintained the enthusiasm for adventurous training in the area. The CCF has also run regular weekends for the RAF section cadets involving orienteering and many other activities, and there has been an annual Signals training weekend at Farchynys since 1975.

One of the outstanding experiences for many boys was the Farchynys Run, and for a few years also there was the Cycle Ride. The run, initiated by Mr Michael Jackson when in charge of school cross-country in 1969, was a circuit from Farchynys to Barmouth Bridge along the north side and then back eastwards along the south side of the estuary and over Penmaenpool Bridge on the return leg. This run

Top
Getting ready to go: view down the drive with Farchynys Hall in the background

Lower
Teaching in the workroom

In the Rhinog Mountains

lasted for many years, and records were kept, and broken. The existing record for the Run is held by Nick Toone (1984) at 1 hour, 14 minutes, 18 seconds. The staff record is held by Philip Davies (PGKD), and is 1 hour 29 minutes, 36 seconds.

The Cycle Ride was conceived by Mr Steve Law and first ridden in 1983, and continued annually until 1994. With the advent of the off-road mountain bike and the decline of cycling among boys in the school, it became more difficult to attract sufficient numbers to tackle the 46-mile course. The course went west to Barmouth, north to Harlech and Maentwrog, the five-mile hill to Trawsfynydd, then south to Llanelltyd, and back to Farchynys. There were 147 riders in the 11 years, many riding more than once, and they tackled the course in all weathers but snow. The fastest time was 2 hours, 4 minutes, 4 seconds, by Daniel Gambles in 1991. 23 individual times below three hours were recorded. The staff record is held by Peter Green in 2 hours 17 minutes. Steve Law rode most often – 9 times! The record for a tandem is held by Chris Taylor and Geoff Hall in 2 hours 41 minutes. These two were on the inaugural ride. Another of the originals was Yossi Brain, an old boy and distinguished climber, who died sadly a few years ago in a climbing accident in the Andes.

In the seventies and eighties there were regular music weekends at Farchynys, each culminating with a concert in Barmouth, often in St David's Church. Some of these are detailed in the Music chapter, and they did provide a valuable link between Queen Mary's and the local community.

From the beginning, one major feature of the school calendar has been the First Year Weeks at Farchynys. Every year in May – July, six weeks out of Summer term are chosen to avoid Exams, Sports Day and the Wreathlaying, and in each of the weeks a party of 16 first-year boys (now Year 7) with two staff and two prefects go to Farchynys on a Monday morning and spend the week there, returning to school at lunchtime on Friday – ready for the weekend party to load up and depart at 2 o'clock. During the week a mixture of study and games, together with the experience of residential living away from home, has become a valuable part of the experience of the young Queen Mary's boy.

Other weekends – war-gaming, History Society, Year visits – have all allowed very many boys with varied interests to enjoy and benefit from this immensely successful initiative of the Darby headmastership of the early 1960s. There have been three Wardens since Farchynys opened: Phil Bull, Stuart Holtam, and Steve Law who took over as Warden in 1995. Each has been totally dedicated to the success of the Welsh Centre, and each has had a vision of the value of this amazing centre for outdoor study and enjoyment, which many schools established, but of these few were retained. The future of the Centre depends entirely on the willingness of school staff to give up weekends in the service of the school and its pupils

The Welsh Centre, showing the workroom, drawn by Adam Draper, A-level Art student 2002–04

7

THE BOARD OF GOVERNORS AND THE SURVIVAL OF THE GRAMMAR SCHOOL

As David Fink says in his Queen Mary's Grammar School, *'when the 1944 Act was passed QMS was a Direct Grant school (or schools), i.e. they received various grants direct from the Board of Education, and not through the local authority, though both county and borough paid for places in the schools for their scholars....QMS applied to continue as a Direct Grant school'. Ellen Wilkinson, the Minister of Education refused the Governors' request and refused to receive a deputation. The status finally adopted was 'Voluntary Aided', but the Grammar School still ranked as a public school because Mr Butler was a member of the Headmasters' Conference.*

Setting up a Voluntary Aided School

The government of the schools was agreed in three documents: an Instrument of Government and Articles of Government, both of 1948, and a Scheme agreed with the Charity Commissioners in 1951. The main effect was that the two LEAs, county and borough, paid for the internal workings of the schools, staff salaries, books and equipment, furniture and maintenance of the interior, while the Governors maintained the external structure, and, at that stage, paid 50% of the cost of new buildings.

By clause 11, the arrangements for admission were agreed between the Governors and the Local Authority, to take into account … the general type of education most suited to the particular child. 'An agreed number of places may be filled by the Governors from amongst candidates who, in the opinion of the governors, possess the requisite educational qualifications, and who make a special claim for admission to the schools by reason of their residence in the County Borough of Walsall, or on other grounds. Subject as aforesaid, the Local Education Authority shall determine which candidates are qualified for admission by reason of their having attained a sufficient educational standard.' From the beginning there were doubts about the efficacy of the intelligence tests used, which might fail to pick out the steady as opposed to the quick boy, or as David Fink said, quoting Ascham: 'the "hard" wits as opposed to the "quick" wits.'

Opposite
Queen Mary's Club Dinner Programme 1979, depicting SL Darby as St George using the 1944 Education Act, which set up selection, to kill the Comprehensive Dragon

GODFREY CADDICK OBE, TD, DL: CLERK TO THE GOVERNORS 1947–1974

Born in May 1912, son of a Walsall doctor, he was educated at Malvern College and Emmanuel College, Cambridge. He qualified as a solicitor in Walsall, and was a member of the TA before the war. In 1939 he was commissioned into the Royal Artillery, serving with the British Expeditionary Force in France. He led his unit back to Dunkirk, and to England. He served subsequently in Egypt and Iraq. In the war he transferred to the Staffordshire Regiment, becoming a full colonel, and then for a time Honorary Colonel of the Regiment. He served as Deputy Lieutenant of Staffordshire and the West Midlands.

In 1947 he became Clerk to the Governors. His service to the schools is detailed in Chapter 6. In his years as Clerk until 1974, he played a crucial part in working with the Headmaster, Sam Darby, and with David Jeffries, when he was Chairman, during the long and gruelling period when the survival of the schools as Grammar Schools was under threat. The battle was won.

At his funeral in the autumn of 2003, Mac White, long time colleague and friend at St Margaret's, Great Barr, recalled that Godfrey Caddick judged his service to QM to be the most satisfying of all the things with which he had been involved. In writing this book, he gave me the benefit of his memories with clarity and enthusiasm, and I enjoyed the warm hospitality of Kath, his wife, and Godfrey himself.

Adapted from tribute given by MF (Mac) White (1935 – 42)

Before the new Articles of Government was set up there were 14 governors appointed by Walsall and Staffordshire, and one by Birmingham University, and only three independent Foundation governors. There was still one Board of Governors for the Grammar School and the High School. The Voluntary Aided Instrument said that the foundation governors could appoint two-thirds of the governors of the schools. There were therefore to be 12 Foundation governors including a representative of the Queen Mary's Club and one from the Old Girls' Association, a representative from Birmingham University, and one from the Birmingham University Institute of Education. There were then six representative governors, four from Walsall, and two from the county.

In the 1950s Walsall provided about 60 of the places at the Grammar school each year, while the County could fill up to 30 places. The remaining places were offered to borderline candidates who came to the school to sit the Governors' Place examination. As fewer Staffordshire places were offered from 1956, about ten Governors' places were filled following examination. Then, as now, a full entry would be 96 boys. Many of the best boys academically came to Queen Mary's in the fifties, sixties and seventies as borderline Governors' Place entrants. Study of Governors' minutes clearly shows this with lists of the Governors' entrants.

Top
WH Cozens

Lower
Judge HA Tucker

It was new to have a separate independent Clerk to the Governors, which office had been held by Mr V John Moore, the Director of Education since 1936. Mr Godfrey A Caddick OBE, TD, DL was appointed the new Clerk to the Governors in 1947, and he remained Clerk until 1974. He died last year in 2003, but he clearly remembered how he was entrusted on appointment to enable the new Board of Governors of the Queen Mary's Voluntary Aided schools to establish a fresh and more independent relationship with the Local Education Authority.

WH Cozens, Chairman 1949 - 1955

The Chairman of Governors (since 1949) was W Henry Cozens. Godfrey Caddick remembered him as a delightful man, not interested in detail, but determined that all the changes of school government should go through smoothly. An Old Marian, he had been secretary of the Queen Mary's Club since 1897. A Governor since 1934, ill health forced his retirement in 1955, and he died in 1961.

Judge HA Tucker, Chairman 1955 - 1963

His Hon Judge Harold A Tucker, a foundation governor, became Chairman. Judge Tucker was an Old Boy, remembered as very straightforward, most interested in the schools and an excellent chairman. He had been at QM from 1900–05, and was called to the Bar in 1922. For many years he served as Chairman of the Staffordshire Quarter Sessions. An ardent cricketer with Walsall Cricket Club, he was also President of the Walsall Golf Club for many years. He died suddenly in 1963, and was succeeded as Chairman of Governors by Mrs Howard Keay.

Circular 10/65: Selection threatened

During these years the new buildings at Mayfield were going up, and this great development in the history of QM has been fully detailed in Chapter 5. The Governors had fully supported Mr Darby, Headmaster, in his drive to re-house the school on its new site. Scarcely had the dust settled on the last brick though, than the Department of Education and Science issued its Circular 10/65. This ushered in the Labour Government's determination to establish Comprehensive Secondary schools throughout England and Wales. The tripartite pattern of secondary schooling, established in the 1944 Act, was challenged, and schemes allowing Grammar Schools to select suitable pupils at 11+ were rejected. Local Authorities were required to submit plans to establish Comprehensive Schools, and this was to mark the end of all local authority 'maintained' Grammar Schools. It was less easy to deal with partially independent schools like Queen Mary's. In the last resort, if agreement could not be found, a local authority could 'cease to maintain' such schools, which therefore would have to capitulate or go fully independent.

In 1966 a major furore developed in Walsall as elsewhere. By the summer discussions were under way and by September the Governors 'were stunned' by proposals that were under consideration. A partial comprehensive scheme already existed in Walsall: the 1960 Scheme which kept the Queen Mary's Schools as Grammar Schools. The Chairman of Walsall Education Committee was Councillor Peter Musgrove and the proposal now was to close QM High School and to set up a combined six-form mixed comprehensive school in the new boys' buildings. Opposition in the council was led by Councillor Bert Smith, who was to be a strong ally of the Governors in the years to follow. In October 1966 the Governors issued an open letter to 'the citizens of Walsall' stating that the Queen Mary's Schools already were fitting into the developing pattern of comprehensive schools in the borough; that by its form of intake they were markedly comprehensive from a social point of view, and that there was real advantage in preserving two of the best schools in the land. It drew attention to the sentence in Circular 10/65 which stated that 'it is important that new schemes build on the foundations of present achievements and preserve what is best in existing schools.'

From 1967 onwards for nearly ten years, scheme after scheme was produced and the pressure to abandon selection was maintained. It was a serious battle. The nature of the Queen Mary's Schools was continually under threat. A 'Friends of Queen Mary's Liaison

F DAVID JEFFRIES FCA
CHAIRMAN OF GOVERNORS 1969–1978

Captain of cricket at QM in 1937, he scored 130 not out against Dudley Grammar School, and 100 plus against Wednesbury. He played Rugger for the 1st XV, and whilst in the Corps he commanded the Recruit Platoon of 70 boys in the post-Munich atmosphere of heightened tension. He left school after School Certificate as very many did, to become an articled clerk as the route to Chartered Accountancy. He was articled in January 1938 to TC Pepper of Herbert, Pepper and Rudland, where he worked, in Walsall,

all his professional life, being senior partner for many years.

In 1938 he joined the TA as a 2nd Lt in the 8th Bn The Royal Warwicks Regt but was subsequently transferred to the 9th Bn in the 61st Infantry Division on the doubling of the TA, which was embodied into the Regular Army in August 1939. For much of the war the Division was stationed in Northern Ireland as part of a very considerable force defending against a possible German invasion through the Irish republic which was neutral. A recent newspaper report in November 2003 refers to released MI5 documents linked to this IRA-Nazi plot, which remained a serious concern to the government throughout much of the war. David emerged from the war with the rank of major.

From 1946 he resumed his career in Walsall, passing his final accountancy exams in 1950. By that time he had played several seasons for the Walsall RFC 1st XV as a second row and a place kicker. He also played for Walsall Cricket Club's 1st and 2nd XI s. Since then he has been one of their vice presidents. In the Queen Mary's Club he became joint Hon Sec in 1946, and, under new rules, their first Chairman in 1956. He has been for very many years a Trustee of the Queen Mary's Old Boys' Scholarship Fund.

Appointed a governor in 1955, he became Chairman of the Property and Finance committee during the appeal before the start of the new buildings at Mayfield. He was appointed Chairman of Governors in 1969 when the future of selection for the school was of deep concern, due to the government's desire to stop selection for schools on academic grounds. The work of the governors at this time is fully detailed in Chapter 7. The Board was responsible for the High School and the Grammar School, and during David Jeffries' chairmanship the High School increased to 3-form entry on its expansion throughout all the Lichfield Street site when the boys moved out. He retired as Chairman in 1978, and as a governor in 1981. His time as chairman was the most difficult in recent times, and his service was most distinguished.

Since 1981 he has continued with his wide interests in rugby and cricket, in the Walsall Golf Club where he is a Vice President and former Captain, in the Walsall Society for the Blind where he is a Vice President and past Chairman and Hon. Treasurer, and in St Margaret's Church, Great Barr, where he has been both Treasurer and Church Warden. He is married with two daughters and four grandchildren.

JSA

Committee' with parents, Old Boys and friends, was set up. A Development committee was organised comprising some governors, the Headmaster, and the Headmistress of the High School, which worked out strategy, and also decided how best to deal with the constant enquiries made by the local press and others, and the intense interest in the town. For quite a period regular early Monday evening meetings were held at school. These were normally followed by informal gatherings at the 'Broadway' pub attended by the male members of the committee, which did a great deal to keep up morale at a time when the Foundation was under great duress. Mrs Richardson, the Headmistress, was always invited but she always graciously declined. After one of the school's most illustrious sons, the venue was dubbed the 'Lord Somer's Bar'.

One Foundation Governor from this period deserves mention for her longevity of service and devotion to the three Queen Mary's schools. Mrs Dawn Carter, a parent and Old Girl of QMHS and daughter of Hubert Plant an Old Boy of QM, became a Governor in 1969 during the chairmanship of Mrs Keay. She remained a Governor until 1993, when the Boards were split, and she continued as a High School Governor until 1998, and since then has stayed on the Governors Committee for Mayfield School. She is, in 2004, Vice-Chairman of the Mayfield Committee. Her enthusiasm for the schools is undiminished, and her contribution to Mayfield School remains valuable.

Selection defended

David Jeffries, Godfrey Caddick and Sam Darby were the central trio after David Jeffries became Chairman of Governors in 1969. Occasionally they met at Jack Aspinall's house. At one point they went to London to consult with Leon Brittan. David Jeffries remembers that special Foundation Governors meetings had to be held in the interest of confidentiality. It was a very stimulating and time-consuming business, but Headmaster Sam Darby had the political instincts and skills to keep the campaign on track, and avoid pitfalls. David Jeffries says that his political feel was brilliant. Bob Christie, architect and governor, remembers being co-opted for a period on to the Education Committee and this seems to have been invaluable for QM.

One of the schemes which reappeared in various forms during the ten-year period was to turn Queen Mary's into a Sixth Form College, or to create for it an enlarged sixth form. These schemes foundered on the deep and vocal objections from local Heads and supporters of the new 11 – 18 Comprehensive schools, who desperately wanted to keep and build up their own sixth forms. Another major problem facing the planners was that it was very difficult to adjust the catchment areas of new secondary schools to prevent Queen Mary's gaining the cream of the intake. At one point an idea was to carve out catchment areas for secondary schools in the borough with Leamore as the centre rather than The Bridge. There was real alarm when the catchment area was altered to the detriment, for example, of Joseph Leckie School which lost its intake from more affluent areas in the south of the borough where the secondary age children were then to be bussed to the new Barr Beacon School. Above all, it was necessary for the Education

Opening the Squash Courts with David Jeffries, Chairman of Governors, Jack Aspinall, governor, Gordon Foster, architect, and fifth from left, Richard Cooper, Director of Physical Education

Committee and the Queen Mary's Governors to consult on the way forward but their diametrically opposing views made agreement impossible.

As a result of the difficulties, schemes for Comprehensive education throughout the borough which left only the Queen Mary's schools with continuing selection, were proposed in 1968, and again in 1970. Pressure lessened during the Conservative administration of Edward Heath (1970–74), but with Labour strong on Walsall council the problem was never removed. In 1973 a proposal to turn the Queen Mary's schools into a Sixth Form College was again mooted, resulting from an invitation from the Education Committee to the governors for them to produce further proposals. Cllr Phil Wood was a staunch supporter of the school at this time. Then, with a Labour government again in power in 1975, proposals for the schools to become fully comprehensive with an enlarged sixth form were again the subject of detailed discussion. As a result of this scheme, Queen Mary's came closest to changing its character. This was the most dangerous time for the schools. In 1974, Godfrey Caddick retired as Clerk to the Governors. He had been appointed in 1947 and had advised the governors through years of development, over Voluntary Aided status, the new buildings, the acquisition of Farchynys and so on. He had been a tower of strength. He said that he found the work 'absolutely fascinating'. He worked with three Headmasters. His successor was Mr BGW (Barry) Rogers (QM 1945–56), referred to elsewhere for his considerable batting prowess while at school!

The Grammar School Saved

In an open letter in September 1975 the Governors stated that the continuance of Voluntary Aided status was the cornerstone of the proposals, 'whereby we retain control of the policy of the schools and assume responsibility for admissions subject to agreement with the local authority.' After consultation, the Lichfield Street buildings were to be replaced at the cost of relinquishing the single-sex character of the schools. The Governors went on to agree to the creation on the Mayfield site of one mixed Comprehensive school of 1300 pupils including an enlarged sixth form. The admissions would be controlled by an Allocation Board of the Head, a Governor, and an LEA representative. Out of 180 children each year, 120 would be from the southern half of the borough; there would be a social and ethnic mix; preference would be given to those whose parents undertook to support them fully to the age of 18, with priority for those with connections with the school, and priority also for those who could make a special contribution to the school other than on grounds of academic ability. Subsequently, in 1976, Mr Sam Darby was designated Head of the new school, and in consultation with the High School he interviewed all staff from both schools who applied for senior posts and Head of Department posts. Detailed plans were drawn up for new buildings to incorporate the requirements of the enlarged school. Within the schools grew an acceptance that change was inevitable.

Then came news which was almost unbelievable! Mrs Shirley Williams, Secretary of State for Education and Science, rejected this Scheme (known as Scheme M). It did not take fully into account the overall requirements of the County Borough as a whole. She required that flaws in the scheme be remedied. By then it was 1977, and no building works had gone to tender, awaiting this government reply. The local authority had no further plans, and within eighteen months and after the Winter of Discontent, the Labour Government was out, and the Thatcher era began. The Queen Mary's Grammar School and the Queen Mary's High School were saved as selective Voluntary Aided schools, and this they remain to this day.

Jack Aspinall, Chairman 1978–1984

In 1978 Mr Jack Aspinall, Old Marian and Managing Director of Walsall Lithographic Company, took over the Chairmanship of the Governing Body from David Jeffries who had had a very difficult eight years in that office, giving tremendous support to Mr Darby in the defence of the school. Mr Darby retired in 1979. His achievements are listed elsewhere in creating the new school buildings at Mayfield, setting up Farchynys, overseeing the enlargement and modernising of the sixth

Sam Darby with Jack Aspinall

form, but above all he is to be remembered for his tenacious and highly skilful defence of the academic character of the Queen Mary's schools.

When Keith Howard arrived to take over the reins of Headmastership, the clouds had just lifted, and he was able to move ahead in a new political climate. However as Voluntary Aided selective grammar schools the Queen Mary's schools still faced an uncertain future if the Labour party was to return to power. In Walsall, where the local council could be unsympathetic, the climate remained difficult, and political decisions were often made which favoured some schools rather than others. (It should be said that local authority officers were always models of courtesy, fairness and helpfulness.) Finance was extremely tight. No capital funding for voluntary aided selective schools was available, and funding for pure maintenance was minimal. This is reflected in the section on The Eighties in Chapter 5. Finding new staff was never easy. Young teachers felt that the future lay in the Comprehensive world and that applying to a selective school might not be best for their careers.

WG (Bill) Stephens, Chairman 1984–1997

A change in the composition of the Board of Governors took place in 1985 with the delayed implementation of a section of the Education Act 1980 by which staff and parent governors were elected for the first time. Mr Bill Stephens (QM 1939–49) was Chairman for thirteen most significant years, during which schools began to feel the awakening of a new, more interventionist political climate. Bill's easy charm belies his ability to appreciate problems and give enormous help in providing solutions. Bill Stephens was chairman through major changes to the Board of Governors. He remembers in his early days as chairman that

Bill Stephens, Chairman of Governors, with Keith Howard in 1995 at the latter's retirement

meetings were still at 2pm and stopped for tea and sandwiches at half past three. They were gentle occasions.

After some years of harsh finances but political stability, there came in 1993 a change in the government of the schools which was to be of lasting importance. After some years of increased 'Local Management of Schools', by which funds for the running of the school were passed to the school, while the LEA retained a proportion (latterly about 15%) for centrally provided services, it was increasingly clear that Walsall's funding for secondary schools was poor compared with other authorities, particularly their formula for sixth forms.

Grant Maintained Status 1993

By 1992 the Governors had decided, along with governors of most voluntary aided schools, to ballot parents with the proposal that the schools apply for a new pattern of devolved school government called 'Grant Maintained Status'. By this scheme GM schools were funded from the Department for Education and Science rather than the LEA, they took over control of almost all the functions traditionally performed by the LEA, and could contract out to private suppliers major areas of activity: cleaning, payroll arrangements, school meals, grounds maintenance and so on. For this they received the final 15% funding which under Local Management of Schools had been retained by the LEA. The LEA would remain responsible for certain specialist activities, including school transport.

In December 1992, Mr Stephens, as Chairman of Governors, wrote at length to all parents explaining the proposals. The new arrangements had financial and constitutional advantages for the schools. Each school would have its own Board of Governors and there would be teacher governors and elected parent governors on each Board, instead of the LEA appointees. The Electoral Reform Society conducted the ballot and 61% of those voting approved the proposal. The Secretary of State approved the change of status, and the schools became Grant Maintained from 1st September 1993.

Since 1990 the school has been responsible for arranging its own admissions. A major concern for the Governors had been the refusal of the LEA to play its part in the admissions procedures, so that the schools had resorted to taking applications direct from parents. Along with the High School, it set up its own admissions testing. Open Evenings in the Autumn attracted large attendances, and following application, between 500 and 700 candidates have come to the school each year for the 11+ testing, as a result of which the school offers 96 places. Many candidates apply to other schools as well, so that many who are offered places decline them, so that boys further down the list receive offers until the places are filled. An independent Appeals Committee is responsible for ensuring that difficult cases arising from this procedure are fairly and fully considered. Candidates are not restricted to the Walsall Metropolitan Borough, and increasingly they come from the surrounding areas.

Queen Mary's Grammar School Governors 1995

Back row L to R: Andrew Phillips, John Anderson, Stuart Holtam, Dr Alan Cunnington, Ken Jeffrey

Middle Row L to R: John Punch, Tom Perrett, Roger Metcalfe, Barry Sanders, Paul Nowell, David Large, Roy Meller, Chris Shaw, Barry Sims

Front Row L to R: Brian Edwards, Joan Archer, Bill Stephens (Chairman), Elsbeth and Keith Howard, Jeff Tromans (Vice Chairman), Michael Goold, Gill Columbine (School Administrator), Barry Rogers (Clerk).

This pattern is being reformed as the government introduces a centralised allocation system for secondary places in each local authority area, a reform which began in 2003/4.

The separate Governing Bodies for the Grammar School and the High School were set up in 1993, with their parent and teacher governors. This meant that the Foundation governors were divided between the two Boards with a few serving on both. The Foundation Trustees met separately. Anomalies were made more apparent by this, and this matter will be dealt with later. Since 1993, the LEA has been contracted in to supply cleaning and the operation of the payroll, while private contractors supply grounds maintenance, and school meals.

In the summer of 1995, the schools were shaken by the sudden death of BGW (Barry) Rogers, Clerk to the governors since 1974. He had advised the governors through the latter stages of the attempt to impose comprehensive education, and had been a tower of strength to two Headmasters.

His funeral filled St Matthew's Church, a measure of the regard in which he was held in Walsall. In his tribute, Keith Howard said that Barry was a man of cast iron integrity, loyalty and probity, getting on with all sorts, seeking and finding good in other people. Angry sometimes on matters of principle, he never bore malice, but showed kindness and good humour. He loved cricket (he had been a superb attacking batsman at school – see Chapter 13), golf (handicap 17), music and his garden. Serving the schools, he was outstanding in his store of knowledge, his expertise and his wisdom. After school and Birmingham University, he was articled and served with Loxtons, solicitors, in Bridge Street. Barry Rogers' death at the early age of 58 was a great loss to his family and to the school community.

He was succeeded at short notice by Mr Ian S Smith, (QM 1964–71), who speedily grew into the job most effectively The schools had to develop their financial expertise, and appoint Administrators (mini-bursars) who had to undertake considerable training for their task. Mrs Gill Columbine has served as Grammar School Administrator since 1993. She has served both as Headmaster's Secretary and School Administrator. In these roles she has displayed enormous loyalty for and love of the school. All the school finances being the sole responsibility of the Governors, active Finance and Property Committees were required. The advice over recent years of Foundation Governors Paul Nowell and Terry Luckin over finance, and John Punch on property, has been invaluable. A Foundation Governor for many years, Michael J Goold (QM 1939–45) has given the most valuable service to the Queen Mary's Schools, as a result of his financial experience and acumen.

Jeffrey AF Tromans, Chairman 1997–2000

Mr Bill Stephens handed over as Chairman to Mr Jeff Tromans in 1997. Mr Tromans had been a parent and governor for many years. His service had been notable with long service in the QMA, and latterly he had been Vice-Chairman of Governors. His particular strength had been his cautious financial approach which fitted so well in the difficult times of the early nineties. Sadly his illness led to his early retirement as chairman in 1999, and he died early in 2003.

JAF Tromans

GM funding was not generous and the Grammar School fought to reduce an outstanding deficit for the first years which led to a reduction in staffing from 41 back to its traditional 38. However, the amount available for capital work and maintenance on the buildings became significant, in the nick of time, as the 1960s buildings began to show serious weaknesses! Laboratories were refurbished, window frames replaced, and much needed minor maintenance was carried out.

When Mr Stuart Holtam became Headmaster in 1995, he established the Development Campaign, and as a result, with parental funding, the Sixth Form Common Room was converted into the school's first modern computer room. All the detail of these developments may be read in Chapter 10.

Reversion to Voluntary Aided Status

The pattern of school government was changed by the Labour Government of 1997 which abolished the GM system, and the school reverted to Voluntary Aided status in 1998. However, in practice the clock was not put back. The funding came via the LEA again, but as much came to the schools as under the GM system. The Governors retained all the responsibilities which they had acquired in 1993. The constitution of each Board of Governors was changed again to reduce the number of parents, to include a non-teaching staff governor as well as teacher governors, and to include two LEA governors. As the scheme settled down it became necessary to review, with the Charity Commissioners, the government of the Foundation. The Foundation Governors of the Grammar School (those not in the employ of the Foundation), had become, after 1993, by default, the Trustees of the Foundation. This clearly was indefensible in the light of the existence of Foundation Governors of the High School who were therefore not eligible to become Trustees. A new scheme was devised to operate from 2004.

Judge PJ Stretton

Judge Peter J Stretton, Chairman since 2000

His Honour Judge Peter Stretton took over as Chairman of the Trustees, and of the Grammar School Board of Governors, in 2000. As Chairman he shows a gentle, careful and incisive touch. In 2003 the Clerk to the Foundation, Ian Smith, resigned when he moved to take up a new position as HM Coroner for Stoke on Trent and North Staffordshire. His interest, legal skills and enthusiasm had been invaluable over the years, and during his time the proliferation of governors' committees had extended the work considerably. He was succeeded as Clerk to the Foundation in September 2003 by Mr Charles Underwood, who has shown remarkable understanding of and support for the schools since his arrival.

It is ironic that by 2004 the Grammar School was more independent financially than it had been since 1944. It also has been the recipient of capital grants of a kind that could not have been considered possible until recently. The school has had to raise its own funds also, and a major Development Appeal was launched in 1996. Many grants now come on the basis of match funding, and the school can only benefit as it able to add its own funds to those grants made available. This has enabled the Language College extension to be built and the Sports Hall planned, as well as major redevelopment of classroom areas within the school, above the Library and in the D room corridor. Detail of all these developments may be found in Chapter 10. At the same time the ability of the school to control its curriculum and the substance and method of its teaching has been almost completely removed. Such a major shift of control could not have been foreseen fifty years ago. The school does retain its right to set its entrance test and to determine which candidates shall enter the school.

A Free Grammar School

Despite increases in government control over education, the governors of the Queen Mary's Schools, once again Voluntary Aided Schools, retain their independence over all policy, appointments and the maintenance and development of the buildings and lands of the schools, according to the Instrument of Government of each school.

Personal seal of Queen Mary I, used as school badge prior to 1907, when EN Marshall introduced the first 'rose and arrows' badge encircled with the motto 'Veritas Temporis Filia'.

8

SCHOOL LIFE

A day at Queen Mary's

School starts at 9.00 am. It has for many a year, despite an attempt by Keith Howard to get us up a little earlier! The school day did not vary greatly between 1965 and 2004, except that in the final few years boys have had to know which week it is – week 1 or week 2 – of the timetable. Boys now get to school earlier on the whole because so many are dropped off by parents on their way to work, or by early school buses. Hardly anyone cycles in. As discussed in Chapter 1, the school now serves a wide region and not the local town, so that very many boys now come by car.

The Head and Second Master meet the gowned Duty Member of staff, the Captain of School (and, now, the Vice-Captain of School for the week) and the Duty Prefects at 8.40 am outside the Head's study. The previous day's report is read out and points made about the new day. It is an unchanging routine. It may go back to Hamilton or be a Darby introduction, but it goes back a long way.

Registration is at 9.00 in form rooms, except on Wednesday when some Year assemblies are at 9, with form registration afterwards. Assemblies have their mention later, but the formality with boys rising in silence for the entry of the gowned Headmaster is a discipline marker and focus at the start of the day.

Boys still rush or dawdle from room to room between periods, sometimes going straight into a room, sometimes having to queue outside. Whether classes stand for the entry of their teacher depends on the decade. Some lesson breaks are marked by the sounding of an automatic electric bell, as is the end of break and lunch, when three bells sound as always was to tell everyone to leave the field for registration.

The field is in bounds in the summer, but out of bounds in wet months. This as always puts pressure on rooms in the winter, but the school has always had an open door policy for form rooms where so many schools lock pupils out of them. The Handbell (which came up from Lichfield Street) is still rung to bring boys in from the field at the end of the lunch hour.

At lunch time many eat sandwiches in the Dining Area or Hall, but there is continuing demand for school lunches. The content of

Top
Caretaker Peter Buckley opens up the school at 7.30 am

Centre right
The 8.40 am daily briefing with Mr Michael Lax, member of staff on Duty (gowned), The Duty Prefects for the day, Steven Smith, Captain of School, Headmaster and Second Master who reads the previous day's duty report.

Centre left
Assembly in the 1960s

Lower
School Assembly at 9.15 am. Address by Mr Tim Lawrence, with Mr Roger Metcalfe Senior Master and Mr Tim Swain Second Master, Headmaster, and Mr Bev Wragg at the piano.

'SOME LIKE IT HOT'
MRS JENNIE LOVATT – DINNER LADY

Jennie Lovatt retired in July 1993. She represents the kind and devoted ladies who have served staff and boys with their school meals over the years. QM, like many schools, is very fortunate in the quality of those who work in the school kitchens

When Mrs Jennie Lovatt started working at QM in 1968, veg were veg. They didn't come pre-washed or pre-cooked in polythene bags; they arrived at the kitchen door in sacks and crates: fresh. There were 10 sacks of taters every day. 'First we set George on 'em. Then we had to eye 'em. George was the peeler. Then there was the cabbage to wash and strip. Mind there were twelve of us on the staff then.' For Jennie it was a part-time job: thirteen hours a week, and she did washing-up.

In those days Fusties used to be responsible for collecting up the plates, scraping any waste into the huge slop bowls, and wheeling the trolleys to the kitchens. 'Poor mites. I used to worry about them getting their uniforms dirty.' Typical of Jennie. Up to her elbows in suds and scalding water, and she'd be concerned about the Fusties wheeling in more plates. The Supervisor, Mrs Frances Watkins, who grew the most wonderful dahlias for shows, persuaded Jennie to go full time in 1972. The early system of serving the same dinner to groups of eight sitting round octagonal tables with grace before each sitting, had given way to cafeteria service, for 600 each day.

Towards the end of her time, the number of hours were cut, and menus using ready-to-serve food were imposed. 'There was a lot of nonsense,' she said. 'We'd always made our own pizzas, and then we got the new plastic ones.' They expected big lads to be satisfied with a spoonful of yoghurt and a minute cookie: 'you can make a lot more jam sponge for the same price.' Jennie always had time for a laugh, particularly when they had goggles to wear when opening the ovens, or when the cabbage fell off on to her hair-do.

She had favourites on the staff. Mr Davison always went to Jennie's queue. 'I'd call him Mr Dollop, because he'd always have an extra dollop of mash'. But top of the list was Ken Dodd, alias Mr Brudenell. 'Such a kind man,' she said. Of course Jennie was kind. She got to know the boys, including the fussy ones. She was never shy of work. As the saying goes, if you can't stand the heat, stay out of the kitchen.

From an interview in The Marian, *1993*

these has changed over the years as the reprint from the Marian of 1993 shows. Once there were two sittings with grace said before each. For 30 years there has been cafeteria service with a menu which has changed with the times. Once it was meat and two veg with sponge pudding, now there are more pizzas than pies, and chips rather than boiled cabbage. There is now much more variety and an emphasis on the healthy content of food has returned.

After school there is a detention, for a few! Those put in detention serve their punishment, but now after two days' notice to parents, where previously boys had to inform their parents themselves, and serve detention the next day. The detention run by the member of staff on Duty is still for 45 minutes. A detention in 2004 would be recognised by its conduct and atmosphere by any who were detained in 1954. For others who choose to stay in school, societies meet as they have always done.

When the school moved to the Mayfield site, the teaching lessons were of approximately 40 minutes, and there were 8 lessons per day in a 5-day week. There had been no Saturday morning school at QM since the Second World War. Wednesday afternoon was senior games for the 5th and 6th form, and that fitted the common practice for inter-school sport, as it does to this day. The pattern of the day was and is to have registration and school assembly first, with period 1 beginning at 9.30. Lunch is an hour, and school ends at 4 p.m. Until 1968 the Scouts/CCF option took the last two lessons of Friday afternoon, but then these activities moved out of the timetable and began at 4 pm. Each year had a 'games afternoon' with team games on the field for the last two periods from 2.40 pm. onwards. Though lesson times have changed, this pattern remains, in a two-week timetable.

Outside the Masters' Common Room and the Detention Room at Lichfield Street (scraper board, 1964, by DJ Cockayne)

Detention then and now

Mrs Chris Ward

Private study in the library

Crossing the main quadrangle

The School Library

The school Library was completed in proud style to complement the Hall on the opposite side of the Quadrangle. It was furnished with extra funding from the Queen Mary's Club and it is blessed with fine views of the playing fields to the line of poplars and Barr Beacon beyond. Elsewhere, in Chapter 10, is discussed the problem of the gallery 'carrels', designed for private study, but taking insufficient account of the temperament of the adolescent sixth-former. The Librarian in 1965 was Mr James Jones, and when he retired in 1982, Mr Jim Walker took on the task. The assistants in the Library in the early 1980s were Mrs J Bucknall, and Mr Robert Roe. Though disabled, Robert Roe identified himself with the school and the library, checking books in and out, and helping pupils in the library. He was very knowledgeable, and when he had to retire he was much missed. There had been a fine collection of books, but the annual grant for the Library (even when money from the Scholarship Fund was added) meant that, with inflation, fewer books could be bought than necessary to maintain the quality of the stock. Boys took books and failed to return them, by design or through forgetfulness. It was a depressing struggle.

Two developments helped: the card catalogue was computerised, with much help in the early stages from a parent, Mrs Bloomer, and electronic anti-theft posts were set up by the door. The reduced time available for the Librarian to spend in the Library was compensated for by increasing the hours allocated to Mrs Chris Ward, the Assistant Librarian. There was comment in the Ofsted inspections of the 1990s that the Library should take more account of the younger years in the school, and Mr Robert Champ who succeeded Jim Walker carried out much modernisation in recent years, with the assistance of Mrs Ward. Private Study has been more or less supervised in the Library over the years. It remains a valuable and attractive asset.

Pastoral Care

Pastoral care has become more formalised, and has increased over this fifty year period, and in recent years the school has put in place, at government behest, wide-ranging policies on equal opportunity and bullying for instance, which has made this pastoral work ever more vital. As mentioned elsewhere, Sam Darby abandoned the house system when he became Headmaster, and a horizontal Year pastoral system substituted. After the sale of the junior school house in 1960, the name 'Moss Close' has been perpetuated in the title given to the Lower school, the first two years, now known as Years 7 and 8. Thus there were to be Yearmasters (now Year Tutors) for Moss Close (sometimes for each of the two years, sometimes combining the two years), for the Middle School years, and then a Head of Sixth Form, with arrangements for

Staff Common Room

the sixth form varying through the years. Usually Year Tutors took their Year group through from the 2nd or 3rd year (now Years 8 or 9) through to the end of the 5th Year (now Year 11). This continuity meant that one Year Tutor could be experienced with the induction of new boys into the school (initially Eric Boothroyd, then Phil Bull, and more recently others, including David Hart, Philip Blackshaw, and now Mrs Debbie

Wood), while those who take a Year over in the 3rd year (Year 9), really come to know them over a 3- or 4-year period. In the sixth form, one or more staff can gain experience with the care of sixth-formers and their university entrance advice. From the beginning 'Yearmaster periods' were set aside for pastoral interviews. Brian Archer, Gordon Brudenell, John Dickson, Geoffrey Paxton (for many years Senior Yearmaster), Tim Lawrence, Ian Davison, Dick Cooper, Bob Fletcher – all provided continuous care for generations of QM boys, who look back, years later, to the master who was *their* Yearmaster or Year Tutor. The Year Tutor builds up expertise in solving schoolboy crime, sometimes involving lengthy and difficult investigation. They also make links with the homes of difficult boys, and they were and are fundamental in providing for the welfare of all Queen Mary's pupils.

School Reports and Parents

Over the years there has been resistance to major change. Generally speaking reports have been sent to parents at Christmas and in July (now only in the summer), and there used to be 'selective' reports at Easter for those giving cause for concern. Despite there being pre-prepared computerised comments available, the opportunity to write personal comments has been preferred. Though many schools use report books, and QM has used them in the sixth form, there is a general preference for single sheets so that the comments of one term do not influence the teacher when writing for the next term. Over the years, phrases like 'satisfactory' have been forbidden, and the use of complete sentences with reference to past work, and what is needed to improve, has for long been laid down.

Despite the simplicity of the above outline, many have been the staff sub-committees set up during the fifty years to try to improve the system of marks and reporting. Much time has been spent working out letters for 'progress' and 'effort'. When a letter code is set up there is a tendency to go for the middle letter of number, and much thought has gone into trying to ensure that the full span of letters is used.

Parents' evenings have been held regularly since the arrival of Mr Darby in 1956. Since the move to Mayfield, individual master's desks have been set up round the school hall and parents of a whole year group have been invited from 6.30 p.m. onwards once a year. Now Parents' Evenings begin at 4.30 p.m. Five-minute appointments are made beforehand, boys and their teachers working out a timetable for each class. Parents move around the hall speaking with their son's teachers, and with the Year Tutor if this is arranged. The Head is always available in his study, while parents from the QMA Catering Committee make, and prefects serve, cups of tea to staff and parents. In the interval the Year Tutor makes suitable comments about the problems of the year group, and the co-operation which the school expects from parents if boys are to make most progress. In recent years this process has been adapted for the sixth form, where previously it did not apply. Now pupils of Year 10 and above are encouraged to attend their appropriate consultation evenings with their parents.

It must be added that each of the Headmasters of the last 50 years has been anxious to meet parents who have problems, and parents have always been encouraged to make an appointment and come into school at any time, if they have particular concerns.

Prefects

Prefects 1963;
Back row: D Longmore, DCM Cole, DG Dack, DE Evans, C Swann, GH Evans, CM Fenton, G Lightwood, DJ Cockayne, PV Weir

Middle row; DF Hughes, DH Griffiths, VG Roper, -?-, D Stone, J Taylor, RH Chivers, JW Rodgers, CJ Lloyd, NT Webb

Front row; MR Wootton, AG Warburton, RT Porter, PC Wiggin, CE Nicholls, SL Darby (Head), SN Neville, EJ Parkes, DRN Lane, DJ Morriss, CS Holland

The Senior Prefects 2004.

Standing: Christopher Dudley, Thaddeus Clifton, Gursukhvir Sohal, Alexander Bartlett, Edward Bray, Christopher Devey, Matthew Whitehouse, Ben Johnston, Adam Draper, James Mercy

Seated: Simon Neachell, Iain Green, James Cox, Geraint Davies, Tom Livingstone, Owen Ingram, Jasper Daniel, Steven Smith (Captain of School), Thomas Ashley, Laurence Griffiths, Neeruj Patel, Hana Preese, Keith Leddington, Jinesh Patel, Ravi Pachchigar

Throughout this half century there has been a body of prefects appointed to assist in the supervision of younger pupils and in the day to day running of the school. Fifty years ago the Senior Prefects, or Prefects, wore the same silver badge as their counterparts do today. They are led by a Captain of School, and one or two Vice-Captains of School. The Captain of School presides at School Assembly, and represents the school. His many duties remain the same as they have been throughout the fifty years: he gives the Vote of Thanks at Speech Day; he lays the Wreath along with the youngest boy in the Abbey; he speaks at the Queen Mary's Club Annual Dinner. Senior Prefects are appointed to assist Year Tutors as Year Prefects, and others become Hall Prefects to assist with assembly, Computer Room Prefects, Librarians, and Prefects with other administrative duties. The Senior Prefects used to be assisted by a select band of bronze-badged Prefects previously called Monitors, but for many years now the whole of the Upper Sixth becomes the bronze-badged Prefect body, with its daily rota of duties around the school, including the duty of assisting the Member of Staff on duty at various points during Break and in the Lunch Hour. The school has always firmly believed in the broad educational value of the lead given by senior boys (and girls) to younger boys in an 11 – 18 school. The benefits for all cannot only be seen in the use of prefects, but in the leadership of older pupils given in Games, the CCF and all other extra curricular activities. An 11 – 16 school can never provide that form of leadership education for young adults.

Writing in *The Marian* in 1989, David Swinnerton, Captain of School admitted his pride and apprehension when asked to accept the job. Then there was a Captain of School's Book which was, he says, not very helpful. Many of the tasks are tedious, like arriving at school at 8.30 to find that either the Moss Close or Duty Prefect has not arrived, 'which means ten minutes desperately trying to persuade someone to replace the missing prefects, at least temporarily'. The Captain of School (or a delegated prefect) attends the Fête, Fireworks and Farchynys Committees, representing boys in the school. This is interesting and very valuable. He is invited to the QMHS Speech Day. He has to make a speech at the Old Boys' Dinner, acknowledging the debt of boys to the school and the QMC, proposing the toast to the Club. Then there is Speech Day with its final Captain of School Vote of Thanks. How nervous beforehand, and how relieved afterwards! The job produces feelings of pride and excitement which remain throughout the year.

Uniform

As can be imagined, the school has been conservative in its approach to the detail of academic and pastoral life. School uniform has always been strictly enforced, and although caps completely disappeared only in the mid seventies, the blazer, grey flannels, white shirt and tie have remained standard through the 50 years of this survey. The first slackening of the cap rule occurred in 1958. There is a story told by

The 5th year boy in uniform!

Ian Crossland who had arrived in the sixth form from a northern grammar school, that he refused to wear his cap except on the very back of his head. Admonished several times by SLD, he was told one afternoon while walking in Lichfield Street, and stopped by the Headmaster who was driving his car, either to wear it properly, or put it in his pocket. The following morning, the story goes, the Headmaster announced that boys in the upper 6th need not now wear caps! Certainly on 6th May 1958, this dispensation was reported to the governors.

Since then changes have been few and standards have been high. Shorts for Fusties went out in the late sixties when all young boys went into longs. Trousers have changed leg width, sometimes narrow, sometimes wide. Woe betide the boy who has his shirt-tail hanging out, or his top shirt-button undone. Outer jackets have to be navy blue, single colour. Much effort, through changing fashions, has been devoted to preventing outbreaks of outlandish hair-styles. Girls have adopted a smart, appropriate and similar pattern of uniform.

Entering at 11, Leaving at 18

How do boys (pupils) arrive, settle down, move through the school and leave? For most of the fifty years the pattern has been that new boys are invited with their parents for an interview with the Headmaster in the June before they start. There are not many schools that take this care over an initial meeting with the boy and his family. The school sells uniform and sports equipment to new boys during the interview period. This 'uniform shop' is run by Mrs Gill Columbine, the school administrator, with a team of mothers. The shop operates in June, and then once a month through the year. It is a most valuable service to the school.

Then an afternoon is set aside in July for new boys to come into school and meet their Year and Form tutors, and prefects, and to be shown their classrooms, and the layout of the school. In school assembly Moss Close boys sit in the gallery. The Year Tutor of Year 7 usually keeps that job for several years in order to become expert in the induction of new boys. This is a skill. New boys are not the little innocents once imagined. Clear discipline has to be established, along with a patient and caring attitude amongst staff dealing with Year 7 boys. This is not easy, but, well done, it can help enormously to enable the 96 boys to start their QM careers on the right note.

No longer is it expected that the previous year's 6^2 prizewinners will travel from university to attend on Speech Day. At the end of their school career, pupils leave after their A levels, and return in the December,

after their first term at university, to receive their A level certificates and, if appropriate, a prize. Staff and Governors are present. Their parents are invited and are thanked by the Headmaster and Chairman of Governors for all their support for the school over the seven years while they have been school parents. This occasion, known as the Leavers' Ceremony, then becomes a Buffet Supper evening, when all swap tales of university with each other and with staff, and that particular cohort of pupils is finally sent off with the school's good wishes. This most successful annual event was introduced by Keith Howard.

School Assemblies

School assemblies, since the move to Mayfield, have been whole-school assemblies on Mondays, Tuesdays, Thursdays and Fridays, with Year assemblies on Wednesdays. The school assemblies have followed a pattern which has survived remarkably. On Monday the Headmaster takes the assembly. On the other three days a member of staff or a pupil or pupils carry through a three-day pattern with a wide subject range: religious, musical or philosophical. There is a hymn sung by the school on two days, and prayers each day. The underlying Christian emphasis has been maintained despite the increased number of pupils of other faiths. After a break, the singing of hymns was re-introduced by Keith Howard. Later, Geoffrey Paxton devised a small school hymnbook about 1990. The formality of standing for the Headmaster's entry is respected, and QM assemblies are a 'wonderful start to the day' and the quality of assemblies remains very high. 'Quirky excellence' is how Mrs Janet Martin describes it in her note in this book! A considerable number of staff are involved, along with senior pupils and others, in the course of a year. The quality of whole school daily assemblies is one of the outstanding features of Queen Mary's today. Over the years they have

Upper
Early assembly from gallery, with SLD, DPJF and prefects on stage

Lower
Boys coming off the field after a practice fire drill

impressed visitors. They impress new staff. They remain in the minds of many boys long after they leave school, when they recall Michael Jackson's references to Wolves, Tony Wiggin's black sacks, Tim Swain's cooking on stage, and much else.

Geoffrey Paxton, writing in 1988, said that, for a few minutes each morning there is a chance to learn what old so-and-so actually thinks, or what young so-and-so has to tell the rest of us from his faith or from his heart. These are, he said, often the exciting voice of a school community at thought, as well as at prayer. 'I've always enjoyed our school assemblies.'

Short mention must be made of the whole school assemblies held in St Paul's Church during the split site period while the school moved to Mayfield in 1961–65. Every other Wednesday the whole school gathered in St Paul's Church in Darwall Street, the old school chapel, at 9.00 am with an eye to the 9.37 bus up to Mayfield! Speakers were invited to address the school for five minutes on a theme, and musicians under Graham Rock and Stanley Hewitt formed a Chapel Choir. The Headmaster, SL Darby, found that this did seem to work to unify the split-site school at this time.

THE MARIAN

1998

Speech Day

Queen Mary's Speech Days have retained a pattern and atmosphere throughout the 50 years. In the early years the day was officially called Commemoration, but informally, and soon formally, it became Speech Day. The pattern has been, throughout the period, for there to be an 11.30 am service at either St Paul's or St Matthew's (now at St Matthew's since the refurbishment at St Paul's). Then the school reassembles in the Town Hall for the Presentation of Prizes at 7.30 pm. All day the Senior Prefects wear white carnations, while the Bronze Prefects wear red carnations. In the morning, the format of the service and the prayers of thanksgiving for the school's founders and benefactors has not altered at all. A visiting preacher is invited.

In the evening the Governors are arrayed on the stage; the national anthem is played; the Headmaster speaks (his formal full report being now printed in the Speech Day programme); the Chairman of

Walsall Town Hall,
Speech Day 2003

Speech day 2003. Mr Paul
Walton (QM 1967–74)
presenting the prizes. Second
from Right, Rev Jonathan Ball
(QM 1974–81) who gave the
morning address in St Matthew's
Church.

Governors comments; prizes are presented; the guest presenter of prizes speaks; the Captain of School expresses the thanks of one and all, and the whole company sings the School Song. Guests, parents and the school fill the Hall. The Mayor and Mayoress of Walsall attend. No longer may the speaker grant a half-day holiday, but it is a traditional ceremony, conducted with style, recording individual and school achievements, which now takes place on the Thursday before October Half Term each year.

Wreathlaying

A major tradition of Queen Mary's since 1954 has been the annual Wreathlaying. In 1964 at the suggestion of Mr Darby, Dr Gerald R Shutt JP, Deputy Chief Steward of Westminster Abbey, retired Headmaster of Westminster City Grammar School, and chairman of the London Branch of the QM Club (QM 1912–21), obtained the consent of the Dean to a party from the school laying a wreath on the tomb of Queen Mary Tudor in connection with the opening of the school buildings in 1965. The Dean then suggested that the school might like to hold a short ceremony that year (in 1964) at which he

himself would read the prayers. The Captain of School and a boy from the first form, the Chairman of Queen Mary's Club, Mr Aspinall (Governor), and the Headmaster would go up to London on July 2nd. A luncheon would be held by the London Branch of the QM Club at the Rubens Hotel, Victoria. Thus the tradition began.

The ceremony was held again in 1965 as planned. Then the party was enlarged and the whole first form attended, together with others from the QMC in Walsall. The ceremony has been held every year since. In recent years the Wreathlaying has been held on the Friday nearest to July 2nd. The coaches of First Year boys (now Year 7) with staff and prefects have added a visit to a London attraction

Wreathlaying in Westminster Abbey 1971. Carrying the wreath: WR Holmes, Captain of School, and 1st year boy, DR Howarth

David Preece and Thomas Hucklebridge-Key lay the wreath at the tomb of Queen Mary and Queen Elizabeth

in the afternoon after the ceremony, sometimes a visit to the Tower, a trip on the river, a visit to the London Eye or whatever seems appropriate. The QMC lunch, attended by London and Walsall Old Marians, was for many years held at the Abbey restaurant, and is now held at the Restaurant Sorriso off Victoria Street. The service at Queen Mary's tomb, which she shares with her sister in the Queen Elizabeth Chapel, is a fitting annual tribute to our Founders, George and Nicholas Hawe, and to Queen Mary, our royal benefactor. Gerald Shutt with Leonard (now Sir Leonard) Peach and then the late Col. Jim Hayward made the arrangements for many years. The London arrangements are now made by Mr Jonathan Turton (QM 1971–78). The school is indebted to the Dean of Westminster Abbey for enabling the tradition to continue.

Another annual event which continues is the Christmas Carol Service. For many years it has followed a traditional nine lessons and carols pattern. Moss Close boys attend, while for others it is voluntary. The choir or a chamber choir sings, while lessons are read by a sequence of younger, then older boys, Captain of School, Director of Music, senior master and Headmaster. Geoffrey Paxton, Ian Davison and Tim Swain have trained the readers over the years, and the whole service is much enjoyed by those who help to fill St Matthew's Church.

Careers education

Careers education has a long pedigree. In the seventies, limited to the fifth and sixth forms, Dr Gordon Jameson, then Head of Classics, supported Year and Group Masters in this work. He introduced early questionnaires and then computer programmes to help pupils to identify their career leanings and university courses. Boys were introduced to an enormously expanded world of careers and careers advice. When he retired the responsibility passed to Mr Roy Jones in 1987. In the nineties, the work was expanded to include the 3rd and 4th year (Years 9 and 10), and to bring in a Careers Adviser from outside, with a careers office built in the upper floor well of the science block. Mr Roy Jones has masterminded this expansion of the work as Careers Officer, and Mrs Liz Meager became Visiting Careers Adviser. Mrs Meager's careful work has been invaluable.

Oxbridge candidates have also been provided with thorough advice and encouragement over the years from their Group Tutors, and from Messrs Paxton (Cambridge) and Anderson (Oxford), and more recently from Mr Swain.

Careers Room with Mr Roy Jones

Sixth Form 1981, showing two of the first girls at QM.

From L to R: Fiona MacAulay, Tim Swain (now Second Master), Dr G Jameson, Mr MJ Jackson, Mr JK Warburton, Mr RF Fletcher (master i/c Sixth Form), Mr GM Austin, Mr FG Nash, Mr BJ Edwards, Michael Schorah (Captain of School) and Joanne Elliot.

Girls in the sixth form

Pupils, rather than 'boys' is the word that describes members of the school when the sixth form is included. From the early seventies, girls have been a small but important element in the sixth form. In September 1976 Kate Wyer joined the sixth form to study physics, chemistry, maths and further maths, and then in 1979 Fiona MacAulay and Joanne Elliot joined 6Hc for geography and geology courses. Since then a small number of girls, up to 15 a year, have transferred to QM for their sixth form study in most years, fitting extremely well into the ethos of the school. In recent years several have been Senior Prefects, and most recently a few have joined the CCF. Some excellent boys as well as girls have transferred from other schools at the age of 16, and their integration into the sixth form has almost always been very successful. In the section towards the end of this book on Memories, there is a contribution from Sheba Sergeant (née Jose) and her sisters, on life for girls at QM.

Inspections
One of the ways in which the school is able to assess itself against others is through a school Inspection. When SL Darby arrived in 1956 he arranged for the school to be inspected to enable him to set his priorities alongside those who came to view the school from outside. The Inspection was in 1960. The changes in pastoral organisation, for instance, sprang from the report issued at that time. No inspection of the school was held then until 1992 when there was a short Inspection led by Mr Colin Potts which was generous in its comments about the quality of the school. Then with the introduction of Ofsted, there was a full General Inspection in 1995 at the end of KG Howard's Headmastership. The team of HMIs was again led by Mr Potts. The inspectors were very enthusiastic about the school, its achievements and the behaviour and development of its pupils. They highlighted some areas for improvement including the need to improve the provision of information technology. In September 2000 there was a further Inspection, with a team led by Dr RG Wallace. Again the inspectors were most impressed by the high standards of behaviour and personal development. Procedures which had been lacking in 1995 were now in place. They felt that results at Key Stage 3 (i.e. at Year 9 or the third year where there are external tests) could be better in some subjects, and they felt that ICT (computer technology) could be used more in some subjects. These reports, based on detailed and critical observation and study, show that Queen Mary's continues to be a Grammar School of very high quality.

The Green Book
Before 1966 the School List was a single folded sheet which included boys by form, staff and governors. Annually produced since 1966, the Green Books almost exactly followed the style of the Wolverhampton GS Red Book of that time, and include lists of governors and staff, then the list of prefects, librarians and others, then a list of boys in alphabetical order (first names shown in full since 1983), then pupils by form, then lists of societies, list of school dates for the year, and so on. Recently a section is included on school policies.

'The Marian'

Founded in the latter years of the nineteenth century, *The Marian* (known in early days sometimes as the *QMS Magazine* and also as *The Walsallian*) has been the record of school life. Published twice a year for a while, it has been otherwise an annual publication of record. Usually it has had records of the school year, some literary contributions from boys, and an Old Boys (QMC) Section. The volumes covering the years since 1954 have been invaluable to the author! Bound volumes are stored in the school archives. For many years the format was formal but in the 1970s when Mr Geoffrey Paxton was editor, *The Marian* acquired a new design and format. More photographs were included and, for some years there were centre sections on special topics, written and designed by the pupil editors. Styles changed through the years. *The Marian* was approximately A5 size until 2002 when it was further modernised in size and colour content. It is provided for all pupils in the school, and is also posted to all members of the Queen Mary's Club.

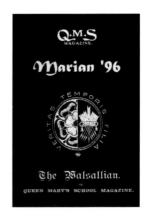

Tomb of Queen Mary and Queen Elizabeth I in Westminster Abbey

9

EDUCATIONAL CHANGE

The school structure

Much of the detail of the way the school was run in the 50s is covered in Chapter 3. The first two years were taught at Moss Close. Then boys went to Main School for 3rd year onwards. The structure of the school by 1966 was to place all new boys alphabetically into one of three 1st year forms. These forms, together with the second year forms 2A and 2, were called 'Moss Close'. Then in the second year the top 32 were promoted to a fast stream form as 3α, while the rest were divided between two 2nd year forms. In the middle school the forms moved on until O levels were taken by 5α, 5A and 5, the alpha form being a year younger. They moved into the sixth form and were divided into sixth classical, history, modern languages, geography, mathematics, science and 'medical'. Those who had come up by the alpha stream could then stay for 6^3, and work post-A level for the Oxbridge scholarship examinations.

In 1971 the last full alpha form was unusually moved en bloc from 5α into a Six 'Transitus', rather than being integrated into the sixth form Groups. This form started a three year A level course in four subjects, and was young enough to stay for post-A work. They were a particularly able group. However the alpha pattern was not continued, and from then the top maths set took O level in the 4th year and then additional maths in the 5th form, but otherwise all the entry progressed up a five-year course, with many subjects being setted by ability. For some years the top French set took GCSE in the 4th year, and additional French in the 5th.

The sixth form titles have not been changed. The sixth form is divided into humanities, maths and science groups, known as 6Ha, b, c, and d, 6M, and 6Sa, b, c, d. With minor modifications this pattern remains today. Traditionally the groups have had subject associations, 6Hc being a geography group for instance. In the lower school, when the alpha stream disappeared, all forms were, and are, known as far as possible by the surname initial of their form tutor. In the main school the old year nomenclature has given way to the national pattern of numbered school years, so that secondary years are numbers from Year 7 upwards, the 5th form becoming Year 11. QM has retained the usage 6^1 and 6^2 instead of the change to Years 12 and 13.

Opposite
Science lesson in Physics Lab at Lichfield Street with Mr LE Kitchen c.1959

Lower
Spanish lesson at Mayfield with Miss B Miranda González in the multi-media lab 2004

Over the years various attempts were made to teach 'General Studies' to the sixth form. All sixth formers took a General Studies A level examination of two papers as they still do. This included a number of language unseen translations, a difficult general comprehension paper, as well as a set of general questions on a wide range of topics, scientific, artistic and social. It was agreed that no one could teach for this exam, but efforts were made over the years to devise general interest courses together with courses at various stages to help scientists with the language element, and humanities sixthformers with the maths/science sections. Pressures on staffing meant that, over the years, fewer of these courses could be offered.

Despite this, many achieved high grades and these, recognised by the Northern group of universities, helped many to be offered their chosen places.

By the 1960s 'new' subjects were well established. Not only were geology and economics now taught in the sixth form and were to be increasingly successful as A level subjects, but the new buildings provided an opportunity for departments to have better resourced accommodation. The new labs were very well

Design Technology class 2003

equipped for their time, while sixth form 'division' rooms, or D rooms were built for the humanities subjects with small sixth-form sets. The only area where the new vision did not succeed was with engineering, where a project to develop technical drawing and engineering failed to create a clientele in an age when the pure sciences retained their cachet. (See also Ch. 11) The TD room became a maths room (and is now a computer room), and the engineering lab became a biology lab, and is now a second design technology room. Perhaps SLD was in advance of his time: engineering in schools is now encouraged, 50 years on!

Private study at Lichfield Street, early 1960s

The Grammar School and the Walsall Boy

It has always been difficult to give just the right amount of freedom to the sixth form to mark their greater maturity, and their development towards the freedoms of work at university. On the one hand there is desire to grant privileges; but on the other the experience is that boys do not suddenly lose their boyish instincts and become mature at the age of 16.

The pressures of staffing and the knowledge that A level candidates should not be 'over-taught', has led to increased amounts of private study being offered. How far should it be supervised, and by whom? Where should sixth-formers work when on their own? Over the years, many solutions have been tried. They had a Sixth Form Common Room when the school was built. Now, when that room has become a main Computer Room, their Common Room facilities have been provided in the Sutton Road houses, as explained earlier. These houses, once used entirely as staff flats, have for many years been transformed and used as small sixth form teaching rooms, with one flat remaining. The sixth form had a short-lived council in the 1970s, and in 1995 one of Stuart Holtam's earliest moves as Head was to institute a School Council which meets in the autumn and spring terms with representatives from Year Councils to discuss with senior staff matters of pupil concern.

The 1970s was a period of teenage rebellion. This has been associated with the development of new universities in the 1960s, the Paris riots of 1968, and a growth of teenage individuality which saw long hair and a lack of traditional respect as outward signs of cultural change. At Queen Mary's a demand for a sixth-form council was accepted, but many signs of indiscipline sadly marred the final years of SL Darby's Headmastership. He, himself, was very exercised over the correct policy to follow. Mr Fink tried very hard to ensure that boys' hair was always 'off the collar', and that 'sideburns' were shaved off. There was minor damage to furniture in the Sixth Form Common Room, and tension over the use of the record player there, and whether

Prefects 1974.

Front row includes SC Homer, MJ Webster, DGM Soutter, DJL Abbot, PP Tredwell (Captain of School), GR Hickinbottom, SI Bateman, PC Walton – Those in the know are challenged to identify the rest & notify the author!

sixth-formers should be allowed to choose to spend private study periods there rather than in the library. It was a difficult period. The retirement of SLD coincided with the arrival of the Thatcher era and an end to teenage rebellion, so that KG Howard, from 1979, was able to re-set standards firmly in an era when short back-and-sides was again in fashion, though his determination so to do earned him the immediate and topical nickname: the 'Ayatollah'! (Mr Geoff Austin was christened, by some, as the 'Lowertollah'!)

In the last 50 years the school has retained its wide social base so that pupils from all backgrounds, and now a wide ethnic base, have equal opportunity to develop all their talents. There are many who have risen from lowly beginnings as FH Hinsley did in the 20s and 30s when he rose from being the son of a caretaker in Birchills to being Master of St John's College, Cambridge. In the last 50 years we have had boys from the New Invention and Bloxwich who have risen to be Headmasters, and in one case a senior tutor at Clare College, Cambridge. A boy from Leamore, for instance, is now a professor and Cambridge 'lead scientist' in Antarctic geophysics. Queen Mary's is a free school with high academic ambition, filled with boys from all backgrounds, including the poorest and most deprived. See Chapter 20!

PROFESSOR SIR HARRY HINSLEY OBE, MA, FBA (QM 1930–1937)

Born in Walsall in November 1918, his father worked as a waggoner with a horse and cart for the coal depot of the local Co-op, and his mother became a school caretaker. They lived in Birchills, and Harry gained a scholarship from Wolverhampton Road Elementary School to Queen Mary's. He walked every day to school from Bentley Lane. Phil Evans remembered him well as a very clever friend at school. In 1936 he was elected to an Exhibition at St John's College, Cambridge. He is said to have arrived in Cambridge 'singularly unkempt' to read History under Geoffrey Barraclough, and to play rugby with long hair streaming in the wind.

In 1939 he gained a First in Part One of the Historical Tripos. After a summer spent hitchhiking in Germany, and seeing the Führer just outside Berchtesgaden, he returned to Cambridge to be discreetly enlisted to the government's Code and Cypher School at Bletchley Park. He became the leading expert on the wireless organisation of the German Navy. At first the Admiralty showed little interest until in 1941 Hinsley concluded that trawlers off Iceland were carrying Enigma coding machines. Within two months, with the capture of a trawler and a U boat, mastery of the Enigma code was complete. This was the intelligence code named Ultra. Hinsley brought his considerable intelligence to the analysis of Ultra decrypts, relying on intuition as well as logic in making inferences about enemy strategy. His own view, developed in later years, was that Ultra intelligence shortened the war by one or two years.

After the war, Hinsley returned to Cambridge, becoming a Lecturer in 1949. In 1965 he was made Reader in the History of International Relations, and Professor in 1969. In 1979 he became Master of St John's College, and for two years from 1981 he was Vice-Chancellor of Cambridge University. He received his knighthood in 1985. His five volume work British Intelligence in the Second World War was published between 1979 and 1990. He also wrote *Command of the Sea* (1950), *Hitler's Strategy* (1951), *British Foreign Policy under Sir Edward Grey* (1977), and he edited *Codebreakers: the Inside Story of Bletchley Park* (1993). He was an idiosyncratic teacher, an inveterate pipe-smoker, an intrepid cyclist, and a witty and sociable man. He presented the prizes on Speech Day at Queen Mary's in 1984. He died in February 1998.

From obituaries in The Times *and* The Eagle *(magazine of St John's, Cambridge).*

QM and the Ethnic Minority

An apparent major change has been in the increase in the size of the ethnic minority intake. Fewer than 15 non-white boys joined the school out of 96 in 1995, the number having slowly increased over the previous ten years. By 2002 the number had increased to 44%, but the percentage varies each year, of course. This is a matter of record. Within the school this change in racial balance has not affected the policies or practices of the school at all. Boys of all backgrounds have been included without any discrimination. There have been two results which may been mentioned. Asian parents are now beginning to take a fuller part in all activities of the Queen Mary's Association and the programme now reflects a new cultural balance within the school. The other is that more boys arrive with a lower standard of English than used to be the case. However this is not only the result of cultural change. Boys from all backgrounds are reading less, and what they read is usually less challenging. Some careful additional teaching has become necessary, and judging by the Key Stage 3 results in Year 9, this is successfully remedying the problem.

An Indian at Queen Mary's, one of the Memories and Reflections towards the end of this book, written by Jude Daniel, is a reflection by an Indian on the integration of ethnic minority pupils into Queen Mary's in recent years.

External examinations

Queen Mary's has always prided itself on its academic achievement. For generations it has been the town grammar school, preparing boys for the professions and for universities. In 1954 all the 5th form took GCE O levels and boys in 62 took their A levels. This pattern had existed since 1949 when the GCE had replaced School and Higher Certificates. The essentials remain today. However there are clear differences when we look more closely. In 1954 most boys left school after O levels and only a minority stayed into the sixth form. Of those that left at 15 or 16, many went into accountancy, law and other professions through articles and so tended to stay in the area for the rest of their lives. Only in the sixties came the vast expansion of the university sector so that almost all boys then stayed on for A levels. As the school moved to Mayfield the sixth form grew to about 170.

In those days, for those going to Oxford or Cambridge, it was still necessary to have 'matric. exemption' which meant having maths, English, and a foreign language to O level, and Latin also, for some courses. These stipulations have been reduced. Those attempting Oxbridge entry then would usually try for a scholarship in the exams which took place at intervals between November and March. Entrance scholarships and exhibitions were awarded until the eighties. Now these awards, where they remain, are made to undergraduates during their courses at university. Sixth-formers going to university gain points according to their A level results. Few are interviewed. They set out their CVs on their (UCAS) application forms, and those that try for Oxford will have an interview and possibly a further test, those for Cambridge will have an interview and may also take extra papers. These arrangements are the subject of review at this time, because of the high number of A grades awarded, so that selection for many courses has become very difficult.

The development of the curriculum

The school in the 50s was responsible for determining its own curriculum. Within each department, masters could decide on the syllabus to follow, which suited their facilities and interests. Generally Queen Mary's moved in the sixties from using the Oxford and Cambridge Board to the Northern Joint Board. When I, as Senior History Master, arrived in 1966, I continued the syllabi I inherited from AE (Nobby) Clark, but subsequently introduced an optional Medieval O level course. In the 70s, with three schools locally, we developed our own 'Mode 3' O level syllabus appropriate to our own needs. Many departmental heads could tell the same story, illustrating the control they had over what was taught, and how it could reflect their own department's teaching strengths.

Sadly control of the curriculum has been lost to central government, so that local skill and enthusiasm now play no part in choosing what is taught. These changes began in the 1980s. The Conservative government began a policy of intervention in education of a kind not experienced before. The aim was laudably to raise standards, and there was much need for this. Teaching methods had barely changed in decades, and could be seen as hopelessly old-fashioned. However, schools were not left to modernise themselves. The independence of schools to make their own decisions and set their own standards came to an end. External control over the curriculum and the testing of pupils brought in the new styles of teaching and new forms of testing. The first departments to be affected at QM were the science departments, and in Chapter 11, dealing with the work of Geoff Austin, the enormity of what was introduced is considered. By the nineties, with the introduction of the National Curriculum, the changes spread throughout all departments. Detailed national syllabuses were issued for most subjects to the age of 16, and with these came external assessments. Years were reclassified in secondary schools as years 7 to 13, with GCSE being taught in years 10 and 11. National assessment in main subjects was introduced in year 9, with assessments also for younger years in the Junior schools.

Over the years the O level was changed along with CSE to the present GCSE, with fundamental improvements in methodology which greatly aid learning. The improvements in French teaching have been impressive! Language teaching has changed totally with the textbook

'Whitmarsh' thrown away, and new direct methods of teaching used throughout all years of study. While this produces excellent results in the early years, changes to the content of the syllabus mean that much grammar that was taught in the middle school in the past is hardly introduced by the end of the sixth form now. This applies in many subjects, not only in language teaching. Course work and modules have been introduced in most subjects, though these can produce problems, including overload. Of recent years a new AS level exam at the end of 6^1 has been brought in, so that the second year sixth exam is now A^2. Extension papers at A level do exist but are not widely used. Thirty years ago there was discussion, initiated by Keith Howard when he arrived as Head, about the introduction of the Baccalaureate in place of A levels, as a more broadly based exam. Cost prohibited its introduction then. Nationally there are recurrent calls for a broader examination at 18.

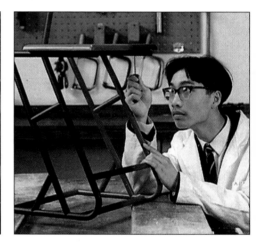

Top
Wooden CDT Chair: Danny Johal (A level student) 2003

Left
The Art Room 2003

Right
Designing and making a chair – GCSE pupil Phutoc Diep, 1991

The imposition of the National Curriculum brought increasing demands on the school and the staff. Throughout the nineties, the National Curriculum had its impact for good and for ill. In many areas of teaching, the new curriculum brought with it more modern methods and materials. In other ways it constrained initiative and personal enthusiasm with its straitjacket requirements. In many teaching areas these factors were not serious where the syllabus was good. Often, however, elements which were believed to be important were left out. In history, for instance, much exciting material was left out, while there was an unnecessary insistence on consideration of the 'provenance' of documents.

In recent years the curriculum content has been increased to include Information and Design Technology, as well as personal and social education including citizenship and careers education. By 1998 it was no longer possible to work with a conventional weekly timetable so that a two-week timetable was introduced with longer lessons, which allowed greater flexibility in timetabling. Sadly pressures on staffing have led to the demise of geology, while finally Classics has succumbed to the pressure to increase modern language teaching for the Language College. More of that later! However, with determination, the school has retained the traditional all-school assemblies, together with an hour lunch break to allow for music rehearsals and other societies, and has kept its 4 pm finish when many schools have opted for an earlier closing time.

Options (Y10,11 only)

GCSE

WEEK 1	1	2	3	4	5	6
MON	I.C.T iT2 M. Holden	Music Music1 B. Wragg	Science 57 D.J.Clough	German Q9 M.Lawson	Maths Q4 P.Elsden	English Q3Read P.Smith
TUE	Science 57 D. Clough	D-T. Design N. Roderick	Art Art 1 D. Wood	English Q3 P. Smith	P.S.M.E Q12 L. Horden	German Q9 M-H Lawson
WED	R.S H1 J. Martin	English Q3 P. Smith	ICT iT2 M. Holden	History M2 D. Rushworth	Maths Q4 P.A Elsden	Music Music 1 B. Wragg
THUR	Physical E Gym G. Taylor	English Q3. P. Smith	German Q9 M-H Lawson	English Q3 P. Smith	Geography 51I S.J Law	Maths M5 S.G. Rout
FRI	Geography 61I S.J Law	German Q.9 M.H Lawson	Games Gym R.A. Francis	Games Gym R.A. Francis	Science 57 D. G. Clough	History M2 P. Rushworth

Week 2	1	2	3	4	5	6
MON	History M2 D.Rushworth	Science 67 D. Clough	Art Art1 D. Wood	P.E Gym G. Taylor	English Q3 P. Smith	Maths Q4 P.A Elsden
TUE	History M2 P. Rushworth	ICT iT2 M. Holden	German Q9 M.H Lawson	Geography 61I S.J Law	English Q3 P. Smith	German Q9 M.Lawson
WED	Swimming Gym G. Taylor	D.T Design2 N. Roderick	Science 57 D.J. Clough	Geography 51I S. J Law	German Q9 M.H Lawson	English Q3. Read P. Smith
THUR	R.S H1 J. Martin	Science 57 D.Clough	German Q9 M. Lawson	Geography 51I 5. J Law	English Q3 P.Smith	Maths M5 S.G. Rout
FRI	History M2 P. Rushworth	R.S H1 J.Martin	Games Gym R. A. Francis	Games Gym R.A. Francis	English Q3. P.Smith	Maths M6 S.G. Rout

6²	2003/2004 FULL NAME	JASPER TIMOTHY DAVID	GROUP	6²SB

Include PS at home (show as HOME) and PS in library (show as PS)

	1	2	3	4	5	6
Week 1 Mon	A P.S.	B MATHS MRRout MS	C CHEMISTRY RM S8	D BIOLOGY RSP S9	E Home	E Home
Week 1 Tue	B MATHS Q4 PAE	C CHEM. RM S8	D BIOLOGY RSP S9	D BIOLOGY RSP S9	A Home	E Home
Week 1 Wed	A P.S.	C P.S.	B MATHS SGR MS	D BIOLOGY RSP S9	E Games	E Games
Week 1 Thu	A G. Studies	B Maths PAE Q4	C CHEM. RM S8	D BIOLOGY A7 S10	E Home	E Home
Week 1 Fri	C CHEMISTRY RY S8	A RM S5	P.S.	D BIOLOGY RSP S9	E Home	B Home

	1	2	3	4	5	6
Week 2 Mon	A P.S.	B MATHS SGR MS	C CHEM RM S5	D BIOLOGY A7 S10	E Home	E Home
Week 2 Tue	B MATHS PAE	C CHEM. RGJ S8	A P.S.	A P.S.	D BIOLOGY RSP	E Home
Week 2 Wed	A P.S.	B MATHS SGR MS	C CHEM RM S8	D BIOLOGY AJ7 S10	E Games	E Games
Week 2 Thu	B General Studies	B Maths PAE Q4	C CHEMISTRY RM S8	A P.S.	D BIOLOGY A7 S10	E Home
Week 2 Fri	B MATH SGR MS	B MATHS PAE Q4	A P.S.	D BIOLOGY A7 S10	C CHEMISTRY RM S8	

Please ensure that you include **SUBJECT** and **ROOM** for each period.

Middle school and sixth form pupils' timetables 2004

Teaching method over the years

I have alluded to the passing of an older generation of masters in the fifties and sixties. Many of these began their careers in the 1920s. Their methods were very old-fashioned by the time they retired. Their lessons were often tedious, dry and repetitive. The discipline of many was often harsh and unthinking. While many were admired for their foibles and their endearing characteristics, others were accepted with ill grace, especially by those who were not very academic, or who rebelled in the atmosphere of the school of those days. The single textbook, the rote learning, the repetitive exercises did not inspire. Not that all their younger replacements were remarkably different, but post-war teacher training did produce better teachers.

Even since the sixties, teaching has, of course, changed, and is no longer dominated by reference to the 'grubby green textbook'. As I have said, pedagogical styles have changed since the days of Clark and Merrett. Then masters wrote on blackboards with dusty chalk. Then at Mayfield on greenboards with the same sort of chalk. Then whiteboards came in with coloured markers. In the sixth form teaching method changed in the sixties as dictated notes fell out of fashion and, using file paper rather than exercise books, the sixth-former had to learn to read and make his own notes, and then discuss work in class.

Lessons are planned more than they were in days when one lesson followed on from the last. The modern textbook is a totally different animal from its predecessor. In colour, it is far more diagrammatic: filled with charts and bulleted explanatory points, questions and answers in a pre-planned sequence as ideas are developed. These books are supplemented by worksheets, and these can be used to stimulate discussion. The use of ICT (information and communication

Mr Bev Wragg with his interactive music whiteboard.

technology) deriving material from the Internet, or recording work by using a PC, is developing as equipment and material becomes more available. Interactive whiteboards are in use in half the rooms in the school, and their use in music education is highly impressive. These whiteboards are linked to a teacher's computer, all written work and display material is projected on to the screen, and during the lesson the teacher can actively write and design new material so that teacher and class can build up their work together on the screen in front of them. Video-conferencing and distance learning are just round the corner.

In the classroom, where all boys in the fifties were addressed by surname only, this style, while remaining for convenience at times, has given way gradually to the complete use of first names for normal purposes. Staff continue to be formally addressed, but their use of the gown for teaching has gone. Except for the Headmaster, Second Master and Senior Master in assembly, the gown is now reserved for use on Speech Day – and to mark out the daily member of staff on duty! With the increase in the number of ladies on the staff the use of the term 'master' has now largely given way to 'teacher', a fact referred to later.

Class work has always been reinforced by homework which has to be marked. Over the years styles of teaching vary, but the recalcitrant boy is given a detention for not working, misbehaviour or persistent disobedience. Detentions are supervised by the member of staff on duty and still last the traditional 45 minutes. Nothing much changes in these areas of school life. However, with the end of the cane (still used occasionally by the Head until the mid 80s, when it was banned nationally) more time has to be spent by Year Tutors and the Headmaster over the more serious offence. Now parents are brought into problems earlier and when necessary boys are suspended from school. On the other side of the coin, there is more care these days to report merit, and teachers are encouraged to pass news of particularly high quality work to the Year Tutor, so that appropriate note can be taken.

Queen Mary's – a Language College

Now that Queen Mary's is a Language College, apart from enhanced facilities, the school has responsibilities for language teaching extending to other schools and the community. The Modern Languages Department now is involved in advising and assisting with language teaching in local primary schools (Bluecoat Junior, Caldmore Primary, Chuckery Primary, Blackwood School and Lindens Primary) and in Bluecoat Secondary School. The school also arranges a programme of 'twilight' lessons for pupils in Punjabi and Gujurati, and evening class language teaching. As has been mentioned in the chapter on 'Masters to Teachers' the advent of a third modern foreign language – Spanish – was part of the Language College package, and this has meant that Latin has very sadly been phased out. Miss Miranda González arrived in 2002 to start Spanish teaching, and by 2004 a second Spanish teacher will be required. It is hoped to accelerate half the year group to take GCSE in Year 10, AS level in Year 11 and possibly A2 level in 6[1].

The building of the Language College wing is described in Chapter 10.

There has also been an increase in links abroad. For very many years there have been language exchanges. Mostly these have been based on links created by the school or by the Local Authority. In Walsall the longest lasting, which goes back to the 1960s, was the Mulhouse exchange in which many QM boys took part. Recently these have been revived, and, jointly with the High School, there is now a French exchange with the Institut S. Dominique in Neuilly, outside Paris. A regular German exchange exists now, also jointly with the High School, to the Lahntalschule in Biedenkopf.

In 1997 Mr Mark Lawson took 45 Year 9 pupils to Andernach in the Rhineland, and in 1998 another similar visit took place. In September 2001 he took 45 Year 8 and 9 pupils to the Futuroscope near Poitiers. In the summer of 2003 Mr Richard Johnson took a similar group on a visit to Normandy. Following a visit with Year 7 pupils to the Christmas market in Aachen, there is now an annual German visit to Cologne and Bonn with a boat trip on the Rhine. The school now takes part in a European Work Experience programme involving sixth-formers spending two weeks with a German company, hosting German boys in the UK for similar experience for them here.

Foreign trips also are run jointly across departments. In 2004 there has been a joint history and Spanish visit to Spain in the February Half term, and an English department war literature visit to France. In addition there has been an A level economics visit to Brussels to study aspects of the work of the European Commission.

Educational change will continue. There is less common ground about the purposes of education than once was the case. The case for a liberal education has been made in which art, music and history are as valuable as science, technology or languages. But this philosophy is continually challenged by philistines at the gate. It may be that basic education has to be geared to training in new apprenticeships for those who should not proceed towards university. Those who govern schools like Queen Mary's must be on their guard.

Proposals for change in the years to come may be benign and reflect new concepts and new understandings. But those who have an independent voice must watch and understand clearly the values which they propound and defend.

Lichfield Street 1954   *Mayfield 2004*

The colours and design of the modern school badge are the subject of not a little confusion! The number of arrows varies: originally there were nine in the 1907 version, including one vertical arrow. Now the number is usually reduced to seven, or even six. Clearly there should be a vertical arrow. More significantly the Tudor rose is shown on all Speech Day programmes correctly as having an outer white rose and a gold centre to the inner red rose, yet when shown coloured the badge used today shows both roses as red, hardly historical! This includes the badge in the Entrance Hall, and that on the 450th anniversary tie! Can we make a plea for a correct revision?

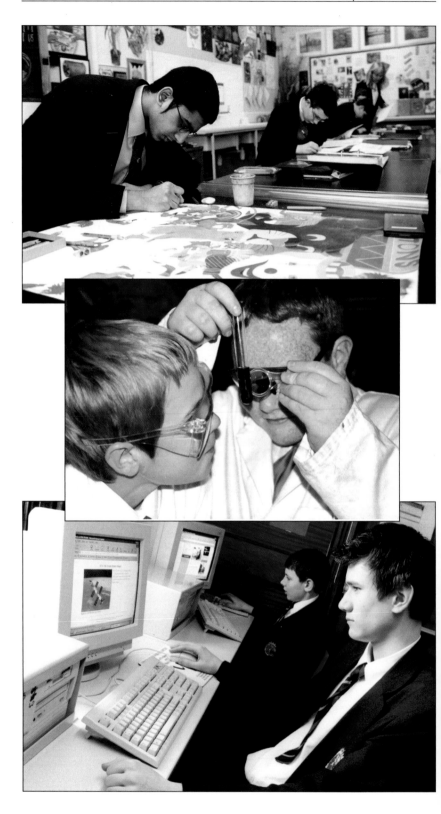

10

QMGS SINCE 1995

In 1995 the present Head, Stuart Holtam, took over the school as Keith Howard retired. Stuart paid tribute to the work of KGH in the academic strength of the school he inherited, and its high level of discipline. Its sport was very strong indeed, as was the drama, music and the CCF. It was a school which was already near the top of the Grammar School national League Tables. A proud school to lead.

Top
A-level Art

Middle
Chemistry

Lower
Using the Internet

It must be said that there remained, and to some extent remains, apprehension about the future of the selective grammar school. However, the ballot scheme enabling parents to vote against selection, set up after 1997, was convoluted and not an actual threat, nor did the abolition of GM status, with the return to Voluntary Aided status, affect the new funding philosophies which enabled the school to manage its own affairs and for the school's capital projects to continue.

Other results of the Grant Maintained period, continuing under the present Voluntary Aided regime, included the privatisation of support agencies. The school meals service was contracted out to a firm now called Sodexho, keeping the employment of loyal staff; grounds maintenance was also the subject of a contract won and renewed by Mr Barry Vernon who has served the school now for 10 years, and the cleaning contract has been kept with the LEA, as have a number of administrative contracts. Setting up and maintaining these contracts between the Governors and private contractors has not been easy, and much credit goes to Mr Paul Nowell, parent and Vice Chairman of the governors, whose expertise has been invaluable.

A Time of Change

A further change must be recorded. In Chapter 1, I have referred to the changes in Borough boundaries and the legal 'Greenwich Judgment', which enables parents to apply for admission irrespective of address, and the greater mobility of the last decades. All this means that Queen Mary's serves a much wider area than hitherto. No longer is QM a Walsall school. It is a regional school, centred on Walsall. Boys come from Cannock and Lichfield (not many), from Sutton Coldfield, from Great Barr and parts of West Bromwich, and occasionally from Wolverhampton. Therefore most boys arrive by car or by bus. One serious effect has been noted elsewhere. Very many families do not identify with Walsall. They centre their lives in other communities. Therefore fewer stand on the touchline on a Saturday. Fewer attend plays and concerts. Fewer come to any but the most popular QMA events. One of the noticeable features of QM in the last fifty years has been that it has been a Community – the Queen Mary's Family. It is more difficult now than it was to retain this sense of belonging to a community when its members are so far flung. This is not to say that that the school has lost the enormous support and respect of its parent body. Indeed the huge sums raised by the QMA in the last year or two indicate the reverse of this. Nevertheless this continuing support comes in spite of the greater dispersal of QM families, and is all the more remarkable because of that.

Less obvious developments of the last few years have included what Stuart Holtam calls a liberalising of the school atmosphere. He says that his predecessor, Keith Howard, had to institute a tough regime when he arrived, and that it was right that it should have been maintained, but by 1995 there was room for a softer approach, though with all the traditional standards kept in place. Indeed when one looks now at the wearing of school uniform, and the movement of boys around the school and in the dining area at lunch, there seems to have been no falling away in standards whatsoever.

New teaching staff

Tim J Swain

Another circumstance of the time which could not be avoided was the retirement of a large proportion of the senior staff. Appointed by Sam Darby in the 1960s to replace the elderly masters from pre-war years that he had found, a strong group of colleagues were about to retire within five years. This was an opportunity to bring in younger teachers, men and women with new ideas, but it meant that those who had led the school to its academic, sporting and other strengths, and who in many ways were the school of 1995, were about to disappear. What a turnover of staff this was to be! It was an opportunity to recruit a new generation with new energy and fresh ideas.

In 1997 John Anderson retired as Second Master. Mr Tim J Swain was appointed in his place. Their contributions are considered in Chapter 11. Tim's grasp of the requirements of school administration at the present time is remarkable, and he has proved to be a strong

Deputy and a determined senior administrator as well as a firm schoolmaster at the heart of a new senior staff team, with many new younger teachers looking for and getting first class leadership, not only from TJS but also from the new senior Management Team of Roger Metcalfe (retiring in 2004), Tim Lawrence, Bev Wragg and Mark Donnan.

The average age of the staff is now very much younger than it was ten years ago! The reputation of the school has enabled it to attract good applicants for the posts advertised, although the national shortage of teachers has meant that fewer apply for any post advertised than was the case a generation ago. That the academic and pastoral work has continued without damage, and has indeed continued to develop and strengthen, is a tribute to the Head, to the quality of the new staff and to the senior staff responsible for the induction of their new colleagues. Notably the number of women on the staff has risen, from four in 1995 to eight in 2003. Details of many of the changes in the teaching staff since 1995 are included in the survey in Chapter 11.

Targets and statistics

The imposition of the National Curriculum since the 1980s had brought increased demands on the school and the staff. This has been discussed earlier in Chapter 9. Now the pressures to appear high in the League Tables, and the development of more sophisticated statistical measurements which ensnared the staff, produced a workload which at least appeared to increase after 1995. Target setting for every pupil in every subject at A level and GCSE was to prove a considerable exercise. Then annual percentages and point scores had to be compared. Then there were targets and attainments at Key Stage 3 and at Key Stage 4. Then these were set against national benchmarks. Then, by 2002, came value added measurements. These showed the difference between actual progress and the average progress made by pupils from the same national starting point. These statistics had to be introduced to an already highly committed staff. However, burdens on the teaching staff are now being reduced as a result of the Teachers' Workload Agreement which is now reducing the clerical tasks of teachers, and the mere supervision of classes and examinations.

Stuart Holtam is now no longer a new Headmaster. He is comfortable with the progress made over these last years. Academic standards have been maintained, which for him, as for his predecessors, has priority. The school remains very high in the national

League Tables, a 'top school'. In 1993 Camp Hill Boys' was the only Midlands boys' Grammar School which consistently scored higher than Queen Mary's, and this is still the case. It has a more professional catchment area and King Edwards' Foundation funding. When, in 2000, *The Sunday Times* ranked the most consistently excellent secondary schools in the country, Queen Mary's was the 9th in the list of boys' schools, and 4th in boys' schools north of London and the Home Counties. A level results have improved over the years: from 42.9% A+B grades in 1993, moving up to 59% in 2000, the figure was 45.9% in 2001, and a very high 66% in 2002. These figures exclude General Studies. At GCSE, 40.7% gained A*+A in 1994, and this figure is up to 56.5% in 2002. There is argument that examination standards have declined, that syllabus content is much reduced, and that pass rates have been dropped to produce results which fit government targets. However, it is also clear that while these factors may apply to a degree, the overall standards at Queen Mary's have gone up and are impressive in any national comparison with schools of like kind. One of the statistics now used where Queen Mary's scores well is that of Valued Added Scores. Assessing pupils at various stages in the progress can indicate whether a school is going beyond the mere line of natural progress. In this Queen Mary's scores highly. In 2002 Key Stage 2 to 3 value added statistics showed the school to be ranked third nationally in terms of its teaching. In the last ten years teachers have clearly succeeded in teaching well, and pupils have continued to be well-motivated. University entrance has been well maintained with candidates achieving grades to enable virtually all to move into their universities of first choice. Six boys have achieved Oxbridge places for 2004.

The need for refurbishment

The immediate problems Stuart Holtam faced had been those brought about by circumstance and time. The Queen Mary's Foundation, with three schools to support, is not financially strong. Indeed, when compared with the King Edward's Foundation in Birmingham, and the foundations which support other ex-Direct Grant day schools in the country, Queen Mary's is financially very slim. It cannot fund the capital developments that the school, and the Girls' High School, now require. The Mayfield buildings, new in 1965, show serious signs of ageing. Roofs, window frames, outside areas, all show serious signs of wear. The wiring and the heating system approach the end of their lives. Work was begun during Keith Howard's headship, when laboratories were outmoded, sports facilities were very poor for the time, and the school looked shabby. This was no reflection on the work of Keith Howard: until the 1990s with its devolved management and then the Grant Maintained scheme, there had been no money to improve matters.

Science labs before and after refurbishment

The Development Campaign Fund and New Building

Clearly a major task was to take the opportunities to improve and extend the infrastructure which was so urgently in need of attention. Some progress had been made in the early 1990s with the refurbishment of two of the science labs (S4 and S7), the planning of the first major computer room (in what had been the Sixth Form Common Room, to replace a tiny facility in S5), preparing the Houses to receive the Sixth Form Common Room, and building a small Careers Room in the Science Block 'well' area. Much had to be made of the opportunities for fund-raising as a Grant Maintained school, and a Development Campaign had to be set up with an eye to the future where already grants were increasingly only available to those who help themselves: that is, matched funding.

In 1996 Stuart Holtam set up the first Development Campaign Fund with the assistance of Mr Andrew Scudamore of South Staffordshire Water, who was seconded part-time to advise on raising funds. Breakfast meetings were held, and plans laid. Advice came in, but searches for sponsors produced little result. In many ways the school was late into this market. However, parents were sent a brochure and letters, as were selected Old Boys, and local firms. Altogether £600,000 has been raised between 1996 and 2003. In all, from the Development Campaign Fund £251,000 was spent on the first computer room; £76,000 was spent on the Design Technology room and computer room 2; £50,000 was the school share of the costs of the Language College wing; over £14,000 went towards the refurbishment of the laboratories S3, S6 and S8; over £13,500 on the replacement of school hall lighting; over £7,500 as the school contribution towards the new seminar rooms in the library and the associated fire escape; and £7,500 to build the conservatory as part of the replacement sixth form centre in the Sutton Road houses. The Campaign Fund balance sheet is shown in Appendix 10. Match funding has played an increasing part, but none of this would have been possible without the drive of the Headmaster and his team, and the generosity of parents, Old Boys and those who hold the school dear.

Computers – The Development of Information Technology

Top
Early BBC computer

Middle
Computers today

Lower
Computer Room 1 (previously the Sixth Form Common Room) with Mr Neil Canning, Head of Information and Computer Technology (ICT)

Queen Mary's had been slow in embracing the Computer Age. Shortage of funds and a touch of conservatism may have been to blame. The reports of Inspectors in 1990 and 1995 indicated that more needed to be done, and quickly. John Farrington had pioneered the work of introducing the BBC series of computers and their use had spread in the teaching of science and in school administration by 1992. JFF had introduced the office staff and senior teaching staff to the need to be trained. The author remembers that he learned from JFF the possibilities of constructing the school timetable, using a computer programme instead of the pencil and rubber method inherited from David Fink. He went on courses, but it was JFF's support which was most valuable. Central Fund was managed with the aid of a computer accounts programme written specifically for it by JFF, and used for nearly ten years. Though his work has been mentioned twice before, I cannot over-emphasise the debt the school owed in the 1990s to the skill and patience of John Farrington as the world of computers evolved within the school. The first computer room, which he designed, had been the converted Science Lecture Room S5.

Then the Sixth Form Common Room was moved to the Sutton Road Houses and the first major computer room was built with 35 RM machines in 1996, and Mr Neil Canning was appointed Head of ICT in 1997. He has grown into the task, and has made an extraordinarily skilled and hard-working leader of this vital area of the school's work. By this time staff training in ICT had begun, but there was still much to be done. There

Mr David Pennington, Head of Craft Design Technology (CDT)

were some subjects where computers were of immediate value, and staff grasped the opportunities eagerly. Other departments did not find that there was appropriate software, or that their subject particularly lent itself to the use of ICT.

To gain further funding a bid was drawn up in 1997 for the school to be granted Technology College status, with the grants and year-on-year funding that that offered. This was to enable development of Design Technology to meet National Curriculum requirements. This bid failed, but the success of the development campaign enabled matched funding to be obtained to complete Design Room 2 (where there had been the engineering/biology lab) and Computer Room 2 (which had been the TD room). This room is now used for work on Computer Aided Design (CAD), which ties in with the original purpose of the room when the school was built. Finally interactive whiteboards are being installed in many rooms – 19 by September 2003. The new interactive equipment installed in the Music Room is of a very high quality and is well used. These whiteboards with their opportunities for computer-based teaching have made possible changes in teaching styles which would not have been considered possible ten years ago.

Building for the Language College

Subsequently another bid, this time for the school to be a Language College succeeded. As from 1st September 2002, the funding came available. This enabled a new impetus to be given to Modern Language teaching. It also produced funds for a modern language wing on the south west corner of the buildings, projecting from the room Q10 which had been a history room, built in 2003, to provide two extra classrooms, seminar rooms, a department store and an office. Also a new multi-media room, with 24 flat-screen monitors, has been created in the D room corridor, combining the previous D2 and D3 rooms. To improve disability access a lift has also been built for easier access from the quadrangle and entrance hall levels to the upper floor level. Aspects of the work of the Language College on the life of the school and beyond are covered in a section in Chapter 9, and its staffing in Chapter 11.

The new Language Wing 2004

Other refurbishment, and the Sports Hall, 2004

At the same time development funds, with matched funding, allowed for a much needed conversion of the 'carrel' area on the library balcony into two soundproofed sixth form seminar rooms, retaining the library store and archive room on that first floor level. A Librarian's office was built on the main Library floor. By stages the entrance hall, and the lobby at the entrance to the school hall, have both been modernised well with curtains and carpeted areas, new furnishings and wall displays. At last the dining area was improved in 2002 with a new wide hatch from the kitchen, and heated serving points. The covered play area was re-roofed and gated so that it was no longer dangerous and open to vandalism. As mentioned elsewhere, the new cricket pavilion was enlarged by the QMC and converted into a bar and social club, while remaining a cricket pavilion. All this has done much to lift the school from the inevitable tired shabbiness of the past.

The approval by the DfES of funding for the Sports Hall provides for the final phase of this modernisation programme with building due in 2004. This will provide indoor courts for badminton and cricket nets, indoor hockey and tennis courts, together with facilities for the range of PE activity. Since the school was built, the gym has always been too small, and although the Covered Play Area has been an incredibly useful space, it has been limited in its use for minor sports.

The future of the Mayfield buildings

For the future, a new classroom block and sixth form centre is needed. In running a school there are many priorities and these development may be a while coming, but Queen Mary's Grammar School needs buildings to match up to its task in the decades ahead. Even more radical thinking is in the air. Keeping, one hopes, the best of the present and the results of recent investment, there may be a move to rebuild the whole school. Classrooms and laboratories built in the early 1960s have a limited life and it may be that the school could be rebuilt within the next decade.

New Sports Hall under construction, March 2004

11

MASTERS AND TEACHERS

For readers who are not 'schoolmasters', I should explain that regretfully the term has largely disappeared. The word teacher is now universally used! Many of us felt that the use of the word schoolmaster was a more complete description of the whole range of service and responsibility involved in that profession than that described by the word 'teacher'. This is a change of usage during the last 50 years.

I have not been able to consider those who were only at QM for a short time. Many of those who served QM over many years gave their time out of the classroom in very many ways. In this chapter individual entries are brief, and in the chapters on school societies, sport, music, drama, CCF and the Welsh Centre, there are further descriptions of the work of those who contributed so much in those areas This cannot do justice to the lifelong dedication of so many. Colleagues and pupils have their own memories too …

Second Masters

When SL Darby arrived at Queen Mary's in January 1956, there was a pre-war generation of masters coming towards retirement. WA Burn and WE Terry had recently retired, and HA Hawkins, FB Shaw, AE Clark, CV Merrett, W Hopkins and JWL Symes were all nearing the end of their careers. Reference is made to many of them in Chapter 3, and that chapter shows the endearing respect in which all are held in the memories of so many! There would soon be opportunities to bring in younger men though there was much to regret over the end of that era. David Fink had been appointed Second Master by Hamilton on WAB's retirement, and he was at the centre of the new team. He had acted as Headmaster for the Autumn Term of 1955. Fred Nash arrived to head Chemistry as SLD arrived, and, over the next years in between 1956 and 1970, new Heads of Department were appointed for Modern Languages, Classics, Mathematics and History.

For almost the whole of SLD's headship, David Fink was Second Master until he retired in 1977. Born in 1914, he was educated at Bancroft School in Essex, and he was a scholar of University College, Oxford. He joined the staff of Queen Mary's for one term in 1940

before enlisting in the RAF. He was commissioned and was stationed in Italy during his wartime service. He returned in 1946 to teach history, and he embarked on writing his scholarly history of the school 'Queen Mary's Grammar School 1554 – 1954' It was, as *The Marian* said, 'a mightily impressive work of scholarship', taking four years to write. It was fluent and comprehensive, and the manuscript was typed by his devoted wife, Gladys. He was an erudite and enthusiastic historian, especially of the Stuart period. Sixth-form boys would distract him into his favourite sidelines of history, giving pleasure to David and to them!

He was a keen and accomplished sportsman, and he coached cricket and rugby; he was a polished pianist and contributed strongly to musical activities, especially to the school Music Club in the fifties and sixties. He was for a while scoutmaster in the school Troop, and he was a railway enthusiast who took parties to Farchynys to travel the narrow gauge railways of North Wales. As Second Master he was an expert timetabler; he was a particularly fair disciplinarian, and he was a warm and faithful colleague, for years being Chairman of the Masters' Common Room. He ran his school life with his diary, filled with his neat spidery writing, and disaster occurred when the diary was mislaid! He maintained an interest in former pupils compiling for many years the '*From All Quarters*' section of *The Marian*. He was a long serving Vice President of the Queen Mary's Club.

Outside school he was a founder member of the Jerome K Jerome Society, and of the Walsall Local History Society. He campaigned for local historical buildings including the Walsall Guild Hall and the old Railway Station. In 1977, when he retired, *The Marian* tribute said: 'David Fink was a schoolmaster devoted to his school who earned the affection of colleagues and boys alike by his wisdom, his kindness and his wit. We shall miss him a lot'. He maintained his enthusiasm for the school in retirement, and died in 2003.

David Etherington (QM 1964–73) remembers David Fink's teaching of A level British Constitution from 1832 to the Present Day. DPJF thought one ought to go further back to understand the Great Reform Act. He went back quite a lot further. He started with the ancient Assyrians, and by the end of the first year Sixth they had arrived at Magna Carta. By mock A levels they had reached the English Civil War. David recalls that they never did get to 1832, let alone the present day, but he still remembers those lessons – a constitutional history of the civilised world, somehow taking in avant garde world cinema, and elements of continental literature and philosophy.

Opposite
The life of David Fink as recorded in The Marian 1978

The following are extracts from a lengthy briefing memo from PA Bull to JS Anderson as the latter took over as Second Master in 1982. They provide an insight into the concerns and tactics of all schoolmasters:

Auditors' Visit: a posse from the Treasurer's office invade the Board Room each year and inspect a number of documents, e.g. D/T sales records, petty cash, registers (what for?), Inventory (and go and ask to see something out of it), car allowance book. I can't ever remember their finding anything seriously wrong. In fact, after constant cups of tea and coffee from Irene, they go away very happy.

Smoking fines: if a boy is reported for smoking I have fined him £1 in the first instance and another £1 for subsequent offences, by which I mean £2 for the second time and so on. I should have kept a list of the offenders, but in lieu I have said to the culprit: 'This is the third time, isn't it?' The boy will say 'No, Sir, only the second' or 'I'm afraid it is, Sir'. However, as I say, a list would be a good idea. The money goes for Cancer Research

Smith owes £3. He went off to CCF Camp before I could chase him up for it!

Corporal Punishment: The book is in the lefthand bottom drawer. As you know, HM's intention is to stop it before he has to. In any case, there's a shortage of canes.

PA Bull

In 1972 Phil Bull (QM 1933–39) became Second Deputy Head, taking some of the pastoral duties from David Fink. PAB was an amazing man, appointed to the staff as a classics master in 1949 after military service in India during WW2, he served the school for 33 years as Latin master, Head of Lower School (Moss Close) from 1968–72, Second Deputy Head from 1972 until 1977, then Second Master until he retired in 1982. He was an excellent disciplinarian; he wielded the cane in an era when it was perfectly respectable and normal so to do; he had a wicked sense of humour; he told fine tales of wartime authority to back up his threats to small boys, and he had a reputation as a teacher of falling asleep in class yet knowing exactly who was translating so that no one dared stop working while he apparently lost attention. He had his little jokes, his plays on hymn lines as with his A level hymn: 'Not for ease that prayer shall be'. He ran the CCF as Major, and then, Lieutenant Colonel Bull from 1950 until 1968, and was Warden of Farchynys from its first days in 1963 until 1979. He retired with his wife, Joan, to live near Worcester. He died in February 2004.

In 1982 John Anderson became Second Master (a post he held till he retired in 1997), and Geoffrey Dunkin was appointed from outside as Second Deputy Head. In 1987 Geoffrey Dunkin moved away to a Headship, and Brian Edwards was appointed in his place. In 1989 on Brian Edwards' retirement, Stuart Holtam became Second Deputy, from which post he was appointed Headmaster in 1995.

JS Anderson

As Second Master JSA worked with Keith Howard during the period of tough management which was necessary following the difficult late seventies with its teenage rebelliousness. It was also a difficult period in the harsh economic climate of that time. When Local Authority funding was very limited, he inherited the management of Central Fund when it was most significant for the life of the school. He took over the annual creation of the school timetable from David Fink. He worked with Yearmasters as the head of the disciplinary chain, co-ordinating with the Headmaster. For a time he managed the school's involvement in TVEI, the Technological and Vocational Initiative funded by government, which provided funds for the introduction of computer technology. There were a multitude of other tasks which fell to the Second Master, from arranging Speech Day, supervising the prefect body and arranging school assemblies, to daily staff cover. It was a fascinating job, alongside a half timetable of history teaching. He also, from 1989 until 1997 commanded the CCF. Since 1997 he has been a Foundation governor, and more recently has become Chairman of the Governors Committee of Mayfield Preparatory School. His successor as Second Master in 1997 was Mr TJ Swain.

Tim Swain was educated at Queen Mary's (1974–81). A modern linguist, musician and actor he gained a place at St John's College, Oxford, where he studied Joint Honours, French and German. He then spent one year teaching in Dijon, followed by a year completing a PGCE at Birmingham University. He was appointed to teach Modern Languages at Queen Mary's in 1987. He was appointed Head of

Modern Languages in 1991, following the departure of Mr Michael Overend. He was appointed Head of First Year in 1989, he became Head of Sixth Form in 1995, and Second Master in 1997. Since his arrival on the staff he has shown himself to be an exceptionally skilful teacher of languages, involving his classes in oral and aural work with enormous energy. He has very great organisational skills which he has brought to the benefit of all the school in the last seven years. As Second Master he has introduced target-setting procedures and school development planning, along with a multitude of administrative tasks inherited from JSA. He is a highly successful Second Master. In 2001 he published '*Tout Terrain*', an A level French Coursebook.

Classics

In 1963 Cyril V Merrett retired after 34 years service to classics teaching at Queen Mary's. A gentle and a courteous teacher, clear and thorough and much respected. As was said when he retired: 'for him the classics was a way of life, able to illuminate and interpret every aspect of human affairs'. He was replaced by Dr Gordon Jameson, second classics master at King Edward VII School, Sheffield. Like Sam Darby, GJ had been a Wolverhampton Grammar School boy, but he had then gone on to Sidney Sussex College, Cambridge. He was a musician, and a man of strong pacifist convictions. He had spent two years in the 1950s lecturing at Cape Town University, and from this experience developed a lifelong commitment to combat racism and injustice. 'Mister-Doctor-Jameson' as he was often known, was a gentle and devoted scholar, a man of common sense and reason. As the years went on, he saw a serious decline in numbers of sixth form classicists, and he considered that classics might not survive. The demise was delayed 20 years, and many boys enjoyed and benefited from their Latin and Greek study in that generation. However, in preparation for an end which did not come, Gordon Jameson studied maths with the Open University, and gained a 1st class degree. He taught sixth form maths in his last years at QM. He was for many years in charge of careers education before he retired in 1987. For all this time he was supported by John Dickson and Phil Bull. JAD was a classical enthusiast, particularly interested in archaeology. He was thrilled to point out to any who might be with him, the line of the Roman Road that could be traced west of Brithdir near Farchynys, and he would explain where the river crossing was where he found the bridge abutment with a marked Roman stone. For two years John Dickson was promoted to Head of Classics, and then following his retirement

G Jameson

CV Merrett

EVENING

The hour when pale-winged mists with cool embrace
Enfold the plain and kiss the sleeping hills;
When beast and bird are hushed, and laughing rills
Seem somehow, though not lessening their pace,
To laugh more softly; when to hide their face,
The night-shy daisies fold their red-tipt frills,
While honeysuckle sweetlier distils
Its stored ambrosia for th'emphemeral race
Of moths to spoil – that blessed evening hour,
Time of tranquillity, what wondrous power
Is hers to soothe the vexed day-weary mind!
So, when the hot noonday of life shall cease
And the long afternoon be left behind,
Still may the evening of my days bring peace!

CV Merrett (classics master 1929 – 1963)

in 1989, Mr JP Blackshaw was appointed. With boundless enthusiasm, Philip Blackshaw taught the classics for its last years until Latin was swept away with the development of Spanish under the Language College banner, and Philip Blackshaw moved sideways into English teaching. The final set takes GCSE Latin in 2004. This is viewed by many with considerable sadness, but the economics are so tight that there seemed to the governors to be no other way if the advantages of the Language College were to be taken up.

History

AE (Nobby) Clark was appointed in 1926, and for 40 years taught History. He came out of the era of the post 1918 world and in the year of his appointment was the General Strike. A left-wing schoolmaster who spread his gospel with a smile, Clark was a kindly, encouraging man who knew his pupils. He retired in 1966 and John S Anderson was appointed as Senior History Master in a department with David Fink, and a young lecturer turned teacher, Mr Bob Leach. For the author to say that John Anderson was an enthusiast or to make other

AE Clark

comment would be improper perhaps! However, a History Society did exist (run by a member of VI Medical), and it was immediately developed with Youth Hostelling weekends (the Welsh castles, Stonehenge, York and Lincoln) as well as Farchynys weekends, and with plenty of West Midlands local history too. At A level there were alternative syllabi for boys to choose, while at O level for many years there was a medieval option. JSA brought from his previous school in Sheffield the pattern of 'work sheets', setting out a plan for two weeks work in the sixth form so that sixth-formers could organise their own reading and preparation, and this pattern caught on as the hallmark of the department. Many bright boys chose the subject and sixth-formers went to Oxbridge and elsewhere to study History or Law. In all this activity the department was well blessed with the vigorous enthusiasm of David Fink and of its younger historians: Philip Done, Clive Westlake, and Tim Lawrence. All enjoyed the history which sometimes involved getting their boots muddy!

In 1978, a year after JSA became Second Deputy Head, Mr John Emery was appointed Senior History Master. When he left in 1980 Mr Tom Perrett was appointed to succeed him. He followed in the traditions established and brought his own scholarship and avuncular style, which endeared him to so many. Tom's rather disorganised enthusiasm belied a very sharp intellect. He enthused many in a lively department. He coached cricket, was devoted to the War Gaming society and to school Table Tennis and Squash. A lively political figure, but always fully sympathetic towards Queen Mary's, he was latterly staff governor, and is now a Foundation governor. Appointed to the staff in 1977, Mr Tim Lawrence took over the Department from Tom Perrett in 1995, when Tom retired. Now an Assistant Head Teacher, Senior Year Tutor as well as Head of History, TL has had a very full career at Queen Mary's since his arrival from Birmingham University in 1977. A Yearmaster for very many years, he is now Head of Sixth Form. He has been an officer in the CCF RAF Section throughout, and since 1997 has been Squadron Leader in charge of the RAF Section. One of many who has given countless weekends to parties at Farchynys, he also has worked with the QMA as staff representative arranging the raffle and ticket sales for the Fête and Fireworks.

TF Perrett

Geography

Mr Brian Edwards was appointed in 1949 to run the geography department to which subsequently was added geology in the sixth form. A Birmingham graduate with enormous enthusiasm for his subject, he has already been mentioned as one who played a vital part in the planning of the new school buildings. He was a Butler appointee, yet one of the new generation with whom SLD could work when he arrived in 1956. When he arrived, he had had great difficulty persuading HMB to give him one slide projector and two blackout curtains for Geography. He overcame physical disability without complaint. He was an enthusiast and a lively teacher. He was devoted to his detailed blackboard work and his red and white mottled covered work diaries. From his entry to his exit, it was 'eyes down', making extensive notes. When the Yearmaster system was established, BJE became responsible for sixth form pastoral work, along with Fred Nash and Howard Chadburn. He was devoted to his department and to those in his pastoral care. In 1983 he became Senior Master, a post he held till he became Deputy Head in 1987. He retired in 1989. He subsequently became a Foundation governor. Earlier geographers in the 1960s and seventies include Brian Hitchens, the eccentric Will Chipchase, and Paul Dean, an Old Marian, who subsequently worked in Wolverhampton Education Department.

BJ Edwards

Mr Stuart Holtam joined the staff in 1972, Head of Geography since 1983, became Deputy Head in 1989, and then, of course Headmaster. Mr Stephen Law (QM 1965–72), who joined the geography department in 1979, became Head of Department in 1989. He followed the line of geologists who taught A geology as well as geography. Deeply enthusiastic, with geology his hobby, Steve Law is attractively unorthodox in many of his ways which makes him a memorable teacher. He has led innumerable Field Courses following the pattern set by Brian Edwards, his mentor, to Wren's Nest near Dudley, and the Daw End railway cutting, to study fossils and strata, in addition to the weekends at Farchynys. He is senior Army Section officer in the C.C.F., and is Warden of Farchynys (See chapter 6).

Modern Languages

FB Shaw

'Fluffy' Shaw had been on the staff since 1926 and reference has already been made to the skill of his teaching, and his Midlands French accent! Known for his rapid walk up Lichfield Street towards Moss Close with right arm bent at the elbow, many will remember lessons beginning with the command, 'Les voyelles et les mots' and the class would repeat their vowel sounds and their associated words. FBS had won the Grande Dissertation Prize at Genoble while working for his *Licencié ès Lettres*, following his Birmingham 1st in French. He demanded accuracy and the use of 'le mot juste'. Mr John Morris was appointed Senior Modern Languages Master in 1964, following the retirement of FB Shaw. A firm, precise gentleman who took a vice-like control over the book and stationery store, John Morris was an enthusiastic linguist who moved on in 1968 and became a Head in Eastbourne. He was succeeded by Mr J Kenneth Warburton, a Cambridge man of vigour, elegance and precision who developed the department and produced linguists of great quality until his retirement in 1987. A very civilised man, a Methodist local preacher, and a theatre lover, he did fine work for the teachers' association, AMMA, of which he was for many years on the executive. For a short period the department was led by Mr Michael Overend, who moved on in 1991, and was replaced by Mr TJ Swain, (QM 1974–81), who arrived as the philosophy of language teaching changed. With extraordinary vigour Tim Swain led the department into direct oral and aural teaching, maintaining and enhancing the scholarly work done in the sixth form. When he was appointed Second Master in 1997, Mr Mark Donnan became Head of Modern Languages, and when the school became a Language College in 2001, Mark Donnan became its manager. From 1974 until he retired in 1992, one of the loyal French masters at QM was John Akroyd. A rigorous, and at times fairly explosive member of staff, John was also a keen supporter of school music and drama, working with John Hutchinson as House Manager for concerts and plays, and then taking over the duties after John's death in 1985. In 1992 John Akroyd's place in the ML department was taken by Miss Leslie Horden, an old girl of QMHS, and a linguist of considerable ability.

Mark Donan

John Lapworth (HJL) had introduced German as the second modern language in place of Spanish after his arrival in 1957. He had inspired and enthused boys; worked on the Fête committee with Brian Archer, and Mrs Lapworth had been one of the first members of the QMA Ladies' committee. An additional teacher of German was Mr Brian Birkby, appointed in 1960. Then after HJL's departure in 1964 came Mr Peter Holgate, a specialist in German and Russian, who built up German until he left in 1971, to be replaced by Mr Ian R Davison, who led the department within modern languages until he retired in 1995. Ian Davison was for many years a devoted Yearmaster, and the latter years he was responsible for liaison with local feeder junior schools, to ensure a smooth entry of boys into Queen Mary's. Mostly IRD will be remembered for coaching and umpiring school cricket, for organising and rehearsing carol service readers, and for his enthusiasm for chess. This aspect of his work is dealt with in Chapter 16. Mr Mark Lawson now co-ordinates the teaching of German; as Miss Miranda González teaches Spanish, now reintroduced. By 2004 a second Spanish teacher will be required.

IR Davison

A great sadness occurred in the summer of 1985 with the death of Mr John Hutchinson who had been second in the Modern Languages Department since 1967. He had contributed enormously to the department, and to the school and its wider community. As is mentioned elsewhere he was for years House Manager for school plays and concerts; he contributed hugely to the reviews and in-house drama, working with Geoffrey Paxton; he gave memorable and scholarly school assemblies; he had run the school bookshop, and he had been for years the staff member of the Fête and Barbecue committees of the QMA, running the annual raffles which, over the years, raised vast amounts for the school. An enthusiastic monarchist, he was a scholar, and a man of amazing literary, historical and general knowledge. A pair of fine wood lecterns in Japanese Oak for use in Assembly were fashioned by David Pennington in honour of John Hutchinson, following an appeal, and were presented to the school in 1989.

Engineering

In 1964 SLD appointed Mr KG Henderson to be Head of Engineering. Grant Henderson had a mining degree (and swimming blue) from Birmingham University, and he had worked for the Nigerian Coal Corporation. He had then entered teaching and he moved to QM from Bridlington Grammar School. The appointment coincided with the opening of the new engineering laboratory (later known as the AB Lab and now Design 2!). The Technical Drawing Office next door was planned as part of the same suite, but known as the TD room it soon became a maths room, and is now a computer room. Sadly engineering did not take off as a new sixth form subject as economics did, for instance. It was the one planning error for the new Queen Mary's, where sixth form subject choices were to remain traditional. Universities continued to look for maths and physics at A level as the preparation for engineering degree courses. Grant Henderson's work was to be in maths teaching, and swimming, as it had been at Bridlington.

Staff at Mayfield, c.1962

l to r: BJ Edwards, GB Archer, BJ Salter, EW Watson, NB Kirby, S H Chadburn, GG Brudenell, EG Law, W Sidaway

Mathematics

One of the bright lights of the early Darby years was EG Law (QM 1937–44), Senior Mathematics Master, who arrived in 1951. An outstanding teacher who made boys think and understand, he moved back, sadly, into university work in 1967. Older mathematicians retired and a clever young man, CD Obray, had stayed for only two years from 1964, so that SLD was determined, by offering good salaries, to attract a new strong team of mathematicians, and in this he succeeded remarkably. In 1966 Mr Michael G Jackson had arrived as No. 2 mathematician and Head of Applied Maths, so that he became Head of Mathematics in 1967. MGJ was to remain at the Head of the department until 1996. A quiet, very determined man, mathematician and Methodist local preacher, (and common room bridge player), his athletics and cross-country organisation was superb. He saw countless sixth-form mathematicians into university, very many into Oxbridge. His direct and homespun Christian assembly addresses were outstanding, and boys always enjoyed his references to Wolves! In 1989 he was promoted to Senior Master. On his retirement, Mr Stephen Rout became Head of Mathematics, bringing enthusiasm and the highest standards appropriate to that department.

Top:
E Foers

Lower:
Dr D Nunes rehearsing Troilus and Cressida *1965*

In 1967, Mr John F Farrington was appointed as Head of Applied Maths; in 1968, Mr David E Pomeroy joined the team, and in 1969, Mr John G Worth arrived. Thus the team of four was set up which lasted until the late nineties. JFF retired in 1998, DEP in 2003 and JGW retires in 2004. DEP has returned as Examinations Secretary. The maths team has been an extraordinarily successful aspect of QM since the sixties. A consistent period of high quality teaching led to remarkable academic achievement. John Farrington became the brains and driving force behind the early development of computers and IT at school, choosing hardware and software, sometimes writing the software himself, advising on the technicalities of setting up a dedicated computer network, and training staff with amazing patience. He advised on all developments until he retired. His school assemblies were clear and came from a devout Christian belief. For years he prepared the annual school Green Book with total accuracy. David Pomeroy's long and distinguished CCF career is dealt with in Ch 15.

English

For many years Mr Eric Foers who had been appointed in 1929, was Senior English Master, and his associate in the department was Mr James Jones who had come to QM in 1947, and who was school Librarian. Eric Foers had been a player of county standard in cricket and tennis, and before WW2 was school scoutmaster for several years. JJ came from military service, having been an AA Gunner in Italy with the final rank of major. For his gun aiming he used an early mechanical computer. For years Eric Foers produced the annual Shakespeare play, which, until he retired had been a task HM Butler undertook himself. The final Foers production was *Julius Caesar* in 1964, the last of the long run of Shakespeares and the last production on the Lichfield Street stage. Then a drama specialist was appointed, the first being Dr Don Nunes, for two years, and then for over 30 years

An American produces Shakespeare

Evening Mail Reporter

Mr Geoffrey Paxton. School Drama has its own chapter: Ch12. Then James Jones took over the department until 1982. He was a wise and careful teacher with a deep knowledge of literature and an enthusiasm for the minutiae of the use of words in texts. He was also a motor racing enthusiast. His successor was Mr James Walker (QM 1944–51), who ran the department and the library (and the Queen Mary's Club) until his retirement in 1996. He inspired his pupils, and in the Library he modernised its content, set up the first computer indexing, and opened up a much wider fiction section to younger readers. His work for the QMC is considered in that chapter. Then GGP became Head of English, yielding drama in 1997 and the department in 1999 to Mr Andrew Maund, who sadly only stayed at QM until 2001, when Helen Field-Mears was appointed to succeed him. Helen has worked to develop the quality of the department, while Mrs Pat Smith, No 2, is now Head of Drama. Both Geoffrey Paxton and Andrew Maund were scholarly English teachers to their sixth forms and will be warmly remembered. GGP was for most of the time second in the English department becoming Head of English only in 1996. Apart from Drama, Geoffrey was for years a Yearmaster, becoming latterly Senior Yearmaster. He edited *The Marian* for many years; and took charge of the Green Book from John Farrington. He carried out a scheme to place works of art in the school corridors, always having a skilled interest in things literary and artistic throughout the school. Latterly, he had worked with the author on historic displays in the entrance hall.

Many masters taught English in the middle school as was common in the earlier days. One of those who was a pillar of the staff in the sixties, and who taught English (and some history) in the lower and middle school for some years was Mr G. Brian Archer who came to QM in 1953, and left to teach in north Wales in 1974. His contribution to the Scout Group, and as one of SLD's original team of Yearmasters is mentioned also in Chapter 16.

Physics

When the first stage of the move to Mayfield occurred in 1961, the scientists took over their new empire with enthusiasm. Science accommodation had been poor at Lichfield Street, and this had been a major argument behind the requirement for new buildings. The Senior Science Master was Mr SH Chadburn, always known simply as 'Chad'. Appointed in 1937 as No. 2 Physicist to WA Burn, Howard Chadburn ran the physics department from 1955 until he retired in 1973. In the

Opening of the First Phase at Mayfield 1962

war he was commissioned into Technical Training Command. In 1961   *SH Chadburn*
Chad became master-in-charge of the Phase One Mayfield site, and
presided very firmly over the work and discipline of those 5th and 6th
formers who now made Mayfield Science Block their school home.
During the split site period, the Mayfield site was referred to on occasion
as 'St Chad's'. In his younger days he coached rugby and cricket; he
assisted with the scouts, and he led the Phys and Chem Society. Above
all he presided over an enormous growth in science teaching,
particularly the increase in the science sixth. His successor as Senior
Science Master until 1985, was Mr Fred Nash, Head of Chemistry. In
1961 Mr EW Watson was appointed No.2 in the Physics department.
An unflappable and gracious man, he was for some years Technical
Director for all drama productions. The school was shocked by his
sudden death in 1974, soon after he retired.

The new Head of Physics (and Senior Science Master 1985–92)
was Mr Geoffrey M. Austin (QM 1952–59) one of Chad's own pupils.   *GM Austin*
He enjoyed being 'Barny', and he met the challenge of the new
curriculum with extraordinary vigour. Science teaching was
revolutionised and, led by GMA, every lesson for every year had to be
planned, and was filed in new filing cabinets. Every lesson included all
the materials required and the preparation documentation. Practical
assessments were set up. Boys who missed these through absence had
to take them later. Records were automated on early computers, and
all marking was recorded. In all this he worked alongside his own
colleagues and Roger Metcalfe and the chemists, and the biologists
Tony Wiggin and Ken Yates. Geoff Austin was meticulous in

establishing this new world of science teaching. No revolution, however, could upset the wonderful tone of strong banter and rivalry between these departments. This maintained sanity among those who taught in the science block. One of the longest serving masters in this half century was Mr Gordon Brudenell. GGB was appointed as a physics master in 1960 and remained until his retirement in 1994, in his last years being Head of Physics. Gordon Brudenell was for very many years a much respected Yearmaster, and he was in charge of school bridge, a flourishing minor sport for much of the time. It is a tribute to GGB that Old Marians ask after him more perhaps than they ask after any other retired member of staff. He was succeeded as Head of Physics by Mr Jim Wilkinson, who has continued to develop the strength of this fine department, and who took over chess from Ian Davison.

Chemistry

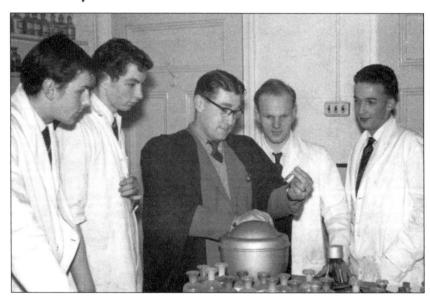

FG Nash

Mr Fred Nash (FGN) ran chemistry for very many years following his appointment in September 1955. He had taught previously at Joseph Leckie Grammar School, in Walsall. In those days he spent much time himself preparing solutions and setting up apparatus in the absence of any lab. staff. When the move to Mayfield took place, Fred advised on the design of the chemistry labs, and oversaw the transfer of equipment, some of which is in use forty years later. Maybe Howard Chadburn, Head of Science, liked the view from the upper floor when the decision was made to locate physics there and leave chemistry on the sunless lower floor – we do not know. However the result was not happy for the physics department. The faulty sealing in the fume cupboard flue from the chemistry lab S7, behind the upstairs cupboards in the physics lab S4, meant that plenty of toxic gas was produced, particularly hydrogen sulphide, smelling of bad eggs, and these gases were blown by the fans directly into S4! This always produced outrage among the physics staff, and wry amusement among the chemists, who had mostly lost their sense of smell anyway! Many investigations into these emanations took place, but the problem was only solved when the labs were refurbished in the 1990s.

Fred was a gifted teacher. His lesson notes were always fastidiously produced with beautiful diagrams of complex apparatus drawn with a ruler and never sketched. Fred believed in the power of humour, and wrote his jokes in the margin of his notes. Fred also exerted an apparently effortless discipline. He often allowed his enthusiasm for a topic to distort his sense of time, extending the length of his lessons often into break or the lunch hour. If Fred returned in 2003 he would notice that the lecture theatre in S8 has been transformed into a small laboratory. S6 has been refurbished with centre benches turned through ninety degrees, and all the fume cupboards work. There are no blackboards with chalk. He would be gratified to learn that some of his technician's cards with instructions for practical equipment are still in use. His legacy lives on.

Mr Roger Metcalfe arrived in 1971, after the departure of Dr Keith Jacques who had been No. 2 chemist since 1967, and it was he who succeeded FGN in 1985, a post he has held ever since. He was Senior Science Master also from 1992 until he became a Senior Teacher, and the post of Head of Science went to Jim Wilkinson. A meticulous teacher, a man of considerable resource, enthusiasm and skill, and wry humour, he has been head of a chemistry department of quality. Roger Metcalfe has taken over curriculum responsibilities since 1997, and now creates the school timetable, a task he performs with breathtaking professionalism! An Assistant Head Teacher, he retires in 2004. Mr Roy G Jones has taught in the chemistry department since 1980, and he has for very many years been responsible for careers education throughout the school.

AJA Wiggin

Biology

In 1957 the young Mr Tony Wiggin (QM 1944–51) arrived to teach biology in the converted PE hut at Moss Close. At that time sixth-form boys went to Miss Eld at the Girls' school for biology where the standard was excellent, while sixth-form girls came round to the Boys' School for their classics! Biology was an infant subject in the Boys' school, and, with a large personality and determination, Tony Wiggin made it an equal science. The opportunity of the move to Mayfield meant that new accommodation was available, but even then he could only

achieve a senior laboratory, with prep room, and share in a general lab. His was an independent department by his choice. AJAW was a memorable colleague and one whose school assemblies, with visual aids taken on stage in a black sack, were most intriguing for all his audience! In 1967 Mr Kenneth Yates arrived as his No.2, to replace Mr Chris Isaacs, and they remained as a team until 1990. For many years they took over the engineering lab as their 'AB Lab' (Advanced Biology), and divided themselves across the Parade Ground, between AB and S9. It was not entirely satisfactory, but they were very keen, and they made it work. Ken Yates was an enthusiast for Farchynys, and he devised A level fieldwork which he conducted there with great skill. He was secretary to the Welsh Centre committee; he was a musician who sang in the school choir for years; he was a well-read historian – a man of many parts. Sadly he was also a lonely man and he could not survive retirement, and he died soon after he ceased teaching. Since Tony Wiggin's retirement in 1990, Mr RS Preese has been Head of Biology.

Economics was introduced with the appointment of Mr Eric Taylor in 1963. He and his successor Mr RF (Bob) Fletcher built up a strong department. Economics moved around, but latterly the department was sited in the Sutton Road houses where Bob Fletcher was also Head of Sixth Form, and could monitor his charges in the common room below. Latterly Bob Fletcher did sterling work as a Senior Teacher organising property maintenance of the school buildings for the governors. He served as a Teacher Governor. When he retired in 2002 as Senior Master, his replacement was Mr Tom Walton who took over economics at the time when the library gallery was refurbished, and he could move economics to one of the upmarket seminar rooms there! Equipped with electronic whiteboard, he has transformed the style of economics teaching.

Mr EJ Kedwards taught **Art** when the school moved to Mayfield. In 1967 he retired after a long and influential career, and was followed by Arthur Hughes who made a considerable impact in his 2 years at QM. Then came Mr PH (Peter) Harman who broadened the subject and introduced pottery. By 1973 he had moved on, and Mr RG Stokes became Head of Art, and he remained at QM until he retired in 1998, to be succeeded by Mrs Debbie Wood. Graham Stokes supported a steady stream of very capable QM artists over the years, with his wide experience and skilled drawing teaching, and he gave an immense amount of help to drama productions. He was also a Form Tutor whose knowledge of boys in his form and year was very thorough, and his comments on them always wise. Seamus Moran (QM 1974–81), a

EJ Kedwards

RG Stokes

'Harlech Castle' painting by RG Stokes.

"The Evolutionary Spiral", Limited edition 1993, sculpture by Seamus Moran (QM1974–1981)

DS Hart

professional sculptor and pupil of Graham's, has allowed us to reproduce a photograph of one of his impressive pieces, while a painting of Harlech Castle by Graham Stokes also appears in this chapter. Since Debbie Wood's arrival, the Art Room has been redesigned and enlarged and the department has grown.

Following Mr Frank Phillips' long tenure as woodwork master (1927–72) – his work is nicely described in Chapter 3 – Mr Neville Cooper ran the department (still technically called 'Handicraft') with charm and skill until 1982. Mr Peter Gordon came to a renamed **Design** department, but in 1987 the school was shocked by his death following a severe stroke. Since 1987 and through a curriculum revolution including the arrival of CAD, or computer aided design, the department, now with two staff and two rooms, has been led by the redoubtable Mr David Pennington, who produces work of outstanding quality.

Mr Brian Bissell (QM 1940–52) taught Divinity until 1966. His successor was the Revd HG Prideaux and, though Humpfrey's stay was short, he did introduce the school memorably to the new thinking paperbacks appearing on the market! By 1969 Mr David S Hart had come to teach what had briefly been Religious Instruction, but which was by then firmly **Religious Education**. David Hart built up a strong department with every boy taking R.E. at O level, a religious and moral awareness course, and then a solid group taking a more biblically based A level. His enthusiastic work in developing and maintaining the Duke of Edinburgh scheme is chronicled elsewhere, and DSH also was a Yearmaster, with many years service as Yearmaster for the 1st year (now Year 7). For many years a part time teacher worked most successfully in the department, firstly Elaine Sturt, and then Marion Butt. Following David Hart's retirement in 1999, Mrs Janet Martin took over the department, and in her own way she maintains the success and high profile of the department.

Music is fully dealt in its own chapter, including the work of the peripatetic music staff. In the chapter on Sport all those who have taught significantly in the PE department have their mention.

Non-teaching staff

The school has been particularly well served by its non teaching staff. For many years Mrs Netherwood was Headmaster's Secretary from Hamilton's days, long remembered for her skills in 'running the school' and after her death in 1966, Mrs Boyd took her place. Subsequently

Mrs Betty Carr (now Mrs Betty Barratt) was secretary to Sam Darby. With her skills and immense knowledge of Walsall and local people she was enormously valuable as secretary. When she retired, Mrs Gill Columbine was secretary, and then, after sound training at Bishop Vesey's, Mrs Mary Matthews worked for both Sam Darby and Keith Howard. When the task broadened to include financial duties and the supervision of a larger office staff, Gill came back to the school as Administrator, which post she still holds. Her service to Queen Mary's has been extraordinary in length, energy, commitment, and cheerful devotion. Mrs Sue Gallier has, for many years, been Headmaster's Secretary, and she has watched over the interests of two Headmasters,

Mrs Betty Carr, now Barratt

Left:
Mrs Chris Radburn

Right:
Mrs Sue Gallier

and has charmed staff and parents alike. In the office for many years Mrs Maureen Fisher was receptionist and clerk, succeeded by Mrs Irene Day. Irene was a legend in her time! When she retired in 1995, her place was taken by Mrs Claire Coleman and most recently by Mrs Lynn Harding. For many years Mrs Chris Ward has been Assistant Librarian and Mrs Chris Radburn has been Resources Secretary, following on from Mrs Dutton and Mrs Mason. All have devoted themselves to their school, and those that have retired have remained loyal to it, attending Speech Days and concerts for years thereafter. We continue to be grateful for their support and interest.

The Senior Laboratory Technician is Mr John Badger who was appointed in 1987, succeeding Miss Sally Owen. Of recent years there have been a series of annual appointments of ICT technicians who have provided essential skills for the smooth running of the school's increasing number of computers. In the kitchens, the Catering Supervisor for very many years was Mrs Frances Watkins until she retired in 1987, followed

Left
Mrs G Columbine

Right
Mrs Irene Day

by Mrs Dot Pritchard, and now, Mrs Kath Wall. Queen Mary's has had a wonderful team of kitchen ladies over the years, and the memories of one, Mrs Jennie Lovatt (1968 – 93), are included as an extract in Chapter 8, and as a tribute to the quality of the people who have worked in the school over all these years. All have been remarkable in their devotion to the school, and many have served for so long.

When the school moved to Mayfield a bungalow was built for Stan Davies, the caretaker, and his wife. Stan remained faithful caretaker till he died in 1991, and his successor Peter Buckley remains caretaker to this day. Unusually Peter serves the school not only through his excellent caretaking and management of the cleaning staff, but also through his Christian beliefs by running Christian Union, and taking regular turns to conduct school assemblies. In 1992 Mr Mike Haig was appointed assistant caretaker and his wide technical and craft skills

Peter Buckley and Mike Haig

have been used extensively in the school, and he is now site supervisor. Both are called upon to support all the evening and weekend activities by opening and closing the buildings at most unsociable hours! Queen Mary's is very fortunate in the devotion of its caretaking and cleaning staff. Irene, Sylvia and Brenda have cleaned the school, each for over 20 years: a wonderful record. After years of service as Groundsman, Barry Haynes left in 1992, and the service went out to tender. Since then the school has enjoyed the skill of Mr Vernon's grounds maintenance business.

In recent years a staff governor has been appointed to represent the non-teaching staff. This governor was firstly Mrs Leslie Jones, then finance clerk, and since 2002 has been Mr Mike Haig.

Staff Wives

One of the features of the first half of our period was the Staff Wives group. Then, with a male staff and most staff wives without fulltime careers outside the home, there was a strong and happy social group of staff wives, led by Mrs Marjorie Chadburn. This was still active in 1980 and regularly wives met for tea in each other's homes. As with the QMA, there was a strong social fabric behind life at Queen Mary's which helped to provide a basis for the various public and cultural activities of the school, and it was also a source of pleasure and friendship. At all plays and concerts and QMA events many school and staff families could be relied upon to attend. With the tendency of staff to live further from school, and for wives to have their own careers, and for this to be replicated in the QMA as families came to live much further from school, so it has become more difficult to maintain this strong core of support which used to be so valuable. The core families are still there, and long may they continue to give support – they book whole tables at the Summer Ball and on Burns Night – but the numbers are not what they were.

School Staff 1992:

Front row: DE Pomeroy, JF Farrington, MG Jackson, JS Anderson (Second Master), KG Howard (Headmaster), SG Holtam, GG Brudenell, GG Paxton, KI Yates

2nd row: SJ Law, B Wragg, DS Hart, IR Davison, JG Worth, RC Cooper, RF Fletcher, R Metcalfe, RG Stokes, TF Perrett

3rd row: JP Blackshaw, DC Isgrove, MC Phillips, MH Lawson, T Lawrence, DJ Clough, DL Pennington, LJ Taylor, RC Champ

4th row: RS Preese, EJ Evitt, PW Green, JP Wilkinson, DJE Appleyard, AH Back, JA Walker, RG Jones

Back row: RJ Wilcox, Miss L Horden, Miss M Williams, Miss C Mellor, TJ Swain

12

DRAMA

The Annual Shakespeare Play

In the 1950s, Queen Mary's drama focused entirely on Shakespeare, and as David Fink's history showed in his Appendix XXIII, the annual Shakespeare Play went back to 1931, being produced till 1950 by HM Butler, and from 1951 until 1953 by RET Everton, who himself played in *Julius Caesar* in 1931. In 1954, a well-reviewed but abbreviated *The Tempest*, was produced by the Headmaster, AN Hamilton. From 1955 until 1964 Eric Foers produced the Shakespeare Play. In *The Merchant of Venice* in 1955 and *Much Ado about Nothing* in 1956 leads were played by Neville J Ellis, NJF Dodd, Bob Porter, JM Lambert, John Bruce, Bob Bradshaw and Barry Rogers. The cast at this time was a particularly able team of actors. The orchestra was conducted by EG Boothroyd, with Russell Green, music master, and Miss EM Flint playing along with boys. Then and for many more years the finances of the Dramatic Society were in the hands of SH Chadburn, Senior Science Master.

The detailed *Marian* review of the 1957 *Richard II* by Miss Emma Flint showed the enormous problems faced by the producer in those latter Lichfield Street days: the temporary stage and lights, the poor acoustics, the use of costumes – and wigs – hired for the purpose, as well as the fact that in 1957 Eric Foers was working largely with an inexperienced cast. In 1958 Bob Bradshaw's final performance was as the King in *Henry V*. 1959's play was *Henry IV Part I* with the orchestra now controlled by GF Rock. Early 1960 saw the production of *Hamlet; Macbeth* in 1961, and *Richard III* early in 1963, with a superb performance by BJ Holmes as Richard.

New Plays for a New Stage

Fittingly the last production on the Lichfield Street stage in the spring of 1964 was again *Julius Caesar*, produced by Eric Foers. Michael Whiston was Brutus and Michael Duffy played Antony. The music was composed and directed by Andrew Parrott and Desmond Burton. In those days a major feature was the Play Supper, with its printed menu, held

Top
The Tempest 1954

Lower
Beggar's Opera 2003

Eric Foers

Troilus and Cressida 1965 in the new quadrangle

after the production. In 1964 Dr Don Nunes, an American from the Wesleyan University and the College of William & Mary in Williamsburg, Virginia, was appointed to teach English and Drama, and his first major school production in May 1965 was *Troilus and Cressida*. It was staged out of doors in the brand new quadrangle at Mayfield with the builders still in residence. David Cockayne returned as an art student to design the set, with help from Andrew Wright. Major parts were played again by Michael Whiston and Michael Duffy with Paul Dean and others including, for the first time, four girls from the High School. Women's costumes were devised by Mrs Frances Gallivan along with a team of enthusiastic mothers. Music for these productions was by FS Hewitt who had arrived as Director of Music in 1962.

Don Nunes' second major play in March 1966 was Philip Massinger's *A New Way to Pay Old Debts*, the first break from the Shakespearian tradition. It was a delight with the frolics and the vigour, the bright costumes and the set. Whiston, Duffy and Dean again played leads, now with Richard Evans, Peter Ladkin and Barry Westley. The Prefects' summer production in 1966 was a first rate performance of *For Pete's Sake* by Leslie Sands, produced by Philip Sturrock.

Geoffrey Paxton

Geoffrey Paxton

By 1966, Geoffrey Paxton was appointed Head of Drama, to succeed Don Nunes who moved to the West Midlands College as a senior lecturer. In the spring of 1967 Mr Paxton produced *She Stoops to Conquer* and that summer the Prefects' Play was *Post Horn Gallop*, produced by Malcolm Heeley and Nina Athersmith. 1968 was the year which showed more of the vigour of drama to come. In March a group of staff and pupils researched and produced, under GGP's direction, the first anthology *1908*. This was a light-hearted picture of England, and Walsall, 60 years earlier – the year the School Song was introduced. Then followed, in July, the second outdoor production in the quadrangle: an adaptation of *The Birds* by Aristophanes, a highly imaginative production with a new generation of actors including David Etherington and Philip Cummings as well as the established figures of Guy Williams and Barry Westley, all aided by fantastic masks by

Macbeth 1968

Arthur Hughes, briefly and memorably Head of Art, and fine music by David Mee, the new Director of Music. In the following term there was a second anthology *Crime and Punishment* (including, as the author clearly remembers, much personal research by boys involving even confessions of shoplifting!), and then, in December 1968, came *Macbeth* with Barry Westley in the title role, and David Etherington as Lady Macbeth and Peter Ladkin as Banquo. For this major production the team of mothers, now led by Mrs Mildred Gilbert, was again involved in the production of costumes. As *The Marian* reviewer said of the production (Act V Scene 3) 'I would applaud thee to the very echo, that should applaud again.' The drama technical director at this time was Mr EW (Ernie) Watson, long-time member of the physics department.

Enormous research, writing and preparation went into Geoffrey Paxton's work. His drama had an originality without parallel in school drama. *The Birds* was a new adaptation from the Greek; *Caviare for the General* required Black Country dialect (checked by Phil Bull), and then he took the script to London to a Jewish friend so that the dialect of Bobchinsky and Dobchinsky could be checked. *Three Men in a Boat* had to be written as a drama, while *The Italian Straw Hat* was a new translation from the French. There were original lyrics for many productions including *The British Life, Liberty and Pursuit of Happiness Show*, and musicals written with Bev Wragg of which *Liberty Hall* was the most significant. None of this could have been translated into quality stage performance without the planning, the running orders and schedules, the briefings and the sheer drive and discipline which aroused total loyalty among not only the players, but the vast technical crew behind each show.

Left:
Man for All Seasons 1972. David Etherington, Paul Mason, Malcolm Webster

Right:
David Etherington, Murray Writtle, Neil Parkes, Chris Holmes

Opposite top to lower:
Caviare for the General 1973

Malcolm Webster and Alec Miklaszewicz

The set

Neil Parkes and Malcolm Webster

David Etherington as the Mayor

Anthologies and Summer Productions

In 1969 the last summer Prefects' Play was *The Happiest Days of Your Life*, produced by Lynn Stanley and Paul Dean, and the main autumn production was Geoffrey Paxton's condensation of the two parts of *Henry IV*. Prince Hal was played by Philip Cummings with a performance considered thoughtful, impish and fluent. Mr Peter Harman, new Director of Art, designed the 'pewter' set. Accompanying the production was an exhibition mounted by Peter Fryer, with the assistance of the history department, on Shakespeare and Henry IV. For some years these exhibitions, associated with the main productions, became essential, and gave an opportunity for boy historians and artists to be associated with Mr Paxton's work. 1970 began with an anthology entitled *The Thirties*, devised by Mr John Hutchinson, with much nostalgia and pre-war music, readings and drama. Then came the April Plays by the junior four years, with *Cider with Rosie, Androcles and the Lion, The Long-Distance Cyclist* and *Maria Marten*, each produced by a different member of staff. Then followed in July, Geoffrey Paxton's summer production of *Oh! What a Lovely War*, a serious attack on the First World War from the point of view of the common soldier, with songs appropriately sung by the end-of-term chorus of 'Roosters'. Though this was a GGP production, it was devised as a Prefects' Play giving Jonathan Phillips a lead as Captain of School. Each year that followed included anthologies in the autumn, with the main play moving in to the Easter Term and a (usually) home-grown summer production also. The idea of the prefects' play was lost. *Journey* was the 1971 anthology, while the main production was *A Man for All Seasons* in February 1972, followed by *The Critic* in July.

A Generation of Talent

Girls from the High School were again admitted to the cast in 1974 for *Romeo and Juliet*, though from 1972 Margaret Hayden, now Margaret Anderson, from the High School, with a team of girls, took over the costume design and making. Materials were bought from Eric on the market. Tudor 'skirts' made for the men in *A Man for All Seasons* were tucked up to make Elizabethan breeches for the play within a play in The Critic. Malcolm Webster's tailor father made a wonderful check suit for him for *Caviare for the General* (1973) which was GGP's adaptation of Gogol's *Government Inspector*, and that suit turned up again and again for years. Otherwise every costume was freshly made for each play, despite the electricity strikes of the 1970s! For *Romeo*, at the start the actors wore modern clothes; then after a drumbeat and flurry of movement, suddenly the whole cast were in collars, capes and cuffs of Cavaliers and Roundheads! Then from 1976, for years plays benefited from the wonderful designs and colours of the costumes produced by Ellen Smith. Her colour contrasts added an extra dimension to the productions, especially of the *Shrew*, *Rivals* and *Bourgeois Gentilhomme*. When he retired, Geoffrey Paxton said that he had been blessed with wonderful costume teams, and he thanked them for their 'sparkling hard work'.

QM's finest two actors of the early 1970s were David Etherington and Malcolm Webster, who, with Alex Miklaszewicz as a fine Ossy, led in *Caviare* in 1973, while Malcolm remained as Romeo in 1974. Malcolm went on to a life on the professional stage. In July 1974 Geoffrey wrote a complete summer show: *The Great Nineteen Twenties Fairground*. This revue looked at the decade with the stalls, rides and songs of a fairground. Tommy came back from the trenches; then came *Housey-Housey*, the *Peace Conference*; the *Tug o' War of the General Strike*;

and *The Nippy's Crossword* in which a waitress in a Lyons Cornerhouse fell in love with a customer doing his crossword! The music was by Jethro Ingram, then music adviser for Walsall, and the whole fantasy had a legacy seven years later in *The Thirties Department Store* (1981) where that epitome of thirties living became the focus of a glorious gaze at the other pre-war decade.

By 1975 in *Julius Caesar* there was a new generation with Paul Tait, Robert Haden, Ian Trow, Andrew Turner and David Roberts. By then Graham Stokes had taken over the art department from Peter Harman and, for many years to come, devised the décor. 1976 was Brecht's *Galileo*. Then in 1977 one of the most memorable shows: *The British Life, Liberty, and Pursuit of Happiness Show* was full of delights as the audience enjoyed the 'inexhaustible pleasures of national self-examination'. Produced by GGP who wrote the sharp lyrics with music 'of great theatrical charm' by Jethro Ingram. Michael Ratcliffe, subsequently to be Drama Critic for *The Observer*, thought it 'terrific fun, and much matter for thought all round'. Then came the memorable *Hamlet* in early 1978 with an outstanding cast including Lloyd Allington, Ian Trow, and Tim Jarman. Michael Ratcliffe said that Allington's was a remarkable performance as Hamlet showing natural dramatic gifts. In 1979 there was *The Beggar's Opera* with Peter Taylor, Andrea Gray and Jonathan Birt and the music arranged by Bev Wragg. 1980 was the year of *The Rivals* and 1981 *Taming of the Shrew* with Henry Summers, Tim Swain and Miranda Lapworth as Kate. 1982 was Thornton Wilder's *Our Town*, and in 1983 the main production was *The Bourgeois Gentilhomme*. Matthew Smith and Simon Stephens led in *The Alchemist* in 1984; and Mr Kenneth Warburton, at the end of an enthusiastic review, praised the addition in the Hall that year, of tiered seating. This was to be used for very many years and it improved the total view of so many in the audience.

By 1974 Bev Wragg had arrived as Director of Music, and he and Geoffrey collaborated on many productions where Bev found GGP to be a 'professional in every sense of the word'. Their first production was in the summer of 1975 with *Three Men in a Boat*, with music written by Jethro Ingram. The highest level of skill and commitment was expected and achieved, and there was always a last-minute spontaneity as quick changes were made to the script or music just before each performance! Never satisfied, both BW and GGP would make changes each night of a production. Beverly Wragg composed all the incidental music for later shows, and together they wrote the full length *Liberty Hall* and the oratorio *Seven Deadly Sinners* composed for the concert of 1995, and much more in the 25 years.

House management of drama and concerts was for many years run devotedly by Mr John Hutchinson (see also in Ch. 11). After his sad death, this work was carried on by Mr David Appleyard, and more recently by Mr Philip Blackshaw.

The Puppet Show

In the years 1976 – 82 there was a Puppet Show at school events, with the script and design developed by actors in school, and led for a time by Ian Trow and Paul Wood. The Puppets were taken out to local schools and churches, and there were Christmas parties with puppets at school. The 'Huppits' were devised, with the Captain of School as the villain to be booed by enthusiastic young audiences. The anthologies continued throughout, usually in the autumn, and *Poets' Corners* in 1983 is a good example. A verse anthology of town life and people, with an opportunity for the audience to write their own limericks on Walsall placenames during the interval. Here with Jeremy Bull, Roger Geiss, Jonathan Nunes, Adrian and Gerald Powell, those not necessarily at the head of the major production cast list developed their talents in shows which provoked great enjoyment.

Costume designs for Hard Times by Mrs Ellen Smith

1985–1997

In 1985, the main production was an adaptation of *Hard Times* with Jeremy Bull and Lee Roberts giving 'bravura performances'. They also led in *The Italian Straw Hat* in 1986 in which a new generation of performers first appeared including Tim Bryars. 1987 saw a new production of *The Tempest*. In 1988 GGP produced *The Captain of Köpenick* by Zuckmayer, a difficult satire which was performed with great skill in another fine Ellen Smith setting, with Gerald Powell giving a convincing lead supported by Matthew Holden and Roger Geiss. This company showed its experience again in 1989 in *Much Ado about Nothing*. During the late eighties performances were enhanced by the stage constructions of Joe Franklin and John Bateman, whose Sicilian villa was the centrepiece of *Much Ado*. A review of 100 years was the heart of *Café Chat*, with a new setting, to be repeated, when the whole Hall became the café and centre of the action. The convincing *First Mysteries* in 1990 was presented in a year devoid of experienced lead actors. Fine music for the *Mysteries* was written by Lawrence Oakley, a pupil at QM at the time. Ellen Smith designed an amazing ark, constructed within a set of boxes by Joe Franklin. A striking production in 1990 was *Oedipus*, produced and directed by Mr Philip Blackshaw, Head of Classics. James Wilkinson played Oedipus, John Manning was the Priest of Zeus, and Teiresias was played by David Huntley. The most ambitious stage set, in what seemed afterwards to have been a golden era, was the set for Shaffer's *Black Comedy* in 1991. In these years much of the backstage support came from Mrs Jenny Bateman and Mrs Ruth Franklin. Jenny Bateman organised the understage area which became her empire and woe betide actors who forgot their behind-stage discipline, if Mrs Bateman was around! The Batemans and the Franklins were two families who gave service of such quality for so many years for the benefit of the school, and from which they gained so much enjoyment for themselves. *King Lear* in 1992 was a memorable production in the 30 years of Geoffrey Paxton's work at QM. Here was Tim Bryars never appearing to be a schoolboy but totally convincing as Lear in speech and manner, so ably supported by Kathryn Manning as Cordelia, with another superb Paul Hughes performance as Edmund, and the first appearance of Richard Nowell, as the Fool. Many of the later shows in the summer centred on the floor of the Hall, and around tables the audience was offered refreshment as an integral part of the show. The provision of refreshments in or out of the Hall, according to the nature of the production, arose from the co-operation between Geoffrey Paxton and Tim Swain. Geoffrey, throughout the years, had found benefit from support from Paul Paterson in the early years and latterly not only Tim Swain but also Philip Blackshaw who proved invaluable, for instance in *Lear*.

Liberty Hall 1993

With a 200-page music score, GGP and Beverley Wragg composed and wrote *Liberty Hall* in 1993, as a joint High School/Grammar School musical venture. A critique of the values of the Thatcherite era, and dominated by the trio of Abigail Arnold, Ian Cooksey and

*Importance of being Earnest
1994
Back row: John Manning, David
Huntley, James Ball, Lee Haynes,
Phillipe Ince. Front row: Paul
Hughes, Charlotte Bubb,
Catherine Manning*

Natalie Raybould, it introduced a new dimension to QM drama. That
summer there followed *The Importance of Being Earnest*, with a final
and superbly female Paul Hughes as Lady Bracknell. During the interval
that summer the audience were treated to the appropriate cucumber
sandwiches with their liquid refreshment! In 1995 Richard Nowell
played the title role in *Macbeth*, with Kate Airey as Lady Macbeth, in
a production described as a 'triumph' by David Etherington who himself
had been Lady Macbeth in 1968. *A Midsummer Night's Dream* was
GGP's last Shakespeare in 1996 with a cast led by John Baker and a
fine Puck by Vicky Mama and Bottom by Alex Bailey. This was a truly
joint production with the High School, with actors throughout both
schools and joint direction by Geoffrey Paxton and Pauline McIldowie.
GGP's long and distinguished drama career closed with a show written
and composed by Bev Wragg and himself *Aesoplutely Fabulous* in July
1997. In July 1999 to mark Geoffrey Paxton's retirement from the
school, Tim Swain, colleague, former pupil and actor, produced the
celebratory performances of *The Everything Must Go Show*. The
understage area was swept for memories which were metaphorically
loaded on to a cart before our eyes. There were sketches from the past,
and songs of the homegrown shows of thirty years were brought out
and sung with gusto. A booklet was produced which showed the
enthusiasm and affection for GGP. The audiences showed their warm
feelings for this remarkable man.

Andrew Maund

Andrew Maund was Head of Drama for only three years, but during that time the quality of his work showed clearly in Brecht's *The Resistible Rise of Arturo Ui* in 1997, with Peter Bradbury's memorable rendering of the title role. Then in 1998 we were treated to another challenge in Arthur Miller's *The Crucible* which warned of mass hysteria and the dilemmas facing all who have to make judgements in society. John Twells, Ian Wilkinson, Peter Bradbury and Tina Jones led an assured cast from both schools. Andrew Maund's final production in his all too short reign was *The Taming of the Shrew* in 1999, with Paul Edward's charismatic and impressive Christopher Sly, convincing performances by Inderjit Sidhu, Clare Nowell and Vicky Millward and an essential contribution by Mr Robert Champ's memorable tricycle. By this time Mrs Jill Pollitt and Mrs Helen Scales were making an outstanding contribution to costumes.

Recent Productions

In 2000, Helen Field-Mears gave us *Our Day Out*, and then in 2001 *Jesus Christ Superstar*, a show dedicated to the memory of Nathan Lloyd, who tragically died at university but who had been a mainstay in the technical crew during Andrew Maund's productions. A huge cast in a wonderful performance, directed by Helen Field-Mears, was

The Beggar's Opera 2003

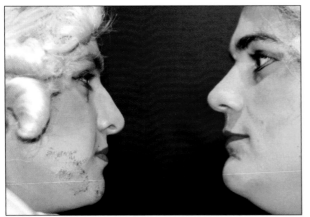

led by a fine group of musicians trained by Bev Wragg. By 2002 the responsibility for drama had been passed to Mrs Pat Smith who produced a much enjoyed compilation of scenes under the title: *Wooing, Wedding and Repenting*. In 2003 a cast of new actors in years 7 and 8, displaying splendid talent and humour, and using sixth-form assistant directors, presented *Treasure Island* with impressive staging and sound.

A recent highly successful innovation has been the school Poetry Competition, for which all years contribute, and which produces a wide range of imaginative work of quality. Winning poetry is read at a evening performance for pupils and their parents.

The December 2003 production by Pat Smith of *The Beggar's Opera* (previously produced at QM in 1979), with the music arranged by Bev Wragg and set by Debbie Wood, was memorable for its musicality and the superbly confident movement of the strong cast led by Keith Leddington, Rachel Kerr and Nick Bridgman. It was a treat, fully in the tradition of Queen Mary's drama.

Paxton, Ingram and Wragg? ('75)

May I take your order, Sir? ('89)

What former colony? ('76)

13

SPORT

Sport has had in one sense the longest continuity at Queen Mary's in the last 75 years. When the school moved to its new buildings, school sport continued on the playing fields as before – except that it lost some of its main pitches and had to adjust to the invasion of new buildings! The old cricket pavilion became obsolete as it faced, not pitches and the outfield, but the parade ground and science labs.

But the Mayfield land could absorb the buildings and still provide playing grounds for the Grammar School and the High School, and all this without encroaching on the land used by Mayfield Prep School. There were now modern changing rooms, those built in the PE Block (and for the girls' school, newly built on the west edge of the site) as well as space on the side of the new buildings to add, a little later, a swimming pool, a new (but small) cricket pavilion and, much later, an indoor rifle range.

Rugby Football – "Rugger" – before 1970

In 1954, Rugby football was the preserve of Dick Hopkins, 'Hoppy' or, later, 'Stub' to generations of boys. A Cambridge Blue who played for Swansea and London Welsh, he took over rugger at QM from WA Burn when he arrived at Queen Mary's in 1935. He was in charge for 31 years, apart from his war service, when Messrs Boothroyd and Burn took temporary responsibility for games. In his appreciation of Hoppy when he retired, DJ Archer said that for him ability in sport was a gift to be enjoyed, and that whoever might have made the touch-down, it was the contribution of the team to the scorer's moment of glory that Dick valued and emphasised.

Fixtures in the mid-fifties were with Adams Grammar School, Lichfield, Bishop Vesey's, Stourbridge, Aston, Burton, Newcastle, Longton HS, Saltley, George Dixon's, Five Ways and Moseley GS, plus a well-established match against Cosford RAF Apprentices which was always the first match of the season. The 1st XV also played Walsall RFC and an Old Boys' XV. In 1955 three boys played for Staffordshire. The needle match was that against Bishop

Opposite
Winners of the 1964 Staffordshire Sevens:
l to r: Chris Nicholls, Peter Lucas, David Stone, John Taylor(with cup), Jan Webster, David Hughs, Clive Hilton – before and after the game

Mr Dick Hopkins

Top
1st XV Rugby Team 1961–62
captain: CC Dodd

Middle
1st XV Rugby team 1962–63
rear: Richard Porter, Garth Evans,
Nick Webb, Chris Nicholls, John
Taylor, David Stone
front: Jan Webster, Graham
Knight, Tim Field, Neil
Copson(Capt.), Peter
Taylor, Tony Cattell, -?-.

Lower
Rugby Sevens with Jan Webster
at Scrum Half

Vesey's. In 1957 the match against Vesey's was lost 0 – 15, but 'it was very fast and clean, and highly enjoyable', according to the captain, P Harris, writing in *The Marian*. After a number of modestly successful years, strong teams produced good results from 1960 for several seasons. In 1961 David Brown played for England Schoolboys against Wales and France, and played for the Staffordshire Senior XV, as did four other members of the 1st XV: Ian Harvey, Ian Brooks, Howard Clews and David Dallow. In the same year Eric Buttery and John Taylor formed the second row pair for the Staffordshire under 15s.

Over the years the quality of the coaching and the team spirit shown gave QM a rugger record of which they could be proud. By the mid-sixties fashion now dictated the game be called 'rugby', and QM had further success by winning the 1964 Staffordshire Schools Seven-a-side Competition. JG (Jan) Webster (1957– 65) emerged as an outstanding player, captaining the Staffordshire Schools side and representing England as scrum-half against France at Poitiers. Jan went on to play for Walsall RFC, to captain Moseley (1971–74), to play for the Barbarians, and to play for England, being capped 11 times between 1972 and 1976. He was in the first English team ever to beat New Zealand in New Zealand in 1973. Back to school rugby, and, by the 1964 season, coaching was in the hands of John Burgess the newly appointed Head of PE. It must be added that without the work of Mr George Crudace with younger boys, coached on Saturday mornings in their first two years, skills and fitness would not have produced such steady results up the school.

Cricket before 1970

Cricket coaching was in the hands of Dick Hopkins and David Fink. For rugby and for cricket (though particularly importantly for cricket) pitches and wickets have to be prepared. In the fifties Mr Toogood was thanked regularly for his work, and for providing refreshments. By the sixties he had been replaced by Alan Roden and then Mr G. Taylor. The general gang mowing was done by the Walsall Parks Department. Cricket fixtures followed something of the same pattern as the rugby list, with the addition of Wolverhampton (who played only soccer in those days), and Bablake. In cricket, the mid-fifties were notable for the skill of BGW (Barry) Rogers, later Clerk to the Governors. Several reports speak of his quick eye, power and timing: clearly an exceptional batsman. JL King and RJ Smith were outstanding bowlers of that generation.

1973. Six England players from Moseley RFU with Jan Webster seated left

By 1958 the young David Brown was emerging, heading the batting averages. In 1959 RJ Smith and D Grainger scored 47 for the first wicket against Newcastle, and then Brown scored 88 in 80 minutes, 72 of his runs being scored off boundaries. In this year the school won the Walsall Knock-out Competition, beating Walsall Trinity in a memorable final. This game is magnificently described in *The Marian* of the day, (October 1959, page 14) with the bowling of David Brown and the batting of Charles Dodd, who completed the victory with two successive eights (equivalent of sixes in normal cricket)! Mention must also be made of the contribution of Terry 'Ticker' Hope in batting and bowling, he and Brown making a fearsome opening bowling pair.

By 1961 after some matches were played away while the grounds were being re-laid at Mayfield, the rugby teams played at Gorway for much of the season until the new pitches were in full use. In the 1961 season with Brown and Dodd still playing, the 1st XI had another fine term. That summer David Brown played for Warwickshire 1st XI against Scotland at Edgbaston, with a match analysis of seven wickets for 110 runs. In the summer holidays he played four county games for Warwickshire. Queen Mary's most illustrious cricketer, he was to go on to play for England, being capped 28 times. There is a further note on David Brown in Chapter 20. In 1962 Dodd was still playing,

Warwickshire six-a-side with David Brown standing left

but by 1963 a new young side only had modest success. However, in 1964, led by DF Hughes and CE Nicholls, QM again reached the final of the Walsall Knock-out. This time, playing Blakenhall in the Final, the team was in sight of victory on the second evening when Rain Stopped Play. By the late 1960s DR Carlile, a very fine bowler, was leading a team including the Duttons, W Bound and FS Orchard, and the coaching, as with rugby, was led by the PE master, John Burgess.

John Taylor completes a cross country run

Other Games in the 50s and 60s

The school Cross Country cup was awarded on Sports Day in the 50s, and one wonders what happened to the Ronald Hayes Cup, newly presented in 1958 with gratitude to the donor. In these years there were regular athletics triangular fixtures and the North West Midlands Schools Sports held at Aldersley Stadium, Wolverhampton. Boys also went on to compete in the Staffordshire Schools Sports (later the AAA Sports) and in 1959 two competitors, Tony Cattell and McKay, went on to the National Championships. In 1961, Cattell's 100 yds in 10.2 seconds and his 220 yds in 23 seconds were outstanding, and in the National Championships that year Cattell jumped 22ft. ½ in, gaining 2nd place in the Intermediate Boys' Long Jump. In 1966 GC Williams won the Victor Ludorum and a National Championships title.

There were of course other sports operating in the fifties and sixties. Apart from athletics and cross-country, there were tennis, golf, swimming, soccer, hockey and sailing. These varied in strength over the years. Walsall Hockey Club provided the pitches, and the musician Andrew Parrott who, for a while, led the Hockey team, has clear memories of the devotion and enthusiasm of his side. He recalls the Saturdays when he played a Hockey match for the school, went on to play the Town Hall carillon, and then on to practise with the Midland Youth Orchestra! Tennis was also keenly played in those days, using the Arboretum courts. Mr Maurice Ebison, a chemist and Cambridge half Blue at badminton introduced the sport in the academic year 1958-59, and two cups – junior and senior – were donated, and the first senior badminton championship was held in Big School and won by Phillip Holmes of VI Modern Languages. Until JAD took over the Sailing Club in about 1970, it had been run with great enthusiasm by Tony Wiggin.

The house system still operated and in the 1955 Sports, Petypher's beat Gnosill's, while in 1958 Docker's won with a narrow margin over Somers'. However with the move to Mayfield, the house system was brought to an end, and was replaced by a horizontal Year grouping. This had something of a negative effect on sports where houses had provided the competitive edge. However houses had little other value latterly, and the Year system provided much needed pastoral care.

Sports memories from those days include the walking to and from Lichfield Street and Mayfield before the new buildings were constructed. Also tales abound of the state of the old pavilion, and especially the colour of the water in the baths after rugby matches!

New staff and new facilities
In 1968 John Burgess was replaced by Mr Richard Cooper, who had trained at Loughborough, and was a rugby player for Leicester and Leicestershire. He came to QM from Birmingham University where he had been a lecturer in the PE Department. He had captained the England Schoolboys side in 1961 with David Brown playing in the team. Dick Cooper was in charge of games and PE as Director of Physical Education at Queen Mary's until 1997. Though his love was rugby, he devoted himself also to coaching cricket with a diminishing team of colleagues for those thirty seasons. When George Crudace retired in 1971, having introduced rugby and cricket to hundreds of young Marians for 25 years, his place was taken by Mr Graham Judd. There was some pressure to reintroduce soccer, but this demand was deflected by bringing in hockey which Graham Judd did with strong support from Brian Archer and, later, Ian Davison. Hockey was later taught with professional skill with the arrival in 1978 of Mr Graham Chesterman. Graham did an enormous amount for hockey and minor sports in the school until he left in 1985, to be replaced by another hockey specialist, Mr Eddie Evitt.

Mr Richard Cooper

Soon after Dick Cooper arrived the final elements of the new buildings were put in place, with the opening of the School swimming bath and later the squash courts. The swimming pool was opened in May 1970 by Mr AD Munrow, Director of Physical Education, Birmingham University. The squash courts and extra changing rooms were opened in October 1971 by Mr FD Jeffries, Chairman of Governors, and a series of exhibition matches by County players was arranged during the week.

The new cricket pavilion was built, which was small but served its purpose. In 2000 it was modestly enlarged by the efforts of the Queen Mary's Club to become a joint clubhouse and cricket pavilion. One of the outstanding occasions in the 50 years since 1954, was the QMC Dinner in 1972 when four main guests were invited: Stephen Hadley (left 1957), winner of a medal in the International Horse of the Year Show; Trevor Homer (left 1960), Open Amateur Golf Champion; David Brown (left 1961), international England cricketer; and Jan Webster (left 1965), international England rugby player. What

Trevor Homer

1st XV 1971/72

Seated: Nick Archer, Mike Dillon, Jeremy Longmore (captain), Brian Causer, Chris Edwards

Standing from left: Les Clives, Andrew Siddons, Jeremy Duckett, Clive Jarrett, Stephen Law, Jonathan Roberts, David Cockayne, Paul Tredwell, Kevin Russell, Jeff Beech, Mr RC Cooper

a quartet from one generation at Queen Mary's! Trevor Homer had been Victor Ludorum in 1960. He went on to win his Open Amateur Championships in 1972 and 1974. He represented Great Britain in the World Cup (The Eisenhower Trophy) in 1972, and he was in the Walker Cup team in 1973.

Rugby with RCC

Rugby has remained the core game in the two winter terms. By 1968 Richard Cooper had begun to instil his fitness regime and skills which produced a deserved victory that year over Burton, though Vesey had too strong a side. Losing Jeremy Lindon-Morris and the Orchard brothers at the end of the season, it was 1971 before training and good attacking rugby began to produce results again. Jem Longmore, Brian Causer, Steve Law and Nick Archer all played for the Staffordshire under-19 XV. Nick Archer, in addition to his cricket prowess, was to play for England Schools Rugby, and to go on their 1973–74 tour of Australia. In 1972–73 training, determination and good backs led to great success, winning nine of the first 12 matches, with MJ Dillon as Captain and Chris Edwards as Scrum Half. Jonathan Roberts, Clive Jarrett, Chris Giles and Rob Haden formed the back line. Much of this team, with the addition of Keith Nangreave and Martin Hunt, were to serve for two or in some cases three seasons. Martin Hunt went on to play for England Colts (the under-19 team). In 1975–76, led by David Sedgwick, the 1st XV had an excellent season with Martin Hunt and Phil Moseley playing for Staffordshire under-19s, and Neil Hunt and Dave Wrighton showing excellent skills.

By 1977 Richard Moon had reached Staffordshire under-16 level, while in the 1st XV John Moore gained a county place, and Gary Taylor (many years later to be Richard Cooper's successor on the staff as Head of PE) was the most improved player of the year. 1979 and 1980 were great seasons with considerable press coverage and cups to the team's credit. Richard Moon and Gary Taylor dominated the team in seasons

1st XV 1980–81

Seated: Saheed Rashid, Jonathan Williams, Richard Moon (captain), Gary Taylor (present Head of PE), Steven Tromans

Standing from left:
Mr RC Cooper, Harvey Sandford, Jeremy Marren, David Ralph, A Moore, Andrew Garratt, Mark Rogers, Robert Fisher, David Land, Andrew Crabtree, Lee Bradnick, Sean O'Brien.

when the fixture list was being expanded, with the encouragement of Keith Howard, the new Headmaster, to include many Midlands public schools for the first time, including Warwick, Solihull, King Henry's Coventry, and King Edward's Birmingham. In the Solihull 7-a-sides in 1979 the team just lost in the final to Cowley, recognised as the top English rugby school of the year. Richard Moon ultimately won a Rugby Blue for Cambridge University in 1984; he played for England A team and for the Barbarians, and then his club rugby was centred on Harlequins and Moseley. He continues to be involved nationally in the game, being a member of the Council of the Rugby Union.

In 1980/81 the 1st XV played 28 matches and won 24 of them with 553 points for and only 165 points against, and anchormen were Saheed Rashid and Jonathan Williams. In 1984 James Walker the captain went on to captain the County side, and in 1985 school rugby benefited from Rupert Moon's two years at QM on his way to play for Wales in the 90s. 1987–88 was a very strong year when the 1st XV was led by Richard Mills.

In 1990 Matthew Holden was captain and Colin Charvis was developing his exceptional skills which would take him to Swansea and to play regularly in the Wales side. He captained the team in 2002, and was

Colin Charvis in action for Wales against Scotland, 2003

Captain of the Wales World Cup team in Australia in 2003. He plays for Tarbes and captains Wales in 2004. In 1992 Nick Rose went on to play for the Midlands and England under-16 B XV, and in 1993 Andrew Pountney reached the England under-18 squad. In 1993/4 the 1st XV had notable victories over Bablake, Henry VIII and Lichfield, and the first team also won the County 7s cup for the second year running. By this time Mr Malcolm Phillips had taken over 1st team training, although Dick Cooper was still Head of PE.

Cricket 1970–1997

Edgbaston Indoor Nets

Cricket in the school went through strong periods and difficult patches. Much of the coaching was by Messrs Ian Davison and Tom Perrett, and then for from 1987 to 1998 by Mr Lloyd Taylor, an enthusiast and coach of great skill. In 1972 Clive Jarrett, Steve Law, Ken Russell and Nick Archer represented South Staffordshire schools. In 1973–74 Nick Archer was outstanding, playing for the County and for England Schools Cricket. In school matches in 1973 he got five half-centuries and a century against Cannock, the first 1st XI century for over twenty years. In the late seventies the loss of senior players during the season as they left school after taking A levels, and the worsening of the condition of the cricket square weakened the morale of the school side. A new square was created and by 1980 conditions improved, led by the skills of Saeed Rashid and Richard Moon but as in rugby, new fixtures with strong schools like Denstone, Wolverhampton and King Henry VIII provided another stiff challenge. By 1983 Sean Wordley was seen as a fine captain in a season dogged by poor weather and modest seasons followed.

From 1987 Lloyd Taylor developed the facilities, adding new nets and an improved square (largely thanks to Barry Vernon, the

*1st XI 1993 with Neil Taylor,
Captain of Cricket*

present Grounds contractor). The acquisition of sidescreens and a bowling machine was made possible by extensive fund-raising on the part of all the cricketers in the school. The Edgbaston Indoor school was used to facilitate winter coaching, to compensate for the lack of a sports hall at school.

It was a period marked by a succession of records for the school. The 1990 1st XI was the most successful for twenty years with captain Ian Wilcox breaking three individual records: most runs in a season (836), most centuries (3), and highest score (191). The defeat of Tettenhall College in that year was by the record margin of 223 runs. In 1991, Faisal Agha took 45 1st XI wickets (second only to David Brown's record in the 1960s).

In 1993 the school staged its first overseas tour to South Africa. It was a resounding success taking in Cape Town, Durban and Johannesburg and finishing with a safari in the Kruger National Park. Neil Taylor was probably the best captain during this era, and he led the 1st XI to the first ever unbeaten season the following year. Andrew Walker, in the same side, scored a record 1563 runs during his time with the first team. Nine centuries were scored between 1987 and 1996. The school produced a steady flow of County players for Staffordshire, together with one, Amit Sharma who went on to represent the Midlands, the NAYC, and then played for Worcestershire 2nd XI. Lloyd Taylor's highly successful coaching era ended with a second tour, to Canada, in 1998.

Swimming, Squash, Sailing and Minor Sports

However one gives pride of place to major games, the development of 'minor' sports was notable. Once the pool opened there was a swimming club run by Mr Grant Henderson, ex-Birmingham University swimming Blue, with John Dickson's help, and a very strong life saving tradition began which lasted for 20 years until Mr Henderson retired. There was success in swimming against local schools. A number of fine swimmers emerged including Paul Stokes and Alistair and Simon Coldrick. In 1988 a school swimming team reached the national Junior Finals at Bury St Edmunds. They came sixth, with Keiran Etheridge, Leighton Williams, Iain Payne and Robert Bough.

Squash, encouraged by Messrs Judd and Holtam, became very popular and a squash club for Old Boys and parents was set up who raised a great deal of money for the upkeep of the courts over the years. Squash was played by many in lunch hours and as a competitive sport and matches have been regularly played over the years. In 1980–81 both Junior and Senior teams in the Squash Club reached the semi-final of the Sportsco Cup. In the Premier Cup the 1st V lost to Aylesbury Grammar School, eventual winners of the national competition. The 1st V were Robert Walker, JM Wightman, David Clift, RC Hodge and Laurence Shore.

Squash team 1981 with Robert Walker, Captain of Squash and Mr Stuart Holtam, coach

Among his many enthusiasms, Mr John Dickson ran the Sailing Club from 1970 until it was taken over by Mr Michael Broom in 1984, though its boats then only survived two more years. Boats were stored and repaired in the Old Pavilion and taken out each season to Chasewater. A sailing party went out each Wednesday afternoon by minibus, and in this way a small group of devotees were taught and encouraged over the years.

In the fifties and sixties there was also a tennis club and a badminton club, each with a master and senior boy encouraging participants and sometimes arranging fixtures. In 1966 there were four tennis fixtures for instance. Tennis was played all through the earlier years, using the courts at the Arboretum. There were three or four matches a year in the sixties when Mr Brian Archer consistently supported the sport for many years, and even in 1972 and 1973 school matches were played against Darlaston, but with the rise of other sports, tennis became only a Wednesday recreational activity, though in the mid-eighties a number of friendly matches took place. More recently, in 2001, two teams entered the Staffordshire Tennis Knock-Out Cup, and reached the semi-final. Minor sports suffered badly in local schools, though not at QM, during the 1980s teachers' dispute, and sadly they did not recover. Local leagues enabled table tennis and badminton players to test their skills and enjoy a few matches each year, though the most memorable table tennis was always that played with saucepan lids on the old table at Farchynys. School table tennis was run by Mr Tom Perrett. Golf was encouraged twice in this period by the two economics masters: why the sport and the subject should coincide I am not sure!

Athletics and Cross-Country

Sports Day was a major feast in the school calendar for much of this period. In 1955 GH Matthews was Victor Ludorum, and RB (Bob) Bradshaw (seen also in drama and trips to Greece and Rome, and for a term in 1966 a temporary master at school) was an up and coming athlete of the middle school. In that summer there were complaints about the lack of refreshments on the field for Sports Day and the need for a marquee with teas. How often was this to be repeated in years ahead? About 1980, the Annual Sports was moved from the grass of Mayfield to the West Midlands College track. For years the school attended compulsorily and in most cases without marked interest. However, eventually a voluntary Sports, with refreshments supplied by David Hart and his team, produced a pleasant atmosphere. From before 1954 until 1966 John Dickson played a major part in both athletics and cross-country. He was then succeeded by Michael Jackson who retired in 1996, but John Dickson's enthusiasm for athletics and his support for colleagues never waned. On Sports Day he was always the chief starter with his starting pistol and blazer. (For many years he served the AAA at its meetings, and was a much-respected national figure in the sport.) For 30 years, with the tireless and efficient organisation of Michael Jackson, the programme of the school sports meeting was carried through impeccably. In recent years Sports Day has moved back to Mayfield. Assisted by others (of whom John Worth

Left
Mr John Dickson in athletics mode!

Right
Mr Michael Jackson

deserves special mention), MGJ and JAD were incredible stalwarts who inspired generations of boys.

By 1969 Jonathan Roberts represented Staffordshire in the High Jump and was 5th in the All-England Championships. Lloyd Peck and Michael Nangreave were then winning at Intermediate level. In the 1971 All-England Championships, Lloyd Peck was 5th in the Junior 1500m in 4 mins. 10.8 secs. Michael Nangreave was 2nd in the Junior Long Jump with 5.92m, while Jonathan Roberts was in the winning Staffs Junior Relay Team. By this time the reduction in the number of local Grammar schools led to the disappearance of most of the triangular matches. By 1973 three boys could high-jump over 6 feet: Mark Savage, Michael Nangreave and Jonathan Roberts. Lloyd Peck

Sports Day 1960.

Peter Radford, Olympic medallist, presenting the Victor Ludorum Cup.

l to r: Peter Thompson, SL Darby, Tony Cattell, James Hicken, Peter Radford, Phillip Sturrock, Michael Hale, John Taylor.

ran 1500m for the West Midlands in 1975 and Michael Nangreave was captain of the West Midlands team.

Inter-school Cross Country appears in the early sixties with the Wolverhampton Schools Road Relay and Queen Mary's developed slowly with the support of Messrs Dickson and Bissell. Messrs Brian Hitchens and Michael Jackson then coached as more races were entered, and by 1967 junior and senior teams were entering a wide range of fixtures, winning the Yarrow Cup at Lichfield as the most improved team, and winning the Walsall Town Championships. 1968 was a strong season when the teams were highly successful in the Tipton Schools meeting, the Rugeley Bowl, and the Wolverhampton Road Relay, and David Everson finished 22nd in the All-England Schools Cross-Country. From 1969 John Worth had replaced Brian Hitchins as a coach. By 1971 the Farchynys Road Race over 14 miles was well established with John Proctor setting a record of 1 hour 20 minutes, and Lloyd Peck, Steve Gould and Chris Florkowski showing their promise. Lloyd Peck came 19th in the All-England Championships in his 4th year at school. In 1974 Peck, Gould and Florkowski travelled to Germany for an International Race and with strong Belgian and German runners, Peck came 1st. In 1978 David Lowen could report again that the teams won the Most Improved Cups. The Under-16s won the West Midland Championships, led by Neil Appleby and including Denzil Homer and Julian Masters. A new generation had emerged, including Nicholas Toone who followed a year later. 1982 was to be another highlight year with the senior team winning the league title, the Sutton Park Race, the Lickey Hills Relay and our own Queen Mary's Relay. This latter inter-schools race was organised by Michael Jackson for very many years. By 1988 Paul Ingram was running for the West Midlands during another period of success. In 1996 and 1997 Ivan Wall won the Birmingham League title for two years running. Though names may be mentioned this sport was above all a team effort in which Queen Mary's was very highly regarded throughout this period.

Skiing

Skiing trips abroad were introduced by Dick Cooper in 1970. In all there have been about 30 trips, mostly in the Easter half term. RCC himself ran 26 of the trips, mostly to Austrian resorts. After 1988 there were several run jointly with the girls' High School. A tremendous number of QM boys learnt to ski, many to a high standard. RCC mentions Warren Winfield, Neil Gosling and Nick and Tom Shaw as outstanding among the many, but special mention must be made of two who went on to pass professional examinations and become professional instructors. They were Julian Dilkes and Michael Mullner.

Astroturf hockey in 1980s

Hockey

Hockey first appears in the 1950s, and inter-school fixtures were played throughout the 1960s. Hockey teams were coached by Brian Archer from 1970 onwards with three or four matches being played each year. Led by Phil Westley, the 1972 season showed that an effective side could be created. With Ian Davison now coaching, hockey made steady progress each season, and in 1976 Chris Baker emerged to lead the side and play himself for the county at under-19 level and later at U 21, while the team won the Walsall Schools Tournament. It was difficult, however, to develop the sport in the shadow of school rugby. In 1978 Graham Chesterman, a hockey specialist, took over and by 1980 there was a 2nd as well as an under-16 team, and these began to provide the depth of skill and experience required. By 1983 a fixture list from under-13s upward had been created and the 1st team had considerable success even against Highfields School, Wolverhampton then the best local school side, and national champions in 1981. Five boys represented Staffordshire at under-19 level. By 1984 the team was having greater success using the astroturf pitch at the Alexander Stadium in Perry Barr. In 1984 the under-14s went on a successful tour in Holland.

In 1985 Eddie Evitt took over and in 1987 a Hockey Tour to Holland took place. In 1988, as a result of Eddie's enthusiasm and coaching, the school had its strongest ever hockey side. They won the Staffordshire U18 cup, and only lost in the finals of the Midlands Cup to Nottingham High School in 1989. The leading player was Andrew Gullick, goalkeeper and Staffordshire U18 team member, though the unofficial player of the season was Jonathan Swain who scored 28 goals in all. In 1991 there was another tour to Valkenburg in Holland for coaching and matches, with four teams taking part. In 1993–94 they won the Staffordshire Cup at under-18 and under-16 levels; the 1st XI, led by Neil Gosling, beat Warwick, Bablake, Malvern, Loughborough, and in the Oxford Schools Festival they won against Whitgift, Aldenham and Abingdon, though they were beaten in the final of the Midlands Cup by Rugby School. They had almost as good seasons in 1995, when Stuart Hopley was captain and in 1996 under Marc Sanders, a season which included a highly successful tour of Australia.

This may be a place to mention the expedition of 1995 to the Hindu Kush, led by Mr Eddie Evitt. Ten boys, Eddie and a guide flew to Islamabad in July. They experienced considerable cultural shock as they moved to Rawalpindi and the town nearer to their base, Chitral. Before their trekking began they witnessed a fine local polo game. Then on to the high-level trekking in the Kalash area. They experienced sickness, but achieved their aims, witnessing some amazingly sensational scenery. By the end they felt that the trip had been a great benefit and a privilege for them all.

Dick Cooper was Head of Physical Education at QM from 1968 to 1997. His contribution was enormous in times of financial constraint when the facilities at the school increasingly needed upgrading: the gym was always far too small, the changing rooms became outdated and the drainage of the playing field was always very poor, though work was done on it at intervals. The CPA was invaluable, and the swimming pool and squash courts were excellent. RCC was a tireless worker for school sport. He had the highest standards and enforced them with his tough personality. He was treated warily by boys of all ages. His rugby was his love, and during his stewardship, Queen Mary's rugby was nationally respected, and he produced fine players for the school, and for county and national sides. He himself worked for the game nationally for many years and was an under-19 national selector, and chairman of the selectors for a time.

QM Sport since 1997

Mr Gary Taylor, an Old Boy whose achievements at school have been mentioned above, took over rugby when he became Head of PE in 1997, and in 1998 under Paul Ricketts the 1st XV won the Staffordshire Cup for the first time since 1987, and 25 rugby players enjoyed a challenging tour of South Africa. In 2000, led by Jonathan Pearson, the 1st XV, at the end of a mixed season, beat a tough squad from a Zimbabwean school in Harare, and then, having led for much of the

1st XV 1998 – with Mr Gary Taylor (Head of PE), Paul Ricketts (Captain of Rugby) and Mr Julian Roderick (coach)

Staffordshire Cup semi-final, were narrowly beaten. In 2001 there was a highly successful summer tour of western Canada, in which four matches out of five were won. Their opposition in the fifth game included provincial and international players. Junior rugby teams have had success, particularly the under-14s in 2002 who won their Staffordshire Cup, and went on to win the four matches on their tour of Limerick and Cork.

Coached by Mr Richard Francis, hockey has improved its performances over recent years. In 2000, the 1st XI led by Andrew Cork narrowly lost the U-18 Staffordshire Cup 3-2 against a strong Cannock side. Then in 2002/3 the 1st XI won ten matches and drew four, and this included a 4-3 victory against King Edward's Birmingham, who had scored twelve goals against them the previous year. In the 2003/4 season the Under-14s won all their 18 games, notably beating King Henry VIII Coventry 11 – 2. The 1st XI, Under-16s and Under-14s all reached their finals in their Staffordshire Cup matches, the 1st XI losing to Newcastle in the Final. The 1st XI captain has been Ravi Pachchigar. The most promising school hockey player is Mandeep Johal of Year 9.

In cricket in 1999, led by Andrew Cork, the 1st XI lost only two of their ten matches, while they had another strong season, marred by poor weather, in 2000, when the team was captained by Tom Archer, the third generation of the family. Mr Andrew Thomas, taking on the task of cricket coaching from Lloyd Taylor, has done an excellent job. In 2001 the under-14s won the Walsall Cup, while the under-13s won the Walsall Schools' League and the Walsall Cup. In 2002 the 1st XI had a solid season with good victories against Old Swinford Hospital and King Henry VIII Coventry, which latter match included a superb unbeaten century by Richard Rawlinson. The under-13s of 2001 became the under-15s of 2003 with a fine season's cricket including a hat-trick by their skipper Daniel Hunt against King Edward's, and an outstanding century by Tom Pinnegar against Sir Thomas More.

In 2001 Mark Joyce played snooker for a three man team in the European under-19 championships. In the final he met the Welsh under-19 champion, and though he trailed in part of the match, he won 6 – 3! QM has not had a snooker star before.

In 2002 the athletics team took part in the Walsall Schools' Championships held at the Alexander Stadium, winning the boys' championship, and with the High School, the boys'/girls' championship. The Cross-Country team, run by Messrs Michael Lax and Richard Johnson (QM 1984–91), also performed its best for some years, both in the Birmingham Schools League and the Walsall Championships, where Peter Mellar was placed third overall. An increasing number of runners train with Birchfield Harriers, and represent Walsall in the West Midland Championships.

School indoor sport will benefit immeasurably when the new sports hall is built in 2004. Reference to this project has been made in Chapter 10. As I write in March 2004, the foundations are dug, and the structure is being built. The new sports hall is on its way.

After some years at West Midlands College, Sports Day has returned to Mayfield

14

MUSIC

The early development of School Music

In the early 1950s the musical director, Mr Russell Green, who had joined the staff in 1931, was only part-time. He was much involved with Edgbaston Old Church where he was organist and choirmaster. The school orchestra was conducted by Mr EG Boothroyd ably supported by both Mr Green, who played cello, and Miss Emma Flint with her viola. The orchestra played music for the annual Shakespeare Play, and occasionally gave recitals which sometimes including playing Russell Green's own pieces.

A choral society, first formed in 1953 under the guidance of Mr Green, sang carols for the Christmas Festival of Nine Lessons in St Paul's. It then practised some harmony singing for the first school concert in Central Hall in March 1954. Much of the enthusiasm at this stage was led by RW (Bob) White (QM 1947–54) who went on to win a Choral Exhibition at Christ's College, Cambridge. The choir practised Stanford's *Te Deum* and Vaughan Williams' *Let us now praise famous men* which they sang at the Quatercentenary Commemoration service in St Paul's that July. The orchestra also played for the music festival which was part of the Quatercentenary celebrations. Thus music at QM began to develop.

Opposite
Ben Sperring, Peter Mellar, Lisa Bull

Left:
Mr Eric Boothroyd

Right:
Mr Wilf Taylor

Recitals by soloists and musical talks were the programme of the music club by 1955. The club had been formed in 1952 by Mr WJ (Wilf) Taylor who was Chairman, and who frequently produced talks to accompany gramophone recitals. David Lyon (QM 1950–56) remembers meetings of the music club, listening to records, with Wilf Taylor and his brown trilby hat on the table in front of him. David Lyon became an army bandsman and studied at the Royal Academy of Music, and then went on to be a professional jazz pianist and a composer. In 1956 Mr David Fink, who gave piano recitals to the music club, gave a demonstration of the new school tape recorder. By 1958 under pressure from SL Darby, the governors had resolved to appoint a full-time Director of Music. Mr Russell Green gained an appointment as Organist and Choirmaster at Trinity Episcopal Church, Watertown, New York, and left at the end of July 1958. Clearly 'R.G.' would be greatly missed. He subsequently moved to Canada, and died there in 1975.

Gordon Rock

Mr Gordon Rock was the first full-time music master at QM though music was only part of his timetable; he took over both the orchestra and choir, and Eric Boothroyd received due thanks for his years conducting the school orchestra. Mr Rock was very informal; he wore sandals and no socks in summer which was very avant garde, and he addressed boys by their Christian name. Thus his approach was fresh in what was still a rather stuffy old-fashioned staff. The choir began to practise more ambitious work for both Speech Day and the Carol Service. A concert was held in Central Hall in May 1959 and a jazz group was formed. Mr Rock took over the music club, assisted by the enthusiastic and very able Glynne Stackhouse, (subsequently Music Director of the British Council), who remembers Gordon Rock and his rigorous sixth-form teaching of music theory. WG Taylor now founded a junior music club with its instigator, Andrew Parrott, then in Form I, as its first secretary. Andrew Parrott (QM 1959–66) still has the minute book, showing that the junior music club first met on 5th June 1959 with 20 boys. It had as many as 54 boys at early meetings, and never fewer than 16. The aim of both clubs was to have as many 'live' meetings as possible, which meant having recitals by members.

Music in the school, and the orchestra in particular, was from now to benefit from the first of many peripatetic teachers to come to the school. The first of these had been Mr Joseph Stones, a violinist who founded the Bromsgrove String Orchestra. Then came Mr Wilfred Goodare, viola player from the CBSO. There were now musical instruments at school for loan to pupils. These developments made possible a full concert in May 1960 at Central Hall, with 250 boys taking part in the choir and orchestra. There was a varied programme in the first half, with the second half given to Bizet's *Carmen* with school choir and the Bromsgrove String Orchestra with members of the school orchestra.

In 1960 an Old Marians' Orchestra was formed, conducted by old boy and past Chairman of QMC, Chad Jackson, and led by Graham Rockett, father of Jonathan Rockett who is now No.2 in the physics department at QM, an Old Marian himself and teacher then at Chuckery Junior School, and supported from the beginning by Fred Hood, one of the viola players. Their first concert was held in November 1960 in Big School.

A tradition which continues began at this time when Clifford Ball, Bournville's *carillonneur* and Andrew Parrott's piano teacher, suggested to Andrew that he apply for the post of carillon player for the Walsall Town Hall. The carillon was set up in the tower in 1953. Andrew remembers well his Saturday lunchtime carillon duty after school hockey matches, and before going to play in the afternoon with the Midland Youth Orchestra. The present holder of the office (2003/4) is Nicholas Bridgman, also a Queen Mary's hockey player!

The 1961 School Concert was held in a well-filled Walsall Town Hall with a second half devoted to a very well-reviewed performance of selections from *Messiah*, again with the Bromsgrove String Orchestra augmenting the school orchestra. From 1962 the music club was organised in two parts: at Lichfield Street and at Mayfield.

The jazz club, led by Messrs Rock and Kirby, continued to flourish, and there was also now a guitar club. The jazz club in particular benefited from the enthusiasm of Messrs Edwards, Hawkins and EG Law, who brought to it their own enthusiasm! Also from this era was David Olney (QM 1959–66) who became a professional jazz player. The local jazz 'star' Ken Rattenbury gave a lecture to the jazz club, and there developed the Merv Poole Trio and a Trad band led by Stewart Greenwell.

From early 1961, with the part of the school now centred on the new buildings at Mayfield, a fortnightly whole school assembly took place at St Paul's. Speakers were arranged and the singing was led by a chapel choir, set up from within the school choir. By Christmas 1961 there was a much more ambitious Carol Service, and in July 1962, Mr Rock arranged his farewell concert in the Town Hall with the second half devoted to a performance of Orff's *Carmina Burana* with the school choir and the CBSO. A young musician at the time, Julian Saney, has an abiding memory of this occasion. Early in the performance nerves overcame the trebles and there was a total silence when Gordon Rock called for their entry. His face was a study of alarm and disbelief. All subsequent entrances were effective and, apart from that one hiccup, the evening was a resounding success. In September 1962, Mr FS Hewitt arrived as Director of Music.

F Stanley Hewitt

The new Musical Director had the benefit of an outstanding batch of musicians in Philip Green, Andrew Parrott and Peter Ford amongst others. A very good violinist, Michael J Smith, was leader of the school orchestra at his time. For the 1963 concert Mr Hewitt was able to use the Old Marians' Orchestra to accompany the school choir in Central Hall. Holst's *Hymn of Jesus* was a challenge for the choir and orchestra in the second half. In 1963 Mr Philip Head had arrived as a peripatetic violin teacher from the CBSO. Mr Head was to outlast all the staff of that time, and, after wonderful service to QM, only retired in 1998. He remains an occasional guest musician.

The 1964 concert was held in the Town Hall. In the second half the choir supported by the Old Marians' Orchestra played a variety of pieces, including Vaughan Williams' cantata *In Windsor Forest*. It is a tribute to the school, and the support in the 1960s, that the Town Hall could be filled for a school concert. Philip Green composed the music for the orchestra to accompany the 1963 Shakespeare Play, *Richard III*,

Mr Stanley Hewitt rehearsing for Speech Day in St Paul's

while Parrott composed the music for *Julius Caesar* in 1964. A connection with Merton College, Oxford had been established under Gordon Rock, a Merton man himself, and Glynne Stackhouse had gone on to study there. Now both Philip Green and Andrew Parrott continued the line of QM musicians at Merton. Andrew Parrott subsequently has become an internationally renowned musicologist and conductor. Another musician from QM at this time was John Bird, author of an acclaimed biography of Percy Grainger, first published in 1976.

The 1966 concert was held in the school hall, with a series of pieces which revealed new talent emerging among the young musicians in the school — Stephen Jaggs, Jonathan Phillips, John Patterson, Alan Taylor and David Lavender — though the school still benefited from the experience of Tim Sutton, Ian Bednall, Peter Ford, PB Langley and Clifford Evans, a distinguished pianist whose post-graduate work led him to study in St Petersburg. Tim Sutton was a superb singer and pianist who gained a choral exhibition at Trinity College, Cambridge and went on to become a professional musician. Ian Bednall went on to study at the Royal College of Music and, having mastered the Walsall Town Hall organ, subsequently gave an organ recital in the Royal Festival Hall in London. The music club was still strong with a visit to the Messiah in Birmingham, a piano recital by David Fink, recitals by pupils and lunch-hour record meetings. The choir, now of a very high quality, performed for Speech Day, the Carol Service, and the Opening of the new buildings. Music still owed an enormous debt to the enthusiastic support given by Mr Eric Boothroyd, as organist in particular.

The new Mayfield buildings provided facilities for music teaching and practice that were of a different scale from those at Lichfield Street. Class music lessons had been held in Big School, excessively reverberent and inconvenient. Music options were in the 'music room', the former kitchen of the Headmaster's house. Small, cramped and very dusty, noise levels had to be watched as it was opposite the Headmaster's study! The new music room at Mayfield and the three practice rooms were palatial for their time. Provision had also been made in the new hall for an organ. Blocks on the wall cover holes which were constructed to bear the weight of an organ platform. The specifications for an organ were agreed, but money has never been available.

The 1967 concert was again in the school hall (or Big School as the contributor to *The Marian* perhaps properly described the new hall), and in the first half the orchestra played pieces by Telemann, Purcell and Haydn. The musicians from 1966 were all available. In the second half the choir, accompanied by an augmented Old Marians' Orchestra, performed Handel's *Acis and Galatea*. At the close of the concert the school paid tribute to the skill and work of Mr Hewitt as he departed to work in Bournemouth after five years at Queen Mary's. Mr David Mee inherited a fine musical tradition and his Easter concert in 1968 again enabled soloists to perform a variety of pieces in the first half, while the second half was given to Vaughan Williams' *Toward the Unknown Region* and *Five Mystical Songs*. In the summer David Mee produced excellent musical accompaniment for the school play *The Birds*. In 1970 the school welcomed a new Director of Music, Mr NRF Jones.

Nick Jones

Mr Jones' first major concert was held in St Paul's in May 1971. This was a most enterprising evening at the heart of which was Hoddinott's cantata *Dives and Lazarus*.

With visiting soloists the choir performed this difficult modern work with great skill which justified Nick Jones's enterprise in choosing this piece. The concert closed with a fine performance of Purcell's *Come, Ye Sons of Art*. Concerts for young instrumentalists began and a brass band also was inaugurated in 1971. The next concert, in 1972, was also in St Paul's where the choir was accompanied by a section of the Old Marians' Orchestra led by Graham Rockett. Their ambitious programme, including Pergolesi's *Magnificat* and Vivaldi's *Gloria*, was also accompanied on the organ by Mr Peter Morris, Head of Music at Bluecoat School, who was to assist in many ways for years to come.

By 1972 instrumental playing had developed so that there were strong brass and woodwind groups, and many solo items in an instrumental concert of quality. Glyn Partridge played piano and bassoon, Christopher Watkiss the euphonium, while Jonathan Turton and Lloyd Allington emerged as younger players. There were very many outstanding contributions recorded in *The Marian* report. In 1974 the third Instrumental Concert allowed a modest audience to hear Christopher Watkiss play Chopin, and contributions by brass, woodwind and jazz groups as well as pieces by a sizeable orchestra. It was the last concert for Glyn Partridge, whose skill with the bassoon was outstanding, and for Chris Dickson, who contributed quality guitar playing.

Bev Wragg, 1974 to the present day

When Mr Beverley Wragg arrived in 1974, he found choral music 'pretty strong'. In three years Nick Jones had built up instrumental

Mr Beverley Wragg

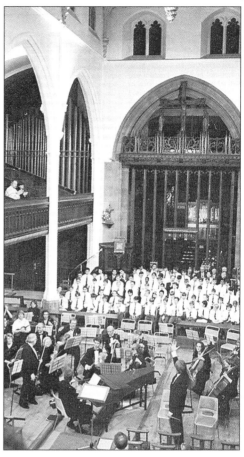

playing considerably, and left a choir of quality. Bev Wragg soon developed the Queen Mary's Schools' Orchestra, later the Joint Orchestra, in co-operation with Mr Tony Lister, Director of Music at the High School. In 1975 they played at a carol concert at Beechdale School in Walsall, and in 1976 there was a concert at St Paul's with the orchestra and piano works played by Hilary Middleton. They put on a concert with St Michael's School choir in Rushall, and it played in the High School Festival in May.

The Joint Orchestra

In 1977 the 'Joint Orchestra' put on concerts at both schools. Lloyd Allington was the leader. By 1978 its solo pieces were played by Lloyd Allington (violin), Adrian Johnson (piano), Louise Andrews (oboe) and Michael Riley (piano). Michael had by then gained his ALCM diploma. At a later concert that year Neil Morley played cello, the horns were Andrew Day, Simon Dilkes and Alison Howes, and Roy Dickinson played bassoon. Roy was later to change to the French Horn, an instrument he was to return to whilst working with the European Commission in Kosovo in 2000, playing with the Kosovo Philharmonic. In 1979 Adrian Johnson gave a performance of Grieg's *Piano Concerto*, and in 1980 he played the Rachmaninov *Piano Concerto No. 2*, whilst the Orchestra supported the newly-formed Chamber Choir with *Joseph and His Amazing Technicolour Dreamcoat*. The Orchestra leader was by then Christina Pritchard. In that year concerts were given in March, July and November – sometimes at the one school and then at the other. In the November concert Neil Morley played the Saint-Saens *Cello Concerto in A minor*. In 1981 the JO put on a concert jointly with

Recent concerts in St Matthew's Church

Shelfield Male Voice Choir in aid of the Mentally Handicapped, at which Michael Riley was the main soloist. There were regular concerts each year in December, at the Grammar School, for Junior school audiences.

By 1983 the co-leaders of the JO were Jane Pearce and Richard Wise. In that year there was a Reunion Concert in Walsall Town Hall with 64 players and a programme including Schubert's *Great C Major* and Adrian Johnson's Rachmaninov. The future was strong with, for instance, up-and-coming trumpets including Martin Shaw and Tom Porter, with Richard Wise and Daryll Prew developing as piano soloists, and, by 1986, audiences being charmed by the classical guitar playing of Simon Northwood. After he left school, Martin Shaw was to rise in the jazz world through playing at Ronnie Scott's. By the mid-eighties most concerts were being held at St Michael's Church, Caldmore which was of a size appropriate for the smaller audiences of that time, and had good acoustics. In 1985, at St Michael's Caldmore, the orchestra performed Bach's *Brandenburg Concerto No. 2* with Martin Shaw, then a member of the National Youth Orchestra of Great Britain, playing the phenomenally difficult trumpet part, two other Bach Concertos and Handel's *Music for the Royal Fireworks*; Bev Wragg recalls there were only three rehearsals for the concert. In 1986 Martin Shaw, having left school, came back to play trumpet in *Zadok the Priest* and *The King Shall Rejoice*. In 1989 Mark Purcell, later Organ Scholar at Oriel College Oxford, gave a recital of Albinoni's *Adagio* on the organ at St Michael's, and in 1990 there was a major reunion concert, at which over 70 past and present members played Beethoven's *5th Symphony*, and pieces by Smetana and Borodin.

But in 1991 the Joint Orchestra was forced to close down. The Borough Youth Orchestra had moved from Saturday mornings to Tuesday evening, and members were unwilling to give up two evenings in a week to orchestral practice. During the years from 1975 to 1991, about 120 girls and 115 boys had played in the JO. Several ex-members had gone into professional music: Martin Shaw and Neil Morley for example. Among the 50 concerts, many were for charity and hundreds of pounds were raised, and some were for Junior schools in the borough. There was an infectious enjoyment about Wednesday evenings in JO, and many past members discovered with disbelief that it no longer existed.

Instrumental Music

Leaving the JO to one side, there was a wide variety of other musical offerings from 1974 onwards. In December 1974 there was a 'Musical

Miscellany' with School Orchestra and Brass Group, Madrigal Group, Junior Woodwind Group, Jazz Group all making their contributions. In 1975 there was an evening entitled 'From Purcell to Pop'. The Grammar School Instrumental Groups and Choir played a full part in the years that followed in the High School Music Festivals arranged by Mr Tony Lister, their Musical Director. A wide variety of song and instrumental solo and group playing marked an ambitious concert 'Music 77', held in the school hall in March 1977. A concert in March 1978 featured the school orchestra in part one, while after the interval the choir performed Christopher Hazell's *Holy Moses*.

In June 1980 the school's Blüthner grand piano was completely restored through the generosity of a Governor, Mr Michael Goold, and his firm WA Goold (Holdings) Ltd in memory of a senior member of their company Mervyn Adams. Mr Adams was a QM parent and had been chairman of the QMA Fete committee 1977–78. A memorial piano recital was held to commemorate the occasion. In the same year a concert at the school by the Birmingham Philharmonic Orchestra saw the beginning of many series of professional concerts promoted by Walsall Music Circle. It brought many world class artists to the school including clarinettist Jack Brymer and Jeffrey Skidmore with members of Ex Cathedra.

Making music in the Music Room

The Jazz Group

At this time many QM boys were in the Midland Youth Orchestra, and in 1981 Adrian Johnson, then at Durham University, played Franck's *Symphonic Variations* at their major annual concert. The distinguished Old Boy, Clifford Evans, came to give a piano recital in 1983. There were several charity concerts at this time. The orchestra and choir in 1983 put on a concert at St Martin's Church for Christian Aid, and this was typical of a time when there were musicians in the school who, with the minimum of rehearsal, could put on an extra concert. In 1982, Music on Thursday was a concert in the autumn with a wide variety of talented musicians from this period, including Gerard Grant, Andrea Gray, Tom Porter and Richard Wise. There were 25 to 30 boys arriving in the school each year with at least Grade One in one or more instruments. By 2002, the number was down to six or seven. Then by the middle school there were as many as 60 instrumentalists, now the figure is more like 35. Then there were quality musicians each year, later boys of such quality were few and far between. Boys live further away from school, the rise of computers has had its effect, while the increased emphasis and greater number of exams has not helped. Parents seem less interested too, and this can be seen in the collapse of the size of audiences.

Following the demise of the Joint Orchestra there have been a series of spring instrumental concerts with a wide number of groups playing. In 1994, Gareth Baynham-Hughes gave a piano recital alongside performances by Oliver Nicholls (cello), Matthew Wragg (violin), Martin Stone (clarinet), Ben Duncan (recorder), with pieces by the brass group, the woodwind group and the jazz group. In 1995 a similar concert took place, with Fauré's *Requiem* sung by the Chamber Choir in the second half. By 1996, Zachary Perry was playing cello, and Richard Till and Richard Hinitt piano. By 1998 the leading pianist was Neil Manchester and Ben Duncan was playing the clarinet. By 2002 the leading instrumentalists were Zachary Perry, Nicholas Hurley (piano) and Ben Sperring (recorder), with Jennifer Bourgeois (trumpet). Since 1982 instrumental competitions have been held each year with outside adjudicators to find the winners of the music batons, presented each Speech Day. In 1982 the batons were presented to ML Shaw and JD Bradbury; in 2003 the winners were Ben Sperring and Adam Sapic. The quality of these competitions reflect also the work of the peripatetic

Concert Programme 1977

music staff who teach in the music practice rooms, week by week, year by year, and who have contributed so much: those who came in the early sixties have been mentioned, including Mr Philip Head. Others include Mr G Nock, Mr A Petrovic, Mrs J Chamberlain, Miss J Blakemore and Mr Stephen Read, who for some years helped to re-start and run the CCF Band arriving at school each week from Wolverhampton at 8.20 am to run a practice before registration.

Choral Music
Choral music has been particularly strong in the last 25 years. Four boys have gained Oxbridge choral scholarships since 1974. In 1974 and 1975 there were choral concerts as part of the High School music festival and the choirs of both schools sang Brahms' *Requiem* in May 1976. In December they sang Britten's *Saint Nicholas* in St Paul's. In 1977, with an invited orchestra

which became the usual pattern, they sang the Mozart *Requiem* in May, and Handel's *Messiah* at Christmas. Soloists were also invited for these performances. Through the Birmingham Philharmonic Orchestra quite a number of players came over the years. Kathleen Washbourne (ex BBC Symphony Orchestra) sang regularly and she was brilliant, with a violin worth as much as a Strad! Links were built up through the Morleys, Dilkes's and Philip Head. For many years Catherine James and John Hawker have been regular soloists.

In 1978 at Central Hall, the choir sang *Carmina Burana*, and later that year Vivaldi's *Gloria* (with boy soloists) and Haydn's *Nelson Mass*. Fauré and Verdi *Requiems*, Bach's *St John Passion*, the Monteverdi *Vespers* – all these were part of the canon of music enjoyed by the choir and their audiences in the Wragg era. In the heyday of music in the late seventies and eighties, the choir took many concerts to St David's Church, Barmouth. The choir would spend a weekend at the school's Welsh Centre at Farchynys, and, with minimal rehearsal, be able to put on a fine concert to the appreciative Welsh audience. These Barmouth concerts are recalled with great pleasure. In 1984, a concert at Barmouth, including Fauré's *Requiem*, was later in the same term, performed again at St Martin's Church, Walsall in aid of the Mayor's Appeal Fund. In 1988 the Chamber Choir sang in St David's Barmouth, with Monteverdi's *Beatus Vir* accompanied by the recorders of Daryll Prew and Andrew Davis. The Head, Keith Howard, frequently sang with the choir, and he retains happy memories of these concerts. In 1988 there was a remarkable concert together with Walsall Choral Society with *Carmina Burana* and *Belshazzar's Feast* being performed in the same concert at Walsall Town Hall. In 1989 the choral concert in St Michael's Church, Caldmore, included a fine rendering of Bernstein's *Chichester Psalms*. In 1994 there was a new departure. As a companion piece to *Carmina Burana*, Messrs Beverley Wragg and Geoffrey Paxton wrote a new choral work, *Seven Deadly Sinners*, which was very well-received piece when it was sung first in Central Hall in May 1994.

2002 saw a new venue for QM music, when a choral concert including the *Bach Cantata No 48* was taken most successfully to St James Hill Church, Mere Green, where the acoustics are excellent. In 2003 there was a fine production of *Messiah* in St Matthew's, and a rendering of Parts 2 & 3 in July, again at St James, Hill. Reference has been made in the chapter on drama to the excellent musicality of the production in December 2003 of *The Beggar's Opera*. In the last quarter of the twentieth century Queen Mary's music, choral and instrumental, has been notable for the variety and high quality of the work it has undertaken. It is only sad that musical talent seems not to be appreciated among Queen Mary's families as it once was, and it must be hoped that audiences may increase to appreciate the quality of what is produced.

15

THE COMBINED CADET FORCE

For a complete record of a century of the QMS Combined Cadet Force, from 1900 to the present day, please refer to Patriotic Scholars, a splendid photographic history, by Bob Cordon Champ, schoolmaster and officer of the contingent, published in 2003. Other references to the early years of the CCF may be found in David Fink's Queen Mary's Grammar School (pages 390/391).

The Compulsory Years

In Quatercentenary Year 1954 the Contingent was inspected by the Colonel-in-Chief of the South Staffordshire Regiment, Sir Guy de Courcy Glover. (See Chapter 3.) This special parade was, however, merely a precursor for the ceremonial anniversary parade on July 2nd attended by the Lord Alexander of Tunis. At this parade, highlight of the Quatercentenary celebrations, Lord Alexander presented to the CCF the London Sword of Honour, gift of the London Branch of the Queen Mary's Club. This sword is used by the senior cadet on all major parades.

As in most other schools of its kind, either entry into the Combined Cadet Force or the Scouts was required for all boys, from 1954 this choice being made for the beginning of the Third Year. Friday afternoon from 2.45 onwards was set aside for the parades, and at QM this pattern lasted until 1968, when a voluntary CCF was established and the parade and

Field Marshal Viscount Montgomery of Alamein reviewing the Queen Mary's Contingent at Annual Camp 1960 at Bourley near Aldershot

Scout meeting were moved to 4 pm, when those who chose not to take part in either activity could go home. The CCF itself was the title for the Junior and Air Training Corps when they had been united into one organisation in 1949. The army section (JTC, and previously, OTC) at QM first paraded in 1900, while the Air Training Corps had been set up at the school in 1944 by F/O JC Barnsley (QM 1917–23), father of Dr Jennifer Milne, until recently Chairman of Mayfield School governors.

In 1954 the Commanding Officer was Major PA Bull (QM 1933–39) classics master at the school since 1949 and CO since 1950, when he took over from Major Price, when the latter moved to Wrekin College. The RAF section was led by Flight Lieutenant

JA Dickson, who also taught classics at the school since his arrival in 1951. Bill Emerson left the school in 1955 and was replaced in the RAF section of the CCF by the remarkable Ken ('Half-pint' or 'Tiny') Thomas. Ken Thomas was as dynamic as he was small in stature. He was a trained navigator and a mathematician who understood that some people have trouble with Maths no matter how intelligent they otherwise might be. Now working with John Dickson and Maurice Ebison (ex-RCAF and another new appointment in the science department), the RAF Section took on a new lease of life.

Phil Bull (CO 1950–68) and John Dickson (CO from 1968), were to take the Contingent through the post-war years until John Dickson retired in 1989, leaving a thriving voluntary Contingent for the future. In 1954 the CFF Instructor was 'RSM' GA Crudace, of whom more later. A cadet of the fifties remembers that the Army Section of the CCF then was very regimented and old fashioned, as indeed its syllabus was at that stage, and, because it was not voluntary, many found it 'a bit of a pain'. Then changes came broadening the Army Section syllabus, and John Dickson arrived with new ideas and began sending people on courses.

Views by the Old Pavilion, then and now. The recent photograph shows Sqn Ldr Tim Lawrence and SSI Bill O'Mara

At this time Army Section training consisted of Part I and Part II of 'Cert. A', followed by more advanced training which could, but rarely did, lead to Cert. B. Most post Cert. A training was undertaken by the 'Cadre Platoon'. One of their operations in 1959 was to construct an assault course in the Moss Close grounds! There was much drill in preparation for Part I, and standard fare was preparation for House Drill Competitions each year. The only modification to the WW II uniform was that the up-to-the-neck serge blouse had by the 1950s a turndown collar and was worn with a tie. The weapon was the .303 rifle. By the 1950s Field Day training in Sutton Park had given way to exercises on Cannock Chase. The 1955 camp was held at Kimnel Park, near Rhyl with 90 cadets, Major Bull being assisted by Lts Allcott and Alexander. The Contingent paraded in Walsall on Remembrance Day and for the Mayor's Sunday Parade. There was a General Inspection each year, when the whole contingent turned out on the field at Mayfield for a drill and turnout Inspection by a senior visiting officer.

The Glider

Corporal David Worrall of the school's combined cadet force, gets some practice on the controls of the school's glider.

The RAF Section's annual camp in 1955 was at RAF Hullavington in Wiltshire, where each cadet had half an hour on the Provost, the RAF's basic trainer. Glider training was at the 633 Gliding School at RAF Cosford. At Cosford, during Field Day in the autumn, cadets flew Chipmunks and Ansons. RAF cadets worked, as now, for Proficiency and Advanced Proficiency examinations. For some 20 years after 1956 the Section maintained a Basic Glider in a Hut at the bottom of the playing fields. In 1956 'F/O Thomas and senior cadets spent the (Field) day at Mayfield, having fun with the glider.' The glider was always a mix between a challenge for those who were the RAF section, and a source of amusement for those who were not! In 1958 Mr Brian Kirby joined the ranks of RAF officers, and camp was held that year at RAF Wattisham with 60 cadets attending.

RAF Section Camp at RAF Old Sarum near Salisbury in 1970 with Flt Lt David Pomeroy

New Training Schemes:
Proficiency and Arduous Training
In 1959 the 'Cert. A' cadet tests were renamed 'Proficiency' tests as they remain today. The cadet training scheme was remodelled as

National Service ended to include less drill and study, and more practical activity and leadership training. This was the year when the first cadets attended a cadet leadership course at the new training centre at Frimley Park, near Aldershot, to gain the Joint Services Cadet Badge. An increased range of cadet courses was now being offered nationally each year. Arduous training entered the syllabus, and in 1960 the first hill-walking expeditions were planned for Easter, to take place in Snowdonia and the Lake District. The Easter Army Section camp in Snowdonia was held jointly with the Scouts, and was led by Major Bull, and Messrs Alexander and Archer (Mr GB Archer was Scoutmaster of the School Scouts, the 13th Walsall.) The RAF expedition was held, jointly with Leeds Grammar School, in the Lakes. An Arduous Training weekend was again held in Snowdonia in 1961.

By 1960 the building works for the new school at Mayfield meant that the Inspection had to take place in the more confined area at Moss Close, where drill was said to be excellent and the RAF Section could show off its wind tunnel and its new Radio Section, the first appearance of a Radio or Signals Section in the Contingent. The Army Section camped at Bourley, near Aldershot, and had the great honour of being inspected by 'Monty', Field Marshal the Lord Montgomery of Alamein. The Army Section Cup was presented to RQMS CC Dodd. The senior cadet in 1961 was AJ (Tony) Phillips who provided his memories for *The Marian* in 1996. He has the sharpest memory of 'Sam' Crudace running up and down the ranks preparing for the Annual Parade. 'That boy in blue, come here' he would yell while 100 boys in blue quaked to know who it was he had spotted. Tony remembers the planks with rows of holes into buckets which were the toilets at Army Camp. He remembers the hours being taught by RSM Crudace how to handle the sword correctly before the big Parade, and that shouting commands to 300 cadets behind him left him with a sore throat for weeks. He went on to stress his conviction of the value of the CCF in training self-confidence, the skills of managing people, and the ability to iron one's trousers. At the 1961 inspection the glider at Mayfield 'FLEW before the very eyes of the Colonel himself.'

George Crudace ('Sam')

One of the deepest impressions made on all QM boys and all cadets in this era was the vigour and personality of the RSM George A Crudace. 'Sam' was an inspiration and a legend in his own time. I would refer readers back to Chapter 3 for earlier references. He had arrived as an ex-Army PE Instructor in 1944 from service with the Sherwood

Foresters, and with experience in approved schools. When he arrived his lessons on the school timetable were called 'Drill'. When he left, they were 'PE' He was responsible for the collection of all dinner money and issue of tickets. He controlled the issue of stationery throughout the school, down to the last drawing pin. He brought in every Moss Close boy for rugger training at Mayfield every Saturday morning in

Left
RSM Crudace receiving the British Empire Medal, with his wife Mary. Five Contingent Commanders are in this photograph: from Left, PA Bull, JA Dickson, JS Anderson, DE Pomeroy, and E Boothroyd

Right
RSM GA Crudace and Cadet CSM Charles Dodd near the pavilion. The CSM carries the London Sword of Honour, gift of the London Branch of Queen Mary's Club

'If you break your leg on the Rugby field, don't come running to me, son.'

the winter terms. And he made the CCF the centre of his life. He ran the stores. He trained the Basic Section, as it was known, in drill and turnout. He acted as RSM for the whole contingent. He was a law unto himself. At camp he did not live in the Sergeants' Mess but slept in his stores with his rifles. He appeared in his pyjamas and slippers in the mornings to issue kit. He loved to have his leg pulled. His phrases were legendary: they were printed as a header on each of half the pages of the prefects' magazine, *Mayfield*, in 1965. 'When I count One, jump in the air, when I count Two, come down again.' Then, 'I'll keep you in five, six, seven, eight, nine days a week, son'. 'Ten times worse than drastic'. 'Those two flags aren't in a straight line, son.' 'You're not here to think, boy. You're here to know'. And, possibly referring to Inspection Days, but on any occasion: 'You'll be there on the day', which left doubts in the minds of the hearers! And best of all: 'If you break your leg on the Rugby field, don't come running to me, son.' He retired to his native Northumberland in 1971, having been awarded the British Empire Medal in 1970 for his services to Queen Mary's and the CCF. The award was made at school. When he retired, the Headmaster, SL Darby, said 'no one has had a more profound influence for good on our boys than he.'

Farchynys and the CCF

In May 1962 the whole CCF was on parade in the Arboretum on the occasion of the visit to Walsall of HM The Queen. By 1963 the Arduous Training Camp was to move into new pastures. The Army, 'at great risk', we read, 'provided us with a one ton lorry, which was driven with great verve by Lt Col Bull (promoted in 1962). Fourteen boys attended together with Lt Col Bull, Lt Bissell and 2/Lt Dunk on the first "Long Field Day". The first two days were occupied by Exercise Mountain Hawk. The final ascent of Snowdon had to be cancelled due to inclement weather. Tuesday, Wednesday and Thursday morning were spent on a cross-country trek to the new School Welsh Centre at Farchynys.' Farchynys was thereafter to be the centre for Arduous (later renamed Adventurous) Training.

As the school moved to Mayfield, the CCF took over its new accommodation there: orderly room, stores and armoury. Numbers in the Contingent were reduced, however, by War Office cuts and then by the move to voluntary membership. In the report of the 1966 Brecon camp we read that Mr Crudace made a surprise visit to supervise shooting on the range, his first sortie from the stores, it was thought, since Mafeking was relieved. The RAF Section continued to sail rafts on the 'shark infested' swamps at Park Hall, while its glider (the 'Grasshopper') was now grounded for re-glueing. Cadets were urged to apply for flying scholarships, while the RAF Arduous Training week was still in the Lake District where cadets competed with those from Leeds Grammar School. In 1968 Lt Col. Bull retired as Commanding Officer and was succeeded by Squadron Leader JA Dickson.

Wg Cdr John A Dickson: the voluntary CCF

John Dickson brought to the CCF a determination to open up its range of post-proficiency activities so that more could be encouraged to join the contingent now it was voluntary, knowing that what was on offer was much more interesting and wide ranging. A start had already been made as Phil Bull had put much CCF support and material into the new Welsh Centre, which was already offering a wide range of cadet weekends as well as Year and society weekends and field courses. For a time since 1963 Field Days had been added to weekends at Farchynys to make Long Field Days, but the limited number of cadets who could be involved soon convinced the officers that they should revert to local Field Days for the whole Contingent. John Burgess was a valued officer at the time, and 'Hamish', his dog, memorably would accompany him to Arduous Training at Farchynys. It was in 1968 that Pilot Officer David Pomeroy joined the contingent in which he was to serve for 35 years, and he assumed command of the RAF section in 1970. He held that responsibility until he became CO in 1997. Lt Colonel Bull ('the Kaernal' to Mrs Watkins in the kitchen!) continued to assist with paperwork and in the stores until he resigned his commission in 1975.

Wing Commander John Dickson OBE

Signal Section

The author remembers joining the CCF as Lt Anderson in 1968 and being soon asked to re-start the Signal Section. The allocation of kit arrived and included radios and telephones, a 10-line telephone exchange, a petrol charger, poles, cables, pliers, screwdrivers, soldering iron and all sorts of belts and hoists. We received permission to join the National Radio Cadet Network in 1970. The radios were on their last legs after many years service (A40 and A41 sets), although the WWII sets (A18, A38) had already gone – just! Within a couple of years we had begun a series of annual Signals training weekends at Farchynys, which still continue. We were supported by a TA Signals Regt at Donnington, and then more recently, by a squadron of 35 Signal Regiment, based at Newcastle-under-Lyme, and NCOs from there have come to help at the training weekends each year. In 1984 the Signal

Section was issued with Clansman radios. This was part of a change of policy: cadets being issued with weaponry, radios and clothing of current army pattern, rather than the hand-me-downs of earlier days.

There was excitement when the new PRC320 radio was first set up on the hillside near the Coach House at Farchynys, and good quality radio communication was established with the cadets stationed in the signals room in the Old Pavilion at school. In 1998 the Signals Section became recognised by the Royal Corps of Signals as a Cadet Signal Troop, entitled to wear the regimental cap badge and belt.

Colour Sergeant Oliver Hawksley receives the Royal Corps of Signals insignia 1999

REME

The old cricket pavilion was a focus for the expansion of CCF activities. Abandoned since the rebuilding and in a dilapidated state, its main room was used by the Sailing Club which JAD took over from Mr Tony Wiggin. Now the CO acquired a an ex-service Land Rover (NDH) and converted one end of the pavilion into a garage for a Motor Transport section. In 1970 a vehicle inspection pit was created in the garage and cadets began to work for the REME trade exam, and Cert T Driver training was introduced. Two Land Rovers were bought. JAD drove NDH and maintained it for years, along with another which was a training engine and bodywork shell.

Hovercraft

The other end of the Old Pavilion eventually became the site for building the first of several hovercraft. The design of hovercraft improved over the years, but the quality of driving (or flying) on the school field was always modest and rugby posts provided unnerving obstacles. On a number of Inspection Days, inspecting officers had the privilege of being allowed to fly the craft while others on terra firma could point the camera and watch. The rooms at the back of the pavilion became the stores and operating room for a new Signal Section. Later, in 1983, a small unused store was converted and equipped as a photographic dark room, and a Photography Section was formed.

As in the past, Old Boy officer cadets came to camps on occasions when at university. In 1968–70 Philip Sturrock, then at Queen's College, Oxford, returned to assist at camp. He brought with him Joseph Gabbott

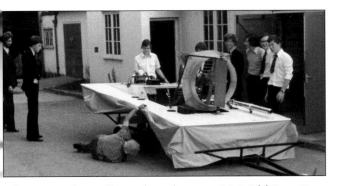

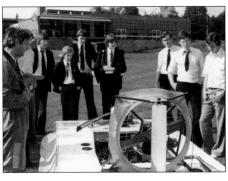

An early hovercraft 1977

who was at his college, though not a QM Old Boy. For very many years Lt Gabbott came to camps and to Farchynys, though Philip Sturrock could not continue. It was only in 1988 that this connection ceased, the contingent having benefited enormously, especially as Joseph was an active member of the TA for many of the earlier years. Many a camp exercise in the seventies and eighties sprang from Joseph's enthusiasm and ability. These camps were memorable for the elaborate 24-hour and 36-hour exercises. That at Sennybridge in 1973 had a Command Post in a 4-ton truck, with a C42 radio through which the whole scheme was controlled, and a 160lb tent in which the officers dined, some in mess dress.

Shooting and the Rifle Range

From 1971 increased shooting skill which developed out of Wg Cdr John Dickson's own energy and enthusiasm enabled the March and Shoot team to win the District competition, while in the first competitive year of .22 shooting the team was 17th out of 38 in the Country Life competition, and rose to the top of its NRSA league. Leading shots in this first year were GM Evans, IL Ross, and CJ Dickson. Shooting continued well thereafter with the team making two visits to Bisley shooting camps in 1972. Preparations

*March and Shoot Team,
21 March 1971*

*l to r: CSM NE Cheadle; Cadet R Owen; Sgt PN Green; L/Cpl M Chester; Cadet DC Atkins; Sgt PR Mason; Cadet CD Lee; Sgt GR Hickinbottom.
(see references in chapter 20)*

soon began to design a small-bore range to be built at school. Funds had to be found both from the Ministry of Defence and the School Governors. It is a tribute to the Commanding Officer's drive that the range was built and was fully in use by early 1984. Immediately it was possible for more teams to enter the cadet competitions and the quality of shooting improved as cadets were trained by Wg Cdr Dickson himself and, after he retired, Captain Law.

The RAF Section continued strongly with cadets winning Flying Scholarships, regular gliding courses, flying at Cosford and with 8 AEF at Shawbury in Chipmunks, paddling the lake at Park Hall on Inspection Day, and flying the contingent's own glider, the Grasshopper. In 1974 six cadets enjoyed an exciting programme at RAF Wildenrath in West Germany, while the main camp was at RAF Halton.

Mount Etna, 1974

In the summer of 1974, after the Nesscliff camp, there was to be a long-planned and much looked forward to adventurous training abroad in Greece, with a two-day (one night) 'assault' on Mount Olympus. As luck would have it, the Turks invaded Cyprus the week before the group was due to leave, while the contingent was at Nesscliff, and the Ministry of Defence said they could not be responsible for the safety of the party. The Ministry said they would approve 'on the nod' another, safer, objective. Hence the idea to climb Mount Etna. Emergency re-planning! The original route was followed by minibus, through Germany and Austria to Yugoslavia. When they got to Split they took the ferry to Pescara, went to the toe of Italy, and across to Sicily. They camped for 8 days at Catania and ascended Etna. They were the only ones daft enough to walk all the way! Most reached the summit by cable-car and a 4-wheel drive bus. The QM expedition returned via Pompeii, Rome, Siena, Venice and the Italian Lakes, all enriched by the leadership of the CO with his wonderful classical enthusiasm, and with 'two burst tyres and numerous camping hazards en route.'

Adventurous training 1996, near Cadair Idris: making for the next campsite

Adventurous Training

The annual Adventurous Training week was usually at Farchynys: a five-day expedition and a day of orienteering or dry-slope skiing. The expeditions for many years involved exercises in the Llanfachreth area including discovering each others' campsites (ex-red Dragon). Many ex-cadets will recall the tins and tokens they had to find and the searching up and down the lanes around the village. In latter years a circular route with four campsites was devised, with tasks for each day, still based on the tins and tokens. Between 20 and 30 cadets would take part and the first evening would be spent issuing instructions and allocating the army rations and cooking stoves, which would be used on the expedition. Every route was carefully planned, and officers would meet sections in the afternoons in their new campsites, with fresh milk and bread supplies to supplement the rations. Some years there was a danger of sunstroke, while Easter in other years was cold and wet! Cadets learnt to map-read, to camp, and to co-operate with each other. Some years there was a senior expedition alongside. This, led by the then Captain Stephen Law, focused on much higher level walking and camping. Some of the campsites were used for up to 30 years, and strong friendships were made with the farmers, stretching to two generations, especially with the Jones family at 'Freddies' (Fridd-bryn-côch), beyond Ganllwyd, and with the Williams' at Ty-glan-afon north of Bontddu. This is also referred to in Chapter 6.

Successes of the seventies and eighties

Much of the progress through the seventies and eighties was built on these successes. Those who were present may remember the climax of the Isle of Man camp in 1976 when it ended in a blaze of glory: such a blaze that the island's part-time fire engines became hopelessly stuck in the sands on the Point of Ayre. Increased efforts went into preparation each year for the District Patrol Competition (now called the Military Skills Competition), and the team came third in 1976. The Signal Section maintained its skills and came first in the radio section of the national Signal View 1976, and third overall. In the same year the QM team won the West Midlands March and Shoot competition again – and the first hovercraft flew! In 1980 a totally revamped 'QM2' with a team led by Sgt Robert Bloomer achieved seventh place in a National Hovercraft Competition at the NEC. In 1980 also, two senior cadets attended a Combined Services Camp at RAF Gibraltar.

A tug-o-war at Proteus Camp

The river crossing

Several senior cadets were sponsored for their commissions and later passed the commissioning board during these years. Peter Lees was commissioned into the RAF and trained as a pilot. He went on to be part of the Red Arrows Team, renowned for its high quality acrobatic demonstration skills. After his RAF career he spent many years as a pilot for Cathay Pacific. Others included Mark Chester, Jonathan Ball and Neil Stanley who went into the Army, the first two becoming army chaplains. Sometimes those not in the CCF at school later entered the services, as did Richard W Jones (1971–78) a senior engineer with the Royal Navy. Several ex-members of the Contingent also rose to high rank in the TA in Birmingham University OTC and in the Staffordshire Regiment, including Philip Jackson and Roger Machin. In the spring of 1984 a team of 4th and 5th year cadets, led by Corporal David Foster, won the Western District Cadet March and Shoot Competition. Then in the same year a ten-man team led by C/Sgt James Walker achieved a long sought after goal by winning the District Patrol Competition. This was a splendid display of ability, character, pride and self-reliance. The cup was presented by Major-General Brendan McGuinness, GOC Western District. 1984 was an outstanding year in the contingent's history.

On Inspection Day 1986, Wing Commander Dickson presented the contingent with its own Banner, which was received, and which has been used since, with great pride.

In the summer of 1986 was the first visit to the 1 Staffords at Fallingbostel in West Germany. Led by RSM David Foster a party of officers and senior NCOs were hosted by the Regiment with competitions, opportunity to drive armoured personnel carriers, a visit to see Challenger tanks in operation, and an impressive visit to the ex-concentration camp at Belsen, as well as a day in Hamburg. The link with the Staffordshire Regiment has always been strong and important. The contingent began as a Cadet Corps attached to the 2nd Volunteer Battalion of the South Staffordshire Regiment, and the Army Section has always worn the badges of the Regiment. Old Boys have belonged to the Regiment, and have fought with the Regiment. The Regiment still looks to QM for officers. The Walsall Branch of the Friends of the Staffordshire Regiment is largely run by Old Marians with regimental connections. From 1986 until 1997 the Staffordshire and West Midlands Territorial Army Committee (TAVRA) was chaired by Colonel WEL (Haggis) Reid (1944–53), an old boy who gave tremendous service to the county of Staffordshire, and to the county's Army Cadet Force in particular.

It must be said that the Royal Air Force gives enormous support to the RAF Section, though its Air Commodore Cadets, and its Liaison Officers and senior NCOs who visit the school and give tremendous support and advice to the RAF Section officers. The 1988 Adventurous Training Expedition to Norway, Expedition Thor, was led by Captain Stephen Law. It was the last major expedition attended by Wing Cdr

Dickson before he retired. In 1987 the school rejoiced to learn that John Dickson had been awarded the OBE for his services, a fitting climax to a fine career, not only as teacher and cadet officer, but also as a national figure in athletics – timing track events for many years all over the country. There was a fine formal dinner to celebrate John Dickson's retirement. Over 100 attended including very many former cadets, officers, visiting regular officers of both services, and former colleagues. It was a tremendous occasion to mark the end of an era of such dedicated enthusiasm. Sadly his retirement was to be short, and he was much mourned when he died in 1991. A refurbished main room in the Old Pavilion, once the base for the sailing club, now a meeting room and office for the CCF and the school, was hung with a painting of Wing Commander Dickson and was dedicated as the 'John Dickson Room'.

Lt Colonel John Anderson

From 1989 until 1997 Lieutenant Colonel John S Anderson, an officer since 1968, commanded the contingent. The Army Section was commanded by Captain Stephen Law, whose arrival not only brought new vigour to Adventurous Training, but also to the training in military tactics. The contingent has been blessed with a high quality of senior cadet, so that officers and senior cadets have worked together year after year as a disciplined team within a hierarchy, but with shared ideals and purposes in a happy

Remembrance Day Parade on the Bridge 1991

Remembrance Day Parade 2000 in Lichfield St. The Contingent Banner in front

comradeship. This has greatly enhanced the training in leadership given to senior cadets. The contingent benefited by recruiting more officers in both Sections. In Sgt Mark Smith we engaged our first SSI (Staff Sergeant Instructor), more recently succeeded by WO2 Bill O'Mara. The work of the Commanding Officer has been greatly aided by having men with military experience in Stores and assisting with training and administration. The pavilion has been centrally heated and has an improved approach with steps and grass bank.

While the Hovercraft Section ticked over, serious attempts were made with the Land Rovers. NDH had to be restored and many hours were put in by Scot Miles and his father, with eventual success. Then another short-wheelbase Land Rover was bought (JSK) which was a

Top
The shooting team which won the National Country Life Trophy and the Assegai Trophy for 25 metre indoor range shooting in 1993.

Seated: Adrian Reeves, Richard Moore, Lt Col JS Anderson (Commanding Officer), Iain Payne, Russell Hinton.

Standing: Capt SJ Law (shooting coach) Kate Lawton, Sqn Ldr DE Pomeroy, Alistair Pritchard, Neil Joynes

Lower:
The Band 1997

roadworthy vehicle. JSK or 'Jessica' was very valuable for a few years, but sadly neither survive as they became too expensive to keep.

The highlights of this period included major successes for the RAF Section in the 1990s. In 1995 the Sir John Thompson Sword of Honour was presented to Cadet Warrant Officer Ian Lakin at RAF Benson, to mark his selection as the best CCF RAF cadet in the country that year. It was the first presentation of the Sword. Led by Cadet Warrant Officer Adrian Reeves the section won the RAF national Air Squadron Trophy in 1996 (QM had won it previously in 1987, the first recipients of that trophy). The award day at RAF Cranwell was a very memorable day. Then, also in 1996, the Queen Mary's Army Section team led by RSM Matthew Punch won the Brigade Military Skills Competition for the first time since 1984, and only the second time ever. The team had determination and high morale. Shooting has always been strong since the range was built. In 1993 and 1994 high quality teams won the national Green Howards/Country Life shooting competition two years running. Several times in recent years the RAF team has won the Section's national Assegai Trophy for small-bore shooting. The enthusiasm of Lt Col Anderson's team of officers and the quality of the senior cadets of those years was memorable. The contingent grew in size, and, building on earlier foundations, the quality was particularly high in this decade.

In 1989 the Band was re-created under the tuition of Mr Stephen Read. With support and training the CCF Band has led all main contingent parades since that year when it was commanded by Drum Major Alistair Pritchard, and, since 1993 it has been the Band for the Aldridge Remembrance Parade each year. In 1995 it provided the main Band, this time led by Drum Major Bernard Scott, for the West Bromwich celebration parade marking 50 years after VE Day.

In 1997 Lt Col John Anderson retired. The Retirement Parade and Dinner were overwhelming in demonstrating the loyalty and gratitude felt among generations of Queen Mary's cadets, officers and friends. He was honoured with the award of the MBE in 1998 for his service to the Cadet movement.

The CCF Contingent, 1997:

Front row seated l to r:
Adam Shipp, James Tomlinson,
Ashley Cunnington,
Michael Kearns, Cadet Warrant
Officer Andrew Smith, Neil Lakin,
Ian Moreton,
Lt RC Champ, Capt AJM Maund,
Capt SJ Law, Headmaster,
Lt Col JS Anderson,
Sqn Ldr DE Pomeroy,
Flt Lt T Lawrence,
Plt Off RJ Hinton, Lt SAS Worrall,
Cadet RSM Gareth Jones,
Tom Moore, Harvinder Bains,
Toby Rhind-Tutt, James Good,
Nicholas Shaw, Neil Hanson,
James Iremonger.

Wg Cdr David Pomeroy

When Wing Commander David Pomeroy became CO in 1997 much of the pattern of the previous 30 years was intact. Overall numbers are now well over 260. Outward Bound weekends at Farchynys, Signals weekends and Adventurous Training continue. Camps at Longmoor, Leek, Nesscliff and St Martin's Plain attract more cadets with numbers up from 50 to nearly 70. The RAF Section was now led by Squadron Leader Tim Lawrence. RAF Camps nowadays take more limited numbers because the capacity of RAF stations is severely reduced, but they are still highly attractive. The Chipmunk has given way to the new Trainer, the Grob, but 8 AEF continues to provide flying opportunity at RAF Cosford as it has done for 40 years, together with gliding and gliding courses.

Each year provides opportunities in the Military Skills Competition, March and Shoot, the Welbeck Pentathlon and many MoD courses. Queen Mary's was 2nd in the national Assegai Postal Shooting Trophy in 2003. The first sixth-form girls have been made welcome and have already contributed much to the contingent. Sadly, Health and Safety factors have made officers' work in recent years more burdensome, and new regulations threaten Adventurous Training and other activities which boast the value of giving cadets opportunity for initiative. Recent ex-cadets who have entered the services include

Daniel Moore and Michael Kearns into the Staffordshire Regiment, and Neil Manchester and James Fern also into the Army; David Huntley, Russell Hinton, and Richard Humble into the RAF, and Matthew Punch and Richard Bowen into the Royal Navy.

Senior NCOs relax at Nesscliffe Camp 1999, with CSM Tom Shaw in hammock and RAF Warrant Officer Douglas Gardner on left

The Centenary: 1900–2000

In 2000 the Contingent celebrated its centenary. His Royal Highness, The Prince Andrew, Duke of York, Colonel-in-Chief of the Staffordshire Regiment, paid a visit to the school and inspected the contingent. It poured with rain but the parade led by RSM JD Pearson was immaculate and the Duke toured the training stands, and spoke to cadets, officers, staff and parents of his admiration for the training of the CCF, and of Queen Mary's in particular. A plaque in the Entrance Hall commemorates this Royal Visit.

Visit of HRH The Prince Andrew, Duke of York, 26th May 2000

In July 2003 came the publication of *Patriotic Scholars*, by Bob Cordon Champ, Army Section Captain in the contingent. This superb record of 100 years of Queen Mary's Combined Cadet Force is very welcome and most impressive. It is a collection of photographs and written extracts which tell the story of a proud volunteer cadet force as it enters its second century.

In 2003 also Wing Cdr Pomeroy retired from the teaching staff of the school but he retains responsibility within the school as examinations secretary. Happily he remains as Commanding Officer. The school was delighted when, in the 2004 New Years Honours List, he was awarded an OBE for his services to the Cadet movement.

16

THE SCOUT GROUP
AND OTHER SCHOOL ACTIVITIES
including the Iceland Expedition 1982

Queen Mary's Scouting

The 13th Walsall (QMS) Scout Troop was founded in 1920 and details of the early years of this lively Troop are given in David Fink's *Queen Mary's Grammar School, 1554–1954* (pages 388/389). By 1954 the Troop had nurtured 48 King's or Queen's Scouts, which is a tremendous record. At the Quatercentenary, the chief scout guest was E Dennis Smith, Imperial Headquarters Commissioner, Old Marian (1922–29), and former King's Scout at QM. The Group Scoutmaster then was Mr RET Everton, the Scoutmaster was Mr David Fink, and Mr Brian Archer, newly arrived at the school, was Scouter in charge of the Senior Scout Troop. Until the 1970s scouting was very popular at school, not only as an alternative to the CCF, but as a lively and respected activity in its own right. The Duke of Edinburgh Award had not stolen the limelight.

Opposite
Scouting at Moss Close in the 1950s - and in France in the 1960's

The Dell at Moss Close

Scouting based at Moss Close: The Dell

The Scout Troop was based at Moss Close. As EJ Parkes wrote in the July 1964 *Marian*, the buildings they used comprised the converted stables and outbuildings of the Moss Close house. The large downstairs room was used as the 'stores', carefully tended by a succession of quartermasters. The upstairs rooms were used for Junior patrol dens and the Scoutmaster's office, while the Senior patrols were housed downstairs. The rooms could be cold in winter! The feature which contributed most to happy Scouting at Moss Close was the 'Dell', a semi-wilderness cherished by the Troop. Here nature provided a perfect camp-fire hollow which was much envied. The dell provided very good opportunities for training in scoutcraft and 'pioneering'.

In 1954 there were seven Queen's Scouts in the Group at one time: a considerable record. They were AG Bolton, AV Hughes, DA Bayley, TP O'Connell, G Bernard Thomas, JB Harden, and JA Cox. In 1956, David W Judson became the Group's 50th Queen's Scout. In 1956 the Seniors camped near Dieppe, while in 1957 they went to the Rhine valley, and 1958 to Brittany. In 1957 two Senior Scouts from QM attended the World Scout Jamboree in Sutton Park, one in the South Staffordshire, and one in the Birmingham Contingent. The camps in Europe at this time were arranged by Mr T Morgan Jones who did a very great deal to assist Brian Archer. In this period other Senior camps were in Ireland, Jersey and Bad Godesberg.

Senior programmes focused on long distance hikes and badge work in preparation for the First Class Badge and the Queen's Scout award. The Scout Troop also had badge work, went to Beaudesert on Field Days, and engaged in Initiative Wide Games. The 1959 Senior Camp was in southern Brittany, while one of their Field Days was devoted to a Cycle Rally. At this time there was a Senior Scout competition in Walsall called the Saxton Sword Competition, and the competition that year concentrated on raft building and rowing in the Arboretum. The Juniors concentrated on competing for the Leckie Shield, a camping competition held annually at Beaudesert. For many years efforts were directed well in advance to ensure success, especially in the Leckie Shield. The Junior Troop went to Ilfracombe for Camp in 1959, and had at least one Field Day in Sutton Park. In 1960 they went to Brockenhurst in the New Forest, a very wet camp. About this time a commando course in the dell at Moss Close was set up by the Senior Scouts and the CCF.

A new Hut at Mayfield

During 1961 the time approached to leave Moss Close. The property was sold as part of the move to Mayfield. Money was raised by the Scouts, and a wedge of land off the bottom of the field at Mayfield, with rough grass around and plenty of training space, was earmarked for two Scout Huts, one for the Troop and one for the Seniors. An appeal was made in the January 1961 *Marian* for £250 towards the huts required, £150 having been raised already. A very successful camp was held that year at Polkerris in Cornwall where there was a fine deserted beach. One night at Polkerris, Brian Archer recalls 'a fearful storm with the scouters spending the night hanging on to the poles of the black store tent, and piling stones from the field wall around the patrol tents as the brailing pegs would not hold. This was David Stevens' last day with us. What a send-off!' Mr Stevens moved away to run a chemistry department in a Gloucestershire school. He had run the Troop since 1956. Brian Archer was now Group Scoutmaster. The Group was much helped at this time by former scouts who came to camps to assist: 'Inky' Ingram (who organised provisions from the big black store tent), 'Ticker' Adderley, and, later on, Des Burton.

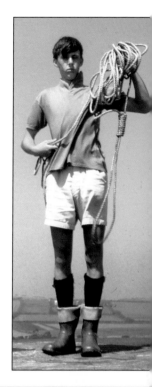

The scouts left their rooms and the dell at Moss Close in the summer of 1962. Their equipment went to the cellars of the Headmaster's house at main school, while the Group moved to the pavilion at Mayfield as a temporary home, together with one red box of kit needed for weekly meetings. There was now one Scoutmaster, Brian Archer, and Seniors and Juniors camped together at Woolacombe in 1962. The new hut was erected in 1963, and storage, cupboards and partitions for the patrols were built. The Group was reunited with its equipment, and a new era could begin. Now they had a home again, the scouts could also enjoy weekend training and camping at Farchynys which had opened that year, and the scout leaders devoted much time running Farchynys weekends as well as the established training. Mr Brian Birkby, and later, Mr Chris Isaacs, joined as assistant leaders in 1963 and 1964. In those years further very successful camps were held at Borrowdale (1963) for the Seniors, and for the Troop: Manorbier (1963) and Polkerris (1964).

There were difficulties at this time with the split-site school, and for a short time there was a Junior Troop at Mayfield, and a Junior Troop at Lichfield Street! Camp in 1965 was in Moelfre in Anglesey. In 1966 the number of patrols was increased to six and the Troop divided into 'A' and 'B' Troop. By this time the canoes were in need of repair and some of the seniors' time was spent in 1967 on this task. The Duke of Edinburgh Award was now incorporated into the programme and some seniors went to Farchynys to complete their 30-mile silver expedition. The Junior Troop had a very varied programme including a theatre performance with local scouts, car-washing for Bob-a-Job week, a Peak District camp, weekend training at Beaudesert, and an assault course construction at Farchynys! From 1968 the scouts moved to 4 p.m. on Friday for their meeting, when the CCF became voluntary and had to move to meet out of school hours. The author

Senior Scouts at Manorbier, 1963

had by this time been drawn into helping the seniors (renamed Ventures) for a short time, while Brian Archer ran the Troop with the assistance of Mr Kenneth McLeish. An outstanding Venture event was a canal trip from Autherley Junction to Chester (and back) which was completed with memorable enthusiasm and panache, during which Paul Dean, leading Venture Scout of the time, with John Wait and others, regaled members with the tales of Winnie-the-Pooh! Richard Hughes gained his Queen's Scout badge in 1968, the first Queen's Scout for several years.

While the school raised money for Farchynys the scouts received a grant from the Consolidated Fund and independent money-raising was frowned on. From about 1968 however, the scouts were asked to go 'independent', and they set up their own subscription and fund-raising with car-washes, jumble sales, sponsored walks, and other efforts which helped to replace tents and buy glass-fibre canoes as well as stoves, flysheets and other kit. In all this they were supported by a Group Executive of parents.

The achievements of Brian Archer

Mr Brian Archer

By 1970 the Troop and Ventures had a wide and varied programme led by Brian Archer, mostly on his own, and for this the scouts were enormously indebted to him. Orienteering had become very popular and provided a new area for training, and an opportunity for training both on Cannock Chase and at Farchynys. Canoeing was also very popular at this time, both at an Easter camp at Gnosall in Shropshire, and on the banks of Ullswater in the summer. Other camps at this time were at Newton Stewart and, memorably, at Llangynidir near Abergavenny, with canoeing on the Brecon–Monmouth Canal. On parents' open days, mums brought goodies for their 'starving' offspring, the spread being supervised by Mrs Archer! In 1972, having just arrived as a geography master, Mr Stuart Holtam offered to help, experiencing his first camp at Austwick, near Settle, Yorkshire, where his driving accomplishments were memorable! He was a Scouter till 1976. Very sadly, in 1974, Brian Archer left the school after 21 years service to the school and the scout group, to move to North Wales. He had been a Yearmaster, a gifted hockey player and coach, and teacher of history and English at all levels. He was very much missed.

New Scouters and new Training

By 1975 the Group had three Scout Leaders, Stuart Holtam, as Group Scout Leader, plus Mr Tom Perrett who had arrived to teach history from Keele University, and Mr Paul Dean, ever enthusiastic Old Boy who was briefly on the staff to teach geography. Camp was at Charmouth, with 'Australian' Games, and the Venture Scout expedition was a sponsored canoe down the river Wye, from Hereford to Symonds Yat. Venture Scout David T Griffiths was Walsall South representative to the World Scout Jamboree in Norway, and he subsequently gained his Queen's Scout badge. By 1978, and following the departure of Paul Dean, Tom Perrett took on the acting leadership of the Group on his own. There was still strong enthusiasm led by a young prefect Assistant Scout Leader Ian Trow, and Quartermaster Julian Masters. After a brief period when the Troop was led by Mr M. Stainforth, Mr Graham Chesterman came to the PE Dept and became Group Scout Leader (1980).

A sad end to the scout hut.

Assisted for a while by Mr Michael Broom, Graham Chesterman expanded the scout programme and for a while there were nearly 40 scouts in the Troop. Fund raising was enthusiastic (many of us remember the beetle drives!), and the Summer Camp was held at Rannoch, Perthshire in 1981 and Holt, Norfolk in 1982. In 1983 scouts camped six times, in Norfolk, at Farchynys (twice), at Beaudesert, at Kinver and at Blackwell Court. They did ropework, mapwork and campcraft. They swam, canoed, hiked and played volleyball, football and cricket. An innovation in 1984 was a very popular Sons' and Dads' Camp on the school field, while 30 scouts took part in a seven-day camp at Farchynys. Then one night the scout hut was burnt down. The fire was ferocious and very little remained. After protracted negotiations and acceptance that the area at the bottom of the field was prone to vandalism, a new hut, out of the proceeds of insurance, was built in 1986 behind the caretaker's bungalow at the foot of the Sutton Road houses garden. Equipment was borrowed and bought to replace that which had been destroyed. There was still considerable enthusiasm, and tribute must be paid to the committee of parents, with the author as Chairman, who led the construction of the new hut.

13th Walsall (Queen Mary's) Scout Group, December 1984.

Rear row: N Newey; B Groves; R Wilson; N Mace; C Law. Fourth row: J Topliss; S Law; D Rowley; R Birch; W Pottinger; D Jones; M Brown; S Davies; P Clews.

Third row: J Baker; J Hartley; P O'Neil; R Siddle; J Blades; W Edwards; R Marsh; H Evans; C Male; S Ingleby; M Gold; A Barnes; C Jones; S Lloyd.

Seated: R Meek; N Gleeson; M Daniels; M Perkins; J Vallance; G Chesterman; M Broom; S Hancock; P Leppington; A Varley; B Moore; T Tolley;

Front row: D Blakemore; A Peach; I Cooper; M Houston; L Axford; O Strickland; P Ward; S Lucas; P Limbrick; P Houston; P Glanville.

By this time Graham Chesterman had left QM for professional hockey work elsewhere, and the Group was led by Mike Broom with help from John Vallance, a Old Boy, Miss Geraldine Brown from the staff and Bill Glanville, a parent. By 1988 the Group was led with much enthusiasm by Dr John Edlin, and then for a short while by Dr Bernard Thomas, an Old Boy and vigorous scout of the 1950s. But it was not possible to find permanent leaders and keep the Group going. By 1991 the decision had been made to close the Group after over 70 years. The hut was handed over to the Duke of Edinburgh Award work led by David Hart. The strong growth of this scheme had played its part in reducing scouting's appeal, while it became increasingly difficult to find staff experienced and willing to take on leadership. However, led by another Old Boy member of staff, John Wilcox, a Scout Club of members of the school who belonged to other Groups met together until very recently for occasional activities and Farchynys weekends. But the 13th Walsall is no more.

The Duke of Edinburgh Award Scheme

The Duke of Edinburgh Award Scheme was founded in 1956. In 1967 school Senior Scouts had begun to work with the Silver and Gold schemes alongside their scout training for the Venture and Queen's Scout Awards. It was not, however, until 1978 that Queen Mary's became fully involved and joined the scheme as a school, led by the enthusiasm of Mr David Hart. David was to lead QM's D of E work from then until he retired in 1999. He responded to the request of Andrew Tanswell and Philip Young, then in the 3rd form, to arrange community work so that they could do the Award. In the first year in 1978 there were 40 boys taking part at Bronze level, including service, interests, physical activity and an expedition. The Bronze expedition is 15 miles long, while the Silver is 30 and the Gold is 50 in wild country. At Gold level there is also a residential project requirement. As time went on, the scheme became more attractive for many boys than scout training which ran in parallel but had a uniform and was based on the Scout Law and Promise. For many the more open D of E scheme had much to commend it.

The scheme at Queen Mary's developed strongly, with Bronze expeditions on Cannock Chase, and police and fire courses held locally. Boys joined in the 3rd year, and were eligible from their 14th birthday. They had till their 25th birthday to complete the Gold. In 1980 eight boys completed their Silver expeditions in mid-Wales. In 1982 the first four boys had gained their Gold awards: Simon Bromley, Robin Dean, Andrew Tanswell and Philip Young, and by this time 80 boys at QM were taking part. At this stage most of those involved were either in the school Scout Group, or in the CCF, but as time went on more were outside these organisations.

In the 1984 *Marian*, Daniel Johnson described a Farchynys-based Gold expedition on the Rhinog Mountains, north of the estuary, and then over Barmouth Bridge, up to the Cregennen Lakes and then, unable to climb Cadair Idris because of the atrocious weather, up the valley north of Dolgellau into the forest, and then back to Penmaenpool by the old railway path. In 1988, when there were 100 in the school involved, Paul Griffiths wrote 'my Bronze was awarded for undertaking a First Aid course, a term of hockey, seven months on ornithology, and an expedition on Cannock Chase. For Gold, I help in the school's camping store and in the careers library. I am now planning my residential, and hope to complete my Gold in October'. In 1989 Paul, Andrew Freeman and Jonathan Thacker, were awarded their Golds. In 1990 there were five Golds, in 1991 there were 11. In 1992 sixteen

Duke of Edinburgh Award Scheme – Expedition Log extract

TUESDAY 1 JULY
Drinking water came from a tap in the wall of the grimly bleak farmhouse, and the lavatory was evidently shared by both campers and sheep for the same highly draughty purposes. At twenty pence a night each we couldn't complain, but camping 'wild' was in fact a lot less effort in many ways.

WEDNESDAY 2 JULY
By 3.15 the sun had gone completely and rain clouds were gathering in the N.W. It was still warm and windy, with 7 Oktas cloud cover, and the next part of the route followed a path along the edge of the Hurst Moor valley ... It turned into a very pleasant evening but by this time we were far too exhausted (mentally and physically) to appreciate it.

THURSDAY 3 JULY
Black Hill turns out to be a highly appropriate name. Struggling to the Trig Point was a bit like walking on the moon or on sand covered with oil. It is pretty weird up there, especially the silence, with no animal or bird life and only scrub grass vegetation: no other land form can be seen from it.

We spoke to a woman who strode off into the distance to a small fenced area containing three poles with dark brown bottles clamped to them. She told us she was testing for pollution; this area is badly affected, surrounded on all sides by major industrial towns and the large amount of acid in the rainfall is adversely affecting the type of vegetation to be found here. We said good-bye and set off again only to be called back 400 yards later to pick up Martin's sleeping-bag ...

FRIDAY 4 JULY
The top (of Far Small Clough) is extremely bleak; all four of us fell victim to the bog and by 1.20 we were all thoroughly wet, thoroughly exhausted and thoroughly fed up. The alternative route down Abbey Brook didn't turn out to be a soft option, it is very steep and the grass was very slippy. We got down quite quickly, stopped for a rest and finished our lunch.

SATURDAY 5 JULY
The road wound out of view up a steep hill, the top of which looked a long way away. The area is pretty and obviously more accessible as there were a lot of people about, especially on the rocks of Stanage Edge. The worst part came after the road junction at Hooks Car where we had a massive climb. Going so fast at the beginning we didn't have much left for this stretch. We had a long rest...had it been a nice day the view from here would have been really good, because we could see for miles.

EPILOG(UE)
It would be difficult to say that we enjoyed our expedition, but we all agreed that we had achieved something valuable. The real test of the expedition is not physical - most reasonably fit people could manage without too much difficulty - but psychological. There were several occasions on which each of us could have happily given up, but we did not and that was our major achievement.

Philippe Bacon, Jonathan Birt, Mervyn Craddock, Martin Perrett, July 1980

members of the group joined 44 others from Walsall schools in Bavaria for activities at Silver and Gold level. The scout hut became a base for the scheme. So the achievement continued: in 1996 there were 139 boys and girls involved, and Queen Mary's pupils had achieved over 50 Gold Awards. In 1999 David Hart retired after 21 years' service to the scheme and to the hundreds of QM pupils who had participated. Hundreds of lunch hours, dozens of Bronze expeditions on Cannock Chase, so very many memorable Gold and Silver weekends at Farchynys. So many have memories for so many of the great crimson reception rooms at St James's Palace, and the warmth of the Prince Philip's comments of congratulation to the successful. The work was taken over by Mr Julian Roderick who had assisted for a few years previously. At present the scheme is sadly in abeyance at QM awaiting new leadership.

Chess

At the time of the Quatercentenary the school was pursuing a moderately successful course in the Wolverhampton Schools League, with JM Davies who never seems to have lost a match for the school. Soon there came into prominence JM Withnall, later secretary of the Staffordshire Chess Association, and much later a local headmaster and politician. His nephew Robert Withnall was top board when QM won Birmingham League Division One for the first time in 1975, three seasons after the school's first entry. Results immediately prior to this success had included good performances in *The Sunday Times* Tournament, although, as *The Marian* reported, 'chess had become something of a chore rather than a pastime of pleasure'. Then from 1974 chess was supervised by Mr Ian Davison, Head of German. His devotion to school chess was outstanding and he ran chess when some fine chess players were at Queen Mary's. For many years Ian Davison administered the Birmingham League as well as QM chess. He cared very much for the proper hosting of all chess matches at school and he was widely known nationally in schools' chess for his work in the Midlands and at Queen Mary's. Since his retirement school chess has been run by Mr Jim Wilkinson.

The Chess Team 1983.

From the top:
David Burton, David Young,
Paul Burton, Paul Metcalf,
Mark Wheeler, Darren Wheeler

    Mark Wheeler arrived in 1980 as joint under-11 British Champion, and his brother Darren two years later, having won the under-11 title in 1981. Mark subsequently won the under-14 title, while Darren was Staffordshire Senior Champion at 13. Both were later

selected for the Glorney Cup Junior Internationals. It was a huge advantage to have such talented players, and with David and Paul Burton providing powerful support and administrative skills, Queen Mary's became one of the leading schools in the country in the mid-1980s. QM won *The Times* Tournament, the national championship for schools, in 1983 and 1987, and had a string of successes in the Birmingham League Division One.

If these years were the high point in terms of playing excellence, the succeeding years saw a strength in depth which was scarcely less impressive. Paul Limbrick was Chess Secretary for four years from 1987, and contributed a very great deal to school chess. Four times in succession in the nineties the school were the Birmingham League champions, and there was consistent success in the lower divisions as well. In 1993 the Staffordshire under-19 team which won the Minor Counties Championship contained eight QM players in a team of 12. Michael Gough, Neil Clarke, Michael Denny and Christopher Bell were significant in this period and not only within the school. Eight times the National under-16 Team Tournament was played at the school. Gradually in the later nineties there seemed to be fewer potential chess-players in the intake, but more recently there appears a richer prospect in view. In 2003 six young players took part in the Staffordshire megafinal of the UK competition, and in the subsequent national Gigafinal Christopher Bellin, of Year 8, came joint first in his age group, and ranked 60th out of 67,000 players. A player of great promise!

Other Clubs and Societies

There is not enough space to deal with the myriad of other clubs and societies which had their long and short lives during the 50 years. In 1954 there was a Field Society, a Debating Society, a Chemical and Physical Society, an Archaeological Society, the Inter-School Christian Fellowship, the Chess Club and a Model Club, this in addition to the sports and music societies which are featured elsewhere. In 2002 there was a Chess Club, a Debating Society, a Joint Christian Union, a Science Society ... Clubs rise and fall, but the essential extra-curricular life of the school has changed less than one might imagine, given also the continuity of music, drama and the CCF. There were societies that had a short life, a few became outmoded, and several depended on the enthusiasm of individual members of staff. Examples of the latter were the Archaeological Society of which Mr John Dickson was President; and the Campanology Society which had two lives, one in the 1950s at Rushall Parish Church, and one in the 1970s when Stuart Holtam with

David Pomeroy and Philip Davies (nationally known for composing peals) took groups of bell-ringers to local churches to practise the art. That group joined parish ringers to ring the bells at the author's wedding at Brewood Parish Church in 1978!

It is difficult to know whether clubs and societies played a bigger part in the 1950s than today. I suspect they did. Interests may have been more modest, while many more boys cycled to school and were therefore independent of buses for going home. Much musical activity in the 1950s was based in the Music Club, with Chairman, Secretary and Treasurer, where today it is organised around the department. Minor sports were arranged as school clubs: there was a tennis club and a badminton club, with their own Captains and Secretaries, with a master as 'President'. Today such games are arranged within the P.E. Department. Reading *The Marians* of the day, I suspect there were also, in some societies, more outside speakers from industry and university, and more serious academic papers written by sixth-formers and presented to larger audiences.

The Physical and Chemical Society, in one term in 1960, had a member reading a paper on 'Titanium', two films – one on the Victor bomber and the other on developments in Canadian nuclear physics – a lecture by Dr Knight of Birmingham University on radiation, and a master lecturing on electrical discharges through gas tubes. The society has had the longest history of all societies outside music, chess and sport. Throughout the sixties and seventies it met regularly with talks and demonstrations from sixth-formers, staff and outside speakers. Led in the early years by Mr SH Chadburn, senior science master, it had a very brief break in the early eighties before it was revitalised by Mr Roy Jones in 1982, and he has led it since. In 1991 the 'Phys and Chem' was united with the Biology Society to form a **Science Society** which has been its name since then. In recent years the emphasis has changed and the society arranges for students to go to useful lectures at local universities, rather than arrange for meetings to be held at school.

A Sixth Form Union emerged about 1970, with a management committee which held meetings with Sixth Form tutors. It arranged a film society amongst other events, and ran a sixth form shop at break in the Common Room. Then in the 1970s the sixth form developed a joint society with the High School: the **Umbrella Society**. This met, not in the lunch hour or at 4 pm but on Wednesday evenings in the Sixth Form Common Room with 30 to 40 present. This all arose during the time of teenage rebellion which affected discipline and standards at QM at the time. Those concerned found it difficult to channel the reasonable

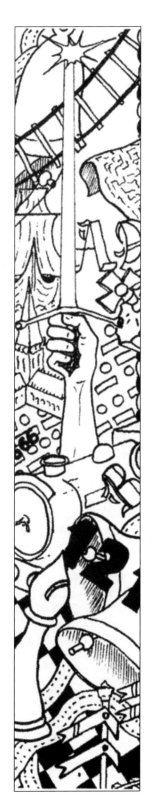

and unreasonable demands of the leading sixth-formers! This is all more fully discussed in Ch. 9. The initiative from the sixth form was supported by Messrs Chipchase and Anderson. Discussion, music and entertainment with many staff involved, including Messrs Paxton and NRF Jones, helped to maintain a good atmosphere and a successful collaborative venture for the two schools which lasted several years, latterly under the auspices of Mr Fletcher.

History Sixth visit to the Open Field village of Laxton 1968

History Society at Winchester 1974 with Messrs Tom Perrett and Tim Lawrence

During the 1980s the **Christian Union** expanded again. For many years under the auspices of Mr John Farrington it met after school on a Wednesday as a joint society with the High School. Other staff gave

LAXTON CHURCH

support over the years: Messrs Chris Cumbers (back in the early seventies), David Isgrove, Ian Bryant (as pupil and master), and then more recently, caretaker Peter Buckley who for well over ten years has given the Society, the Joint Christian Union, consistent inspiration. Now there is a Moss Close Christian Union also. It is noteworthy that the CU has always been a Farchynys user. It has also regularly provided, every term or two, a week of school assemblies.

One of the most successful societies over the years, which I use as an example, has been the **History Society**, developed by John Anderson from that which he inherited in 1966, and lasting through, uninterrupted, to the present. Based on a wide range of talks by boys and staff, quizzes and videos, visits, and very many trips to Farchynys, the society has lasted well, and has more recently been led by Messrs Tim Lawrence and David Rushworth (himself a participant in his school days of the 70s). For years it met in school on Mondays 'at 4.05 in D5' as the assembly announcement had it. Most historical monuments in Central and Northern Wales, and in Shropshire and the Marches, have been studied. In the early years there were also Youth Hostel weekends to York, Lincoln, the Wye valley, the Stonehenge area and Winchester. In these weekends the author was supported by his colleagues at various times including

Trip to Rome: in the Forum with Mr Philip Done

Messrs Philip Done and Clive Westlake. Following a highly successful visit to northern Spain in 1968, there were, during the 1970s, annual Easter trips abroad, usually combining two of Florence, Venice and Rome. These comprised 24 boys with JSA and one or two masters including, on various trips, Nick Jones, Philip Done and Neville Cooper. More recently, in 1998, there was a visit to Ypres and the Somme by a party of 37 boys and staff.

In 1970 the **Debating Society** had a joint debate with the High School with 76 people present. A master, Dr Jacques, led a discussion on the 'advantages of science', there was a debate on the permissive society, and another on euthanasia, while Messrs Hart and Patterson led the debate 'that this House believes that no man is an island'. With the ups and downs found in the life of school societies, the Debating Society, with junior and senior sections at times, has flourished and has entered with some success for regional competitions over the years, more recently led by Mr Lawrence.

The **Bridge Club** began life as a staff bridge club in 1961. It soon spread to the sixth form and remained strong into the 1990s, very much inspired by the enthusiasm of Mr Gordon Brudenell. The best years were around 1980 when the school succeeded in the Daily Mail Schools Bridge Competition (later the English Bridge Union Schools Competition). The school team came 4th, 3rd, 2nd and 1st equal, before winning the Cup, and holding it for one year. The outstanding player at this time was Glyn Liggins (1974–81) who went on to play internationally. The keenest players over the years were members of Walsall Bridge Club. Throughout the half-century bridge has been played in the Common Room by teams of staff, sometimes at one table, sometimes at two!

Of the other societies is this period some of the most lasting include the **Wargaming Society**, led by Mr Tom Perrett, which frequently visited Farchynys over the years; the **Model Club**, and the **Railway Society**, encouraged for many years by Mr John Wilcox. More recently there have been newer groups like the **Cercle Français** and the **Deutscher Club**, the **Maths Club**, and the **Latin Club**. All have contributed to the wider education of the Queen Mary's pupil who is prepared to give up time outside school hours to follow his own interests, and to encourage others. Many have improved their communication skills and have learnt to administer and organise for the first time by helping to run a school society. Oh, that more would take part and benefit thereby!

Charity Fund Raising

Throughout the years there has been fund raising for charities, very often led by Year Tutors and their Prefects. The school has always supported the Poppy Appeal. There have been non-uniform days when boys have come to school in jeans and sweaters rather than uniform, and have paid for the privilege with a payment (usually £1) which would go to charity.

Recently there has been a more concerted attempt to encourage pupils to raise funds for local and national charities. In 2003, approximately £3000 was donated for a number of causes, including the Sister Dora Hospice, Motor Neurone Disease Association, Jeans for Genes Day, The Poppy Appeal and so on. Mr Michael Lax organised a Readathon which raised £1900 for children's cancer charities.

Olympiad, Superschools and Young Enterprise

A development of recent years has been in sponsored competitions of the intellectual kind. The Maths **Olympiad** has been going for many years and many boys have gained bronze, silver and gold certificates. In 2001 in the Intermediate National Challenge three pupils were invited to take part in the National Challenge. In the Junior Challenge that year Matthew Causier of Year 8 was placed in the top 29 of the National Olympiad. In 2002 31 Year 8, and six Year 7 boys took part. The Year 8 boys achieved 11 gold, 13 silver and four bronze certificates, Graeme Cade being invited to take part in the national Olympiad. 15 sixth-formers also took part in the UK Senior Mathematical Challenge, achieving five gold certificates, Jude Daniels being invited to take part in the British Mathematical Olympiad. Some pupils tried their skills in an international website, with their solutions being published with budding mathematicians from Vietnam, Romania and the USA. A Year 11 group won £200 for their success in a National Cipher Challenge. In 2003, 29 Year 11 boys and one Year 10 boy took part and gained 16 gold, five silver and five bronze certificates, four being chosen to go forward nationally.

For the last six years the school has entered the **Superschools** Quiz. In 2001 the team reached the final for the third time in four years, and this time they won against Wolverhampton Girls' High school. In 2002 with a new team they entered against 103 other schools in the Midlands, in the MG Rover sponsored competition. Beating Bishop Vesey's in the Regional Final, the team faced King Edward's Aston in the Final. With Ed Doolan as the usual Quiz Master they edged into the lead by one point at the final whistle, again winning trophies for themselves and £1000 for the school. In 2003 the team reached the semi-finals.

The **LionHeart** Challenge is a new competitive exercise. In May 2003, a team of eight 15-year olds went to Bescot Stadium, and had a day to design a product or service to promote tourism and leisure in the Walsall area. They made a mini business plan, detailing marketing and finance, an IT virtual mock-up of the product or service, a

PowerPoint slideshow, and a three-minute presentation. Their idea was a dance festival at Bescot Stadium and the Arboretum. Experts were available to help, and they were questioned by a panel of judges, including the Chief Executive of Walsall Football Club and the Human Resources Manager of Marks and Spencer. The QM team won the competition and the glass trophy, enabling them to go to a national final.

In the national **Young Enterprise** scheme, the school has set up, for 2003–04, two small Companies of pupils to use their enterprise to raise funds. Each company sells shares (at 50p each), raising capital for their year-long project. The company 'Go Biz' produced the school Christmas Cards for 2003 amongst other schemes, while the other company is raising further funds through car washing so that it can retail 450th school anniversary memorabilia (mouse mats, notepads etc). In order to operate soundly the Company Directors have an external business professional to advise them. The scheme is developed within the school by the Head of Economics, Tom Walton. Those who have success can go forward to a regional and national competition.

School Christmas Card 2003 designed and produced by GoBiz

The Eighties

One conclusion that may be drawn from this study of fifty years in a Grammar School, is that the 1980s at Queen Mary's was a vintage decade. A great deal of talent had emerged in earlier years, especially in the early sixties and early seventies, and there is vitality in the school today. The 1980s remains rather special. As has been said, it was a period of political and social calm, and within the school the new educational trends and demands had made little impact. Though it was a decade of financial stringency for running the school, there was more wealth among many of the school families.

The CCF, in the final years under John Dickson, won the District Patrol Competition and went to visit the Staffordshire Regiment in Germany. In 1988 there was the visit to Norway, Expedition Thor. The Scout Group had its final flourish, led by both Graham Chesterman and John Edlin, with up to 40 scouts in the Troop. 100 in the school were involved in the Duke of Edinburgh scheme in 1988. Chess was in its heyday with the school team winning the Times national championship in 1983 and again in 1987. John Bateman and Joe Franklin enhanced GGP's productions with fine stage constructions while Ellen Smith still produced her quality constumes.

By the end of the decade rugby and cricket were exceptionally strong with tougher fixture lists, the 1990 1st XI being the most successful for twenty years. The 1988 hockey side was the strongest ever. Musically it was the last decade when quality musicians entered the school every year, rather than occasionally. Martin Shaw, Richard Wise, Simon Northwood and Mark Purcell are names from this era. The QMA were expanding their events and the Joe Loss Summer Ball was established. The description of the Iceland Expedition of 1982, below, is a tribute to the enormous vigour showed by members of staff whose experience and energy were at their height, and who were then not worn down by the bureaucracy of modern 'education'. An evocative retrospect in contained in Ian Cooksey's memory (Memories 5) at the end of the book.

Above all, QM was fortunate that in the 1980s it had a Headmaster in Keith Howard who was the ideal Head for those times.

Iceland 1982

This expedition represents the ambitious extra-curricular outdoor activities organised during the last 50 years. Here is an example of a project which was not associated with Farchynys, the Scouts or the CCF. It is an example of the rich life of the school during this period.

After two years as a project and a label attached to a stream of discos, sponsored walks and jumble sales, Iceland had, for all eighteen of us, become something of a fantasy. We talked glibly of driving rain, heavy snowfalls, freezing conditions, without stopping to think what we were saying. As the expedition grew near, apprehension increased. Eventually we boarded the coach at school, and with many a wave, we were on our way.

The adventure, for that was what we wanted it to be, began after our first night under canvas. We had arrived at a tiny farm, and had set up camp. We broke into our food packs for the first time, lit primus stoves, and tried to see into the valley behind the farm into which, next day, we would begin the task of transporting our ton of equipment and food. No one, I think, would deny that those first few days were a severe challenge. Although on one occasion Mr Chesterman was eager to prove his ability by carrying over ninety pounds, most were more than tested by only thirty. After three days moving up the valley, we were at last able to begin the real work – studying a rock glacier 4,000 feet up on the mountain in front of which we had made our main camp.

The previous winter there had been a heavy snowfall, and the mountain stream was still covered with a thick layer of snow. Kicking steps, it was eventually up this that we made our way, after testing it with boulders rolled from higher up. Bright sunlight, dazzling skies and brilliant snow hardly seemed like Iceland; yet when we reached the glacier at the top there was no doubting. A huge pile of rocks greeted us, the glacier's snout jutting violently forward into banks of snow on either side. Stopping to put the equipment we had carried into the shelter of boulders made by a party some years before, we clambered on to make our first inspection. By now the wind was biting cold. The only exposed ice was at the back of the corrie. The rock of the glacier was very fragile. Even huge pieces slid away at the slightest touch. We gathered below the ice, put on crampons and went up to look. The

Surveying

corrie itself formed a vast natural amphitheatre, towering up to the flat plateau of the mountain-top itself.

The fieldwork projects we were to carry out were many and varied. Most important was to survey the glacier, to draw maps of it, and to estimate its melting rate. Five years before, the first school to visit the area used a levelling device to paint a series of straight lines on the rocks across the glacier. We repeated this, and found that in some places it had moved forward as much as a metre. One group climbed to the plateau each day to study patterned ground. They took hundreds of photographs of the huge circles and stripes of stones, which nature, by its own secret devices, had arranged.

During our two weeks in the valley, it was easy to forget that our only relationship was attending the same school – the camp became a community of its own, everyone just belonging naturally to it. Everyone equally dreaded the 'Get-up' orders at 7.30, everyone enjoyed the evenings spent in quiet relaxation – cooking the evening meal and talking.

The most memorable day, perhaps, came when the work was over. A group of us decided to walk on to an ice-field in the next valley. It was a glorious day, and the sun glared down at us as we tried to find a place to cross the river. It took us four hours to climb up on to the snow, but the view when we got there was breathtaking. On either side, rock and ice towered, and far down below, on the edge of the fjord stood the main northern town of Akureyri, a tiny blur of colours. There we found another glacier, massive peaks of ice tearing into the blue sky, plummeting crevasses striking hundreds of feet down into harsh green ice. The sheer scale was frightening. Everything was open. Nothing moved. There was no noise except for the occasional crash of falling snow. It was all touched with red as the sun lowered. In the distance were the grey tops of two ice-caps, a turmoil of dark clouds brooding over them. It was midnight before we got back to camp, lit all the way by the constant sunlight of the Icelandic summer night.

The day we left, the Icelanders at the farm gave a party for us. Sitting in the warmth, our wind-reddened faces stung. Our smiling hosts filled and refilled the table with food. Even Mr Holtam's persistent complaints that this wasn't how an expedition should be, couldn't stop him from indulging. All that was left to us was three days in Myvatn, a volcanic region in the north. Despite the foul weather we were able to visit Mount Krafla, one of Iceland's most active volcanoes, and walk on lava erupted in 1980 (two years earlier). The rain which fell turned to steam on the still-hot lava, and we ate lunch in the midst of a vision of hell. Our enthusiasm for lava was soon dampened by a seemingly endless walk along the lava flow of 1729, but it was easily revived by a trip to the naturally heated swimming baths close to the campsite.

Iceland was an experience I would not have missed for the world.

Adapted from a report written for The Marian *by Nigel Moore (QM 1976–83).*

17

QUEEN MARY'S ASSOCIATION

The First Fêtes

One of SL Darby's lasting contributions to Queen Mary's was the QMA. Founded to assist with fund raising for the new buildings, it became the backbone of parental support throughout the recent 50 years and active families became part of the Queen Mary's family.

The first school Fête was run in 1953 by Mrs Hamilton and Mrs Burn, with other staff wives and parents' to raise money for the Quatercentenary gates appeal. In 1958 parents, Old Boys and friends formed a committee to run a Fête in aid of the school Building Fund. The Fête was held at Moss Close and raised £900. Each year thereafter a Fête has taken place but at Mayfield, run by a most ambitious committee.

In 1963 the Headmaster, SL Darby, pioneered a form of parents' association which has proved immensely successful, and, forty years later, in 2003 it raised, in the one year, £26,000 for the school.

Inauguration of the QMA

Mrs Judy Lindon-Morris remembers the inaugural meeting in the Hall at Lichfield Street. 'Mr Darby said he didn't want to call it a parents' association because it was an association of friends of the school'. Mrs Lindon-Morris remembers also that Mr Bob Christie asked her if she would join the Amenities Committee and she became its secretary. She bought her Olivetti typewriter then. Other early members of that committee included Dr Henry Pollitt, Jimmy Ladkin, Hazel White, and Dr John Weston. Members of the committee became their friends. Mr Darby later rang her and asked her to become secretary of the new Welsh Centre Management Committee, which she did till 1979. She remembers this as a very happy time, and it is clear that the parents who became involved in the QMA did find lasting friends there, and their abiding loyalty to the school was developed in the QMA.

The QMA absorbed the Fête Committee, but the latter retained control of its funds separately for many years. The first QMA Management Committee chairman was Mr Harold Hunter, and its first treasurer, who remained at the helm for 10 years, was Mr CA Hart. The subscription was five shillings a year. Its unusual format, which produced such success, was that it set up virtually independent committees to run individual events and to support the school. These committees were co-ordinated by a Management Committee, but for many years kept their own funds. Indeed there was always reluctance to pool funds into the Management Committee accounts! In this way several groups of parents were involved independently of each other, and the combination of all their efforts was to be remarkable. At the time of its creation the new building fund was the first priority, but Farchynys had just been bought, so that support for the Welsh Centre was important. Headmaster AN Hamilton had set up the Consolidated Fund to which parents subscribed seven shillings and sixpence a term, but even then this was proving insufficient, and the QMA was soon to be asked for items for the school above and beyond that which the LEA provided, or the Consolidated Fund could support.

The secret of success: the separate committees

By 1966 there were, apart from the Fête Committee, six committees: Social Functions, Amenities, Membership, Careers, Catering, and the Ladies' Committee. The Social Functions Committee, in these early days, ran the Barbecue, and, by 1968, was running the annual Valentine Dance. The Amenities Committee ran the Open Day at Farchynys, and the annual Clothing Sale. The Ladies' Committee ran wine and cheese evenings, and coffee mornings. The other three committees were 'service' committees which did not raise funds. The Careers Committee brought ideas for developing careers advice; the Catering Committee served teas, coffees and soft drinks for cricket and rugby matches, and served refreshments at other school events, including some QMA events. The Membership Committee strove in the early years with great success to reach a 90% parent membership, and to add old boy and friends membership as well. Having produced ideas, the Careers Committee ceased to exist by 1968. Following a meeting called by Mrs Darby, the first Plant Sale in 1969, was popular, and Mr Ken Jeffrey became chairman of the new committee. The sale soon became the Homes and Gardens

Ken and Joyce Jeffrey – long serving stalwarts of the QMA

Event, and was to be one of the longest running successes. For years hundreds of wallflowers from a grower near Lichfield were collected for the Saturday morning event.

One of the early ventures which clearly caused difficulty was the provision of a film of the opening of the school buildings, and of QMA activity, made to help to attract new parents. Dr Pollitt was responsible and he worked with Mr Brian Edwards, senior geography master, who had care of the equipment. There is record of continuing concerns about the state of the film and the equipment! Eventually, as Judy Lindon-Morris remembers, the film became very dated! Then records show that in the 1960s events which harked back to the decades before no longer had appeal. Sherry evenings soon became wine and cheese evenings. The idea of a 'Flannel Dance' was mooted and dropped. Arranging dances was difficult: the school dances of the fifties were no longer appropriate, and soon the boys wanted discos where the behaviour was seen by the school to be inappropriate! However, the Fête was a continuing annual money-raiser and by 1970, £1000 was raised by the Fête (including the raffle), and about £1000 was raised by all the other QMA events. In 1970 the 'Roll-a-Penny' stall was bought by Mr RA Wassell, a parent, from his friend Pat Collins. From the first years the Fête Hut was built for the equipment and it has been used ever since.

The early days of the QMA coincided with the Comprehensive threat. The Head used the QMA to gauge parental feeling and encourage support for the governors. In 1968 a defence committee including parents was discussed by the QMA and set up as the 'Friends of Queen Mary's Liaison Committee'. This committee did not last, but it is an indication of the alarm that action had to be taken on all fronts.

Staff & the QMA

Several unconnected aspects of school life were brought before the QMA Management Committee for their support. Mr Peter Holgate, Head of German at the time, set up a school bookshop. This was a lunchtime venture with portable bookcases which were opened up in the entrance hall. The books were supplied by Husdon's, then the leading Birmingham bookshop. Soon Mr John Hutchinson, 2nd in the Modern Languages department took over the bookshop, which was a considerable success throughout the 1970s. The QMA made grants to underwrite the stock.

As time went on, John Hutchinson became a member of the Management Committee and was the school staff member on the Fête Committee, running the raffle for many years. The raffle was, and is, a major money-raising element of the Fête, and involves boys selling vast number of tickets through their families. Tickets have to be collected and folded in a hugely time-consuming manner. Considerable staff organisation was necessary for the barbecue and fireworks as well. After his death, the new staff member on the Fête Committee and the Barbecue Committee was Mr Jim Walker who continued the magnificent work until his retirement, since when the work has been carried on by Mr Tim Lawrence.

The Farchynys Open Day referred to in Chapter 6, was run by the Amenities Committee, now known as the Lower School Events Committee. In 1968 there were 208 who attended, and the numbers varied up to 250. The QMA helped to arrange the opening of the swimming bath in the Spring of 1970, and the squash courts in October 1971. From then on the QMA has supported the Squash Club in increasing and then maintaining its membership. The association also supported the setting up of an Evening Institute in 1973, when all parents were invited to join classes in hobby topics. This was supported by the Education Committee and became the evening classes which the school has hosted ever since.

The QMA and Farchynys

Before decimalization and the oil crisis in the early 1970s which markedly inflated prices, figures of profit seem very small. The annual barbeque (*sic*) raised £126 in 1967, and by 1971 the figure was up to £150. The Valentine Dance in 1971 produced a profit of £75, and the Homes and Gardens £60. The new minibus in 1970 cost £900, given an allowance of £180 on the old vehicle (licence and tax etc included). The whole workroom extension to Farchynys, completed in 1974, cost just over £8400. In 1972, following decimalization, the Consolidated Fund termly contribution went up from 7s 6d, or 37½ pence, to 50 pence which was a reasonable increase and simpler to collect! In 1973 a weekend visit to Farchynys was still £1.75 per head with 80p allowance per boy for the purchase of food.

Inflation, following the oil crisis, caused the QMA problems. By 1976 a minibus cost over £2000 new and the allowance on a one year old vehicle was £1000. A larger minibus cost £3240. Including the depreciation cost of the minibus, Farchynys was now costing £3600 a year to run. The Consolidated Fund and the Scholarship Fund shared

Farchynys Open Day 1964: the first group of parents to admire the headland: seated left is Ralph White. We would be pleased to receive names for others!

this burden with the QMA. In fact Mr Phil Bull, the Warden, ran a sponsored swim in 1976 which raised £1125, and the larger and more expensive 15-seater bus was purchased to last two years. But QMA events now raised more money as the pound changed its value. In 1977 the Fête raised £2000; by 1980, £3500. By 1981 the amount raised by QMA including the Fête was in excess of £13,000.

By 1975 the members of the Management Committee included Messrs Phil Homer, L Carter, H Mullens, Chris Stone, RM Walker, P Quigley, S Palmer, A Boynton, J Sutton, P Day, Ken Jeffrey, Eric Dilkes, and Ted Nightingale, with Mesdames N Homer, M Haggett, Hazel White, Vi Beech, Jackie Dilkes, S Wallis and J Coombs. The Committee remembered two hard-working members who died at that time: Mr P Hunt and Mrs M Weston. The list represents so many who served the school with enormous devotion, and who at this time gave their energies when the future of the Queen Mary's Schools as selective schools was very much in doubt.

Everything ready for the Summer Ball

The Summer Ball

In 1978 it was proposed by Mrs Betty Gray that a Grand Summer Ball be arranged in the Town Hall, with dinner and a bar, and music by Joe Loss and his Band. The first Ball was held in 1979 at school, with decorations by Walsall Parks Department. It was a tremendous success, although its small profit was taken up by the cost of moving a grand piano from the West Midlands College to the school for the evening! Despite this a second Ball was held in 1980, and Betty Gray and her team went on to put in a prodigious amount of work for these annual occasions, which became a permanent part of the Joe Loss calendar as it did Queen Mary's. His two calendar fixtures which he enjoyed most were Queen Mary's and his booking to play for the Queen Mother.

By this time SL Darby had retired, with the QMA clearly yet another of his successes. Before he retired the association was made aware that with the change of government at the General Election the school was no longer under the shadow of threat that had been there since 1965. Keith Howard, his successor, in 1979 welcomed the work of the QMA in his first address to it as President, saying how forcibly he had been struck by the vigour and enterprise of this flourishing association, and that he could not avoid full awareness of the work carried out for the benefit of the school.

One of Mr Howard's early moves was to amend the pattern of the Consolidated Fund which had hardly changed since Hamilton's day. Parents were asked to make termly contributions to what was now known as Central Fund of £1 'or more'. This open-ended request opened the door to greater generosity, and termly contributions rose from £300 to £1400, and soon to upwards of £1600. The author remembers counting the contents of the envelopes form by form, and how, though the younger boys' parents became ever more generous, the parents of senior boys maintained their traditional habits and put only their £1 into the envelope! Then it was cash, but as the years passed, more and more cheques came in the termly voluntary offerings! And how important and welcome this was in the financially difficult years ahead.

Wider demands on QMA fundraising

In the early eighties there were the familiar demands on QMA funds: the library, the Green Book and the regular renewal of the minibus. But there were new requirements: the replacement of the old wooden fire escape at Farchynys; some funding for the refurbishment of the Sutton Road houses (described fully in Chapter 4); the increased expense of coaches for teams travelling to schools in the enlarged sports fixture list; funds for buying the school's first computers, and the QMA's very welcome desire to buy new curtains for the hall, and curtains for the dining area. By this time it had become accepted that all QMA funds were paid annually into Central Fund, but this did not diminish the QMA committees' real and proper desire to know about the projects for which they were raising money.

In 1981 a Crime Prevention Panel was set up in Walsall, and Parents' Associations were invited to send representatives to its meetings. It considered many areas of increasing concern for parents in the rise of juvenile crime, and sought ways of involving parents in helping to prevent young people getting involved. For some years there were reports at every Management Committee meeting about the work of the Panel. When a Junior Panel was set up, a sixth-former took part also.

The pattern of the annual Fête has hardly changed, though it has become more informal. Stalls round the quadrangle, the roll-a-penny in the centre, stalls down the field including archery and coconut shies, usually a tempting stall to soak the captain of school and prefects with sponges of cold water, sometimes special events for the year, and teas in the canteen provide the essence of the event. In years past a local figure opened the Fête, and was entertained to tea in the Sixth Form Common Room or Library, and then guests sat on rows of chairs on the quadrangle steps for the raffle draw. This element has gone, regretfully, but the raffle continues to be a major money-raiser underpinning the whole event. Running the Fête is hard work and the school is indebted to the generations of parents involved.

The Fireworks event

The Barbecue, now the Fireworks event, has been the other long-lasting success. Again stalls around the quadrangle with plenty of soup and hot dogs, and now Indian food, sometimes events in the hall, and the hundreds who line the top of the field beyond the library to witness a rich and well-timed display, usually at 8.30, to the sound of Handel's *Music for the Royal Fireworks*. A simple but very popular event.

By 1984 the annual Fête was raising over £4000. Mr Michael Powell took over from Chris Stone as only the third treasurer in the life of the QMA, and he confirmed that he expected to hand over £10,000 to the Headmaster for the year. By 1986 this figure had gone up to £14,700, with termly parental contributions up to £9000. In 1985 the Ladies' committee jumble sales raised £270, and the fashion show produced over £1000. The Joe Loss Ball had a profit of £2377, including the proceeds of the bar. The Homes and Gardens Event raised £884. Mr and Mrs Ken Jeffrey and Mrs Hazel White retired. They had been on committees of the association from its earliest days, while others who were involved in these years included Mrs Vi Beech, Mrs Betty Gray, Mrs Mary Stokes, Mrs Shirley Motteram, Mr and Mrs Jeff Tromans, Messrs Andrew Waters, George Armitage, Ian Hartley, David Judson, Tom Shore, Alan Jones, Tony Lawrence, and the Revd Michael Metcalf. Mr Ted Jones was Secretary to the Management Committee.

In 1985 the QMA learnt that all parents would be eligible to vote for the first time for a Parent Governor, subsequently Mr Alan Jones was elected as the first. This was the year also when, led by Mr Carl Zissman and Mr Brian Simmons, the QMA acquired a Bar Committee (the Bar team having started in 1983–84), which was to ease the provision of refreshment at future QMA evening events very considerably, and greatly increase the profits. It was in 1986 that representatives of the QMA met with those of the King Edward's Grammar Schools PTAs in order to give them the benefit of the experience of Queen Mary's in gaining support and funds from parents. Another new venture was the creation of 'OMPA', the Old Marians' Parents Association, under the auspices of Mr Ken Jeffrey, who was appointed a Foundation Governor in 1987. For the record, the Barbecue and Fireworks Committee was renamed the Fireworks Committee in 1989.

The Fête, the Fireworks and the Summer Ball were still increasing their profits. Following the retirement and death of Joe Loss, the Band was now led by Todd Miller, but the QM fixture was still one of the firmest in their calendar. The work of the Amenities Committee and the Catering Committee were as important as ever. However the Ladies' Committee and the Social Functions Committee were having to work extremely hard to find support and raise the funds of previous years.

New directions in the nineties

By 1993 the active members of the Management Committee included Joe Miles, chairman, who did so much for the QMA and the Welsh Centre Committee bringing his practical experience and contacts to bear on all occasions, Pat O'Kane, Bernard Shepherd, Barry Sanders, Barry Sims, Mike Yates, Pat and Faith Moore, Bill Coleman, and many others. It is a pity to quote only a few, but equally it would not be right to exclude those who did so much in their era for Queen Mary's. By 1994 Mrs Gill Columbine, school administrator, had become Management Committee secretary. Major events were producing excellent results: the 1994 Fête raised £5825 net, Fireworks raised £2350, and the Summer Ball raised £3500. There was also a barn dance, the toy sale, a sixties evening, the Christmas Bazaar, and a quiz night. For the OMPA membership there was a buffet evening. In these years one important regular fund-raiser was the 200 Club run by Mr W Coleman. In 1995 the VE Dance in May, which was an extra event, raised £600 and the total raised for the year went up to £15,951, despite the difficulties in raising support.

In 1995 the QMA said farewell on his retirement to Mr Keith Howard, Head since 1979, and welcomed the new (and well-known) Head, Stuart Holtam. The first event of any school year was always the New Parents' Film Evening. It was this and the AGM of the QMA that produced agonising discussion. Whether to unite the events; how to prevent new parents being overwhelmed with information about the various committees; how to run the buffet supper, and so on! The film of earlier years had long been abandoned and replaced by a slide and tape show on the school's history. The tape had not survived and by the 1990s Mr John Anderson, as Second Master, (and even after he retired!) gave the historical commentary each year, followed by the Farchynys Warden, Mr Law, who showed wonderfully evocative slides of the Welsh Centre. A new film was discussed, but no progress was made!

1996 saw the launch of the new Development Campaign with an initial target of £150,000. After the launch, the appeal to parents raised £60,000, and when all gifts and tax rebates are taken into account Mr Holtam was able to report by May 1966 that the school was only £35,000 short of the target. Questions were asked about the place of QMA fund-raising in the light of this campaign, but the Headmaster stressed that Farchynys, the minibus and games coaches plus a host of smaller expenses could not be fully supported without the continued work of the QMA. The funds raised by the campaign would enable the first major computer room to be equipped. A further £250,000 would be needed to upgrade facilities for design technology. By 1998 it was clear that a major future project would be a sports hall. Details of this campaign are more fully described in Chapter 10.

The QMA Today

Clearly, however, changes in parental support were occurring. Considerably more was being given directly in termly donations, and to the development campaign. As early as 1990 there had been reports of a decline in attendance for some events, particularly the Saturday morning events, and some had to be cancelled. Fewer parents were coming forward to support some of the committees, and the structure of committees now was revamped, demonstrating the vigour of the QMA at this time, under the chairmanship of Mr Barry Picken. In 1998 the Ladies' Committee was disbanded after 35 honourable years. The Homes and Gardens event had not survived the drop in Saturday morning support, and a car boot sale committee was set up. The toy sale survives. An antiques fair committee had been created, and the Amenities Committee was renamed the Lower School Events Committee, and after a most successful Burns Night, a permanent committee for this event was approved. For some years the Summer Ball Committee was led by Mrs Alison Tomkinson with great success. A major change was proposed when it reported that a new minibus would cost £20,000, of which only £8500 could come from part-exchange. What a change in relative prices since the early days!

By 1999 another generation of parents was guiding the QMA, led by Mr Mike Love, Mrs Yvonne Calogirou, Mrs Janet Bridgman, Mrs Steph Coleman, Mr Nick Chomyk and others. The total number of events had been slimmed down, but the funds raised were still extraordinarily impressive. It had become noticeable that the several major events, other than the Fête and Fireworks, were supported by many friends of friends who were not from the Queen Mary's community. A new venture in 2000 was a joint Cultural Evening with Mayfield School, with Mrs Nicky Watson liasing between the two parents' committees. A further new venture in 2002 was an Asian evening, 'A Taste of the East', which helped greatly to gain the support of many families who hitherto had supported the school in very many ways, but had not supported QMA events. It had seemed difficult to attract parents from divergent cultural backgrounds to attend some events, and it is to the credit of the QMA that they are accepting the challenge and overcoming this problem. At the end of the 2002–03 year £26,000 was handed to the school, over £5000 more than in any previous year. This is an extraordinary achievement. Such is the continuing value to the school of the enormous efforts put in by the QMA.

QUEEN MARY'S GRAMMAR SCHOOL № 0968

SUMMER FETE 1982

№ 045791

FETE GRAND DRAW

FIRST PRIZE: £200
Prize — THEATRE VOUCHERS
Prize — GARDEN FURNITURE
Plus Many, Many More Prizes

Promoter: Mr. S. G. Holtam, Sutton Road, Walsall.
Drawn on Saturday, 5th July, 1997 at the School Fete
under the Lotteries and Amusements Act, 1976 with Walsall M.B.C.
THANK YOU AND GOOD LUCK
TICKETS 20p EACH

Printline Complete Printing Service   Tel./Fax: 0121-352 0331

18

QUEEN MARY'S CLUB

The Queen Mary's Club had been founded in 1874 in the Headmastership of Revd AC Irvine, who was the Club's first secretary, and its progress until the 1950s is recorded in David Fink's Queen Mary's Grammar School, *in Ch XVII.*

In recent memory the Club planted the line of poplar trees at the bottom of Mayfield, and also paid the costs of the War Memorial boards in Big School which were moved to Mayfield to the new hall there. When Farchynys was purchased and its ownership was conveyed to trustees, the Club took responsibility for overseeing the trusteeship and it has annually paid the local rates and council tax on the property since its acquisition. When the appeal was made for the new buildings at Mayfield, the Club's own contribution was to enrich the furnishing of the new library. The Club also contributed in its early days to an old boys' Scholarship Fund, and, together with the scholarship funds which were amalgamated after 1944, this became the fund for travel scholarships which is still administered by its trustees of old boys and governors. More recently the Fund has been most generously augmented with a bequest from the much loved RA (Sticky) Burton (QM 1930–37). This fund makes generous annual grants for books for the library, and makes grants for other equipment and resources for the school, as well as grants for Queen Mary's students while at university.

Mr Phil Evans past chairman of QMA and long serving governor, seen during CCF Inspection 1955

The Club at Lichfield Street

In 1955 the Club devised a new constitution, and 'reconstructed' itself with an annually elected chairman, FD (David) Jeffries (QM 1928–37), being the first Chairman in 1956, and in that capacity he welcomed SL Darby as the new President. He also arranged for regular club gatherings on the first Wednesday of the month, at the Royal Oak, Ablewell Street, now the Royal Hotel. These were most successful with a monthly attendance of 40 and more. It may be noted that the 1956 Annual Dinner cost 14s. a head and 137 Old Boys attended. Annually there was an Old Boys' Cricket Day, and in 1957 a Golfing Society was started. 16 Old Boys attended the Annual Dinner of the QMC London Branch in March 1957. In 1959 the number had grown to 27. In 1958, during the Chairmanship of PW (Phil) Evans (QM 1925–36), two dances were held and the Club joined with parents and the school to make the first School Fête a great success. Readers of *The Marian* were sorry to read of the deaths of familiar figures from the past: Bompas Smith (Headmaster 1897–1906), and WG ('Crop') Thomas (retired Second Master, cricketer, artist and historian).

1959 saw the launch of the Appeal for the Rebuilding Fund for the new school on the Mayfield site. All Old Marians were sent the brochure and the response was very strong along with parents and local industry, so that the Governors could approve the first instalment, and the walls of the new science block began to rise on the playing fields. Sam Darby hoped that the QMC would have facilities in the new school, but that was not to be – at least not for over forty years!

1960 saw the founding of the Old Marians' Orchestra by Chad Jackson (Club chairman in 1957). Chad was assisted in setting up the orchestra by Fred Hood (QM 1925–33), and the first leader of the orchestra was Graham Rockett. The first concert was held in the school hall in November 1960, with the proceeds being donated to the Building Appeal Fund. Further reference to the OM Orchestra will be found in Chapter 14. In addition to the orchestra practices and concerts, there were, in 1961, a motor car treasure hunt, a bowls evening, a ladies' evening, two dances, as well as cricket and golf, and the Annual Dinner. A pretty good programme! In 1962 the Club moved from the Royal Oak where it had had monthly gatherings of about 40 members since 1956, to the Walsall Club in Lichfield Street where rooms were available weekly, and club nights were arranged for the first Wednesday in each month. However, by 1966 it was clear that the Walsall Club had not attracted members, and the monthly gatherings began to fade away.

At this time a representative of the Queen Mary's Club sat on the Board of Governors. Since 1948 Frank Cooper had been the first such Governor, but in 1962, following Frank's death, Phil Evans was appointed in his place. Phil remained the QMC Governor until 1983, when he was succeeded by Roy Meller, who only resigned recently in 2003. The new QMC Governor is John Vallance (QM 1956–63).

In 1962 the Guest at the Annual Dinner (then always held on Shrove Tuesday) was Arnold Fellows (QM 1911–17) who expressed his intention to gift to the school a major part of his art collection as an investment for the benefit of the school.

THE ARNOLD FELLOWS COLLECTION

Arnold Fellows attended Queen Mary's from 1911–1917, and after reading history at New College, Oxford, he returned to the school briefly as a master. Most of his career was spent as a Housemaster at Chigwell School in Essex. He and his wife, Marguerite, travelled widely and collected paintings: oils and water colours, and drawings, and he gave to Queen Mary's the first part of his collection in 1963 so that it could hang in the new school being built. He became a very good friend to Sam Darby. The corridors of the new science block became an art gallery for these paintings, though subsequently many were re-hung in the Board Room. A further part of the collection came to the school after his death in 1973. He also gave to QM a copy of his *"Wayfarer's Companion"* in which he writes of the English countryside and its buildings, the product of a lifetime of travelling and teaching.

He was a true benefactor and a man of learning.

Taken from articles in The Marian.

By 1964 the new buildings at Mayfield were nearing completion, and the school Welsh Centre at Farchynys had been purchased and was refurbished and open. The Club had played a vital part in both projects. For the new school, Old Marians had fully supported the Appeal, and had in particular contributed to the furnishing of the new school library. For the Welsh Centre, the Club had found the first four Trustees, had supplied a representative on the Welsh Centre committee, and had accepted responsibility for paying the annual rates/council tax bill.

During Sam Darby's Headmastership, and since, all the school 1st year (now Year 7), and its staff and prefects attend an annual Wreathlaying Service in the Queen Elizabeth Chapel in Westminster Abbey, along with the Chairman of QMC and representatives of the Club, placing a wreath, with a band in school colours, on the tomb which the sisters Queen Mary and Queen Elizabeth share. The wreathlaying is held on a convenient day near to July 2nd, which is the date of our Letters Patent of 1554. This service was first held in 1964 at the instigation of an Old Boy, Dr GR (Gerald) Shutt, Headmaster of Westminster City School, with the assistance and support of the Dean of the Abbey. For the first year or two only a few boys attended, but the Headmaster then decided to include all the first year, and that has remained the pattern. London Old Boys and a group from Walsall also attend, and have lunch together afterwards. For some years arrangements were in the hands of Len Peach (now Sir Leonard Peach (QM 1944–51) and Col. JS (Jim) Haywood (QM 1921–27). In recent years Jonthan Turton has arranged the lunch. (The annual wreathlaying is referred to again in similar terms in Chapter 8, School Life).

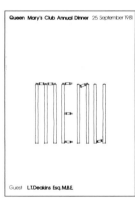

In 1964 also at the last Annual Dinner held at Lichfield Street, the principal guests were former Headmasters HM Butler and AN Hamilton, together with many former masters including WA Burn, former Second Master, and Miss Emma Flint.

Mayfield

On 25th May 1966, the new buildings were officially opened by the Dean of Westminster and the Royal Badge in the Entrance Hall was unveiled. There was a service of rededication in the morning at St Matthew's, and many exhibitions were put on in the afternoon for visitors. The Queen Mary's Club event was a buffet in the evening. The oldest active Old Boy, Frank Cookson (QM 1890–91) planted a red horse-chestnut tree; and the Mayor of Walsall, none other than Cllr Miss EM Flint (Staff 1915–49), unveiled the Marshall medallion in the Administrative Corridor in the presence of Mrs Marshall and Dr W Marshall, widow and son of EN Marshall who as Headmaster had acquired the Mayfield estate for the Foundation.

By this time the Club was closely associated with Sam Darby in the defence of the school's selective Grammar School status, following the issue by the government of the famous *Circular 10/65*, by which it hoped to introduce Comprehensive Secondary education throughout the country. The details of this long struggle are examined elsewhere, but Club members played their part in the defence of the school over the next 12 years.

In 1969, following the death of Emma Flint in 1968, the EM Flint Art Award was instituted. These annual awards to support and encourage students were open to all art students in Walsall, and the adjudicators were appointed by the Queen Mary's Club. Ken Wilson (QM 1927–32) organised the Award for some years until it was clear that the sum being awarded could not attract applicants. Then under Ken Wilson's guidance it became for a while in the 1980s an Annual Festival of Art and Craft work for Junior schools in Walsall. The winning school was awarded a full size framed photograph of an oil painting, *Walsall Market circa 1930* by HW Wright (QM 1923–31). The original painting was given by the Club to Walsall Library.

After the school moved to Mayfield, the annual dinner date was moved from Shrove Tuesday to the last Friday in September to enable university old boys to attend. When the squash courts and swimming bath became available, and badminton could take place in the new gym, these activities became popular and the monthly gatherings dwindled further so that they were discontinued in early 1972.

Miss EM Flint (Staff 1915–49)

Though retired before 1954, Emma still cast an influence until her death in 1968. She remained the first and only lady to be a vice-president of the Queen Mary's Club; she was Mayor of Walsall in 1966–67 and as such was present at Speech Day in 1966, and she was Deputy Mayor at the time of her death; and she worked hard to get support for an art gallery for the town and gave her name to the EM Flint Art Gallery, built in 1963 next to the Library in Lichfield Street. She was 83 when she became Mayor and she performed her duties while resident in a retirement home.

In 1914 she had met EN Marshall and he asked her to take charge of the school Art Department. She stayed for 34 years. She was also for many years the Principal of the Lichfield School of Art, and as an artist of ability she had many pictures hung by the Royal Academy. Shrewd, lively and blunt, she believed in hard work, and those who fell from grace were DFs: damn fools. A formidable character, remembered with affection well into our time.

JSA

Club Centenary

In 1974 the Club's centenary was organised by the secretary, Ray Bull, and the chairman for the year, Douglas Gilbert. On the day of the Dinner, in June, a reception and lunch was arranged. Old Boys and their ladies were welcomed with sherry, and there were tours of the school by prefects. Then an informal luncheon followed with a welcome to guests to which Mrs BE Richardson, headmistress of the High School responded. At the Dinner, the principal guest was Old Boy Sir Richard Powell, GCB, KBE, CMG (QM 1918–27) Vice President of the Club and Governor of the school. The Toast to the Guests was proposed by David Jeffries, Chairman of Governors. On the Sunday, following a

Centenary Service was held in St Paul's Church, conducted by the Revd Charles Lewis. A commemorative booklet (top left at the front of the chapter) was produced in Club colours which contained a full list of members and a history of the first hundred years. The booklet was produced by Jack Aspinall's company, Walsall Lithographic. During the centenary year there were commemorative cricket and golf fixtures, as well as football matches for David Judson's recently formed team, Mayfield 72. Thirty members and guests attended a dinner arranged by the London Section of the club, at the Royal Automobile Club.

Ray Bull and Jim Walker

By 1979, when Bob Wootton took over the chairmanship of the Club from Bramwell Davis, the cricket and golf sections remained strong, the 1972 A and B soccer teams were very active, and, although Chad Jackson was no longer at the helm, the Old Marians' Orchestra continued strongly. By 1983, sixteen junior schools took part in the EM Flint Art Award competition. The Club had taken a lead in raising funds for the Gerald Shutt Memorial Chemistry prizes, and had also given generous support to an appeal for the school's Iceland Expedition. On a sad note, the Club's secretary since 1971, Ray Bull (QM 1938–44), died suddenly on the morning of the 1983 Wreathlaying. The Club owed an enormous amount to his loyalty and enthusiasm. Mathematics teacher and associate editor of the Nuffield Mathematics Course, QMC representative governor, Rotarian and Round Tabler, he had a detailed knowledge of Old Boys of the school, and he was sorely missed.

During the 1980s the Club experimented in various ways to attract more members to its activities but it is clear that with the vast expansion of higher education, the great majority of Queen Mary's boys (and the girls who now join for their sixth form) now go to universities all over the country and fewer of them ever return to live and work in Walsall. The demand, therefore, for club activities seemed to have declined in an age of so many leisure and holiday opportunities. JA (Jim) Walker (QM 1942–50) was Secretary from 1983, and he worked extremely hard to maintain the impetus of Club activities, and under him links with old boys increased as he had a wide range of links with Old Boys of his and later generations. The Club did work very hard to run 'Race Nights', shooting competitions in the school range, Farchynys weekends, and even, for those with young children, a day out on the Santa Special on the Severn Valley Railway. More recently a strong swimming club has been very successful. One major encouragement in recent years has been the increased support for the

Annual Dinner. Largely as a result of the work of Jim Walker as Secretary, from about 120, numbers grew in the 1980s and 1990s until in 2001 the number was well over 200, and attempts had to be made to keep the number to about 175 which was considered reasonable for the size of hall. Jim Walker had resigned as Secretary when he retired from the QM staff in 1996 and he was succeeded by Andrew Mitchinson, while in 2002 Graham Padmore took over the reins.

For many years David Fink compiled the Queen Mary's Club Section of *The Marian*, with obituaries, information and news *From all Quarters*… In recent years, John Anderson has taken over this task.

The Clubhouse and the QMC today

During the last ten years, there has been a renewed drive to secure a permanent base for the Queen Mary's Club. There were many who saw the decline in support for regular activities as a warning that such premises as were proposed would not be viable. Therefore several

The extended cricket pavilion, now also the QMC clubhouse

schemes were considered for premises, and designs were prepared. Ultimately a proposal was accepted to extend the small school cricket pavilion which faces the field. The extended pavilion could have cellarage beneath, and could be designed to have a bar and lounge area, kitchen and toilets, and still maintain its proper facility as the school cricket pavilion. With considerable drive from Peter Lawrenson (QM 1961–66), and his sub-committee, an appeal was made, funds were found from donations, from the Club, and from the School, and in 2000 the Clubhouse was opened.

It is managed by the Queen Mary's Sports and Social Club Committee, and it is a clubhouse facility for all members of the Queen Mary's community. This development fulfilled a wish expressed by Mr Darby in 1959 when he wrote the QMC President's letter hoping that club facilities would be included in the new buildings! A regular programme of events has been developed and income from a regular booking from the Walsall Bridge Club has helped it to pay its way. The clubhouse is available for school QMA meetings, and other bookings, and it also remains the cricket pavilion.

Among the activities of the QMC in 2004, apart from its annual Dinner, there is a golf section, swimming club and a cricket team. The

QMC helps to maintain Farchynys. The Club arranges transport for local members to attend the annual wreathlaying in Westminster Abbey every July, and arranges lunch for them and for London Old Boys after the ceremony. Whilst there is no 'London Branch' these days, a growing number of retired London Old Boys meets for occasional lunches under the lead of MN (Tony) Naylor (QM 1939–43). Finally the annual Leavers' Ball for school sixth-formers from QM and the High School is run by the Queen Mary's Club. The Club continues to enable past pupils, both boys and sixth-form girls, and staff, to maintain contact with each other and the school. It has been particularly pleasing that in 2003 a few of a younger generation of Old Boys who are now in their 30s and 40s have joined the QMC committee, and this is very encouraging for the future.

A List of Chairmen of the Queen Mary's Club since 1956 appears in Appendix 8.

Prospice, Respice

19

THE FUTURE

Asked about the future in 2003, the Head clearly was extremely optimistic. Academic standards continue to be strong and new staff were developing well. The Language College opportunities were good. The new buildings, Language College wing and sports hall, would enhance the facilities, and the school, he believed, should then look forward to a development on the site of the Sutton Road houses, possibly a new sixth form centre. Unseen modernisation remains to be done – the electrical wiring, and the boilers and heating system – together very expensive projects. There is a possibility of a complete rebuild on the Mayfield site at a future stage as part of the government's Building Schools for the Future Programme.

Whilst the school funding formulae adopted by the LEA have not and still do not favour smaller schools, and while there is pressure in various forms for collaborative sixth forms of a kind which does not favour the fairly large, but academic sixth form, there must, however, be some cause for concern. Any demand that all pupils at 16 should have the right to a wide selection of courses must threaten the independence of the sixth form with a relatively small academic selection of courses on offer. Video conferencing and the cautious introduction of new subjects may help. It may be necessary to introduce some form of common timetabling between sixth forms. There is room for further expansion of the sixth form. There is also popular support at present for successful selective schools and this may help Queen Mary's to get funding for the future. The school must continue to raise its own funds for development, trusting that some form of matched funding will be available as has been the case recently.

However, there is always the possibility that political changes may threaten the present moratorium on selection. Selective schools must remain wary of those who may return with threats to academic selection at 11. In the Introduction I made the point that the school is part of a Foundation which is an ancient corporation with liberties which have been and still are respected by the state, even in times when our form of education may not always be favoured by the state. Queen Mary's must remain on its guard, and be ready to defend itself.

One of the areas where the school has been most successful in the past is in absorbing happily the large ethnic minority among the boys who enter at 11. Strong parental support for the school, and its supremely tolerant atmosphere, have ensured success in maintaining a happy and successful atmosphere. There seems to be no reason why this should not continue.

AERIAL VIEW

The rivers are like long blue snakes,
And telegraph wires like string.
Trees like arthritic hands,
Are surrounded by clouds of lambs.

And cars, red like blood,
Travelling the veins of the road,
The eruptions of a chimney pipe,
Are ignored by the ants below.

And at night the dark
Is illuminated by orange fireflies.
Towers like guards spear,
Piercing the blanket of night.

Only I have this view of the world,
Flying in the blue, suspended sky.

Jonathan Farrow Form 7P
Read at the annual Poetry Competition 2003

One of the significant and encouraging achievements during recent years has been the very positive relationship between the school and the Walsall LEA on the one hand, and between the school and other local schools on the other. The development of the Language College with the requirement for collaboration with local Junior and Secondary schools has helped greatly, and Stuart Holtam, as Head, has fostered the good relationships between QM and local schools. QM is teaching French in five local junior schools, and assisting Bluecoat School in its language work at Key Stage 3. As a Language College, the school is already working to enhance its international emphasis across the curriculum.

Within the school there is confidence for the future. Despite pressure on the staff, Queen Mary's can still field five rugby teams, five cricket teams, hockey teams and cross-country teams, can still boast the best CCF in the midlands, can still point to flourishing music and drama, and can maintain a wide variety of weekend activities at the Welsh Centre at Farchynys. Beat that!

Year 7 2003–2004

LIFE IS LIKE A BICYCLE TYRE
TONY BURTON (QM 1963–70)

Desmond and Tony Burton are the sons of RA (Sticky) Burton OBE, JP, (1930 – 37), farmer of Stonnall, Chairman of QMC 1968, and a great supporter of QM, who died in 1992.

Life is like a bicycle tyre in that it goes round and round with the same things reappearing, except that you and the bike have moved on. As I've pedalled through, life influences from my years at QM have kept reappearing like a mark on a revolving tyre.

My earliest QM recollection was being unsure which form room was really mine on my first day at Lichfield Street. Despite being a geographer, my uncertainties about where I am have increased with age. As 1x's resident stutterer, I cultivated the ability to make on-the-run substitutes for difficult-to-say words. Years later the same skill helped me in my Spanish after I had accepted a teaching job in Mexico City.

Geography gave me the excuse to work as a VSO on the Caribbean island of St Kitts for three years. After that assignment I taught for eighteen months in deepest Somerset before accepting that posting in Mexico City. During 17 years in Mexico, I graduated from teaching to full-time organiser of eco-tours and part-time travel writer. In Mexico I met and married Gwen (a half Chinese Canadian born in Australia). Even though we now live on Vancouver Island in western Canada, Mexico still holds a tremendous allure for me. I still organise the tours including one to the over-wintering sites of the migratory Monarch butterflies.

The cartographic skills that Brian Edwards painstakingly tuned have proved invaluable, though the latest edition I have completed includes computer-assisted digital maps, rather than the Edwards variety. Maths has been important to me, and while Messrs Farrington and Jackson would prefer not to believe it, I now teach adult 'Maths Upgrading' courses each year. Even Latin proves useful. My Spanish owes much to Dr Jameson's conviction that everyone needs Latin.

As for Farchynys, my last visit there, in 1970, nearly ended in disaster when the minibus gearbox failed half way up Dinas hill. We were saved from oblivion by the quick reaction and skilful driving of Mr Chipchase! Years later this incident returned to me as my brakes failed in a rented car on the steepest hill in Montserrat. Fortune smiled and after a 90 degree turn through a red light and over a narrow bridge, the car came to a halt outside the local police station. The road now lies buried under tons of lava.

The QM Scout Troop provided me with a headstart in group management skills. Chess and bridge fell by the wayside until now when I struggle to checkmate my 10-year old son. Wednesday afternoon golf at school has enabled me to become probably the only Old Marian to play international golf for a Caribbean island!

The bicycle tyre keeps revolving around............

ADB, from Vancouver Island, 2001

SQUADRON LEADER JOHN BLACKWELL
FLIGHT LIEUTENANT SIMON BEDFORD
FLIGHT LIEUTENANT TONY LUNNON-WOOD   SQUADRON LEADER ERIC STEENSON   FLIGHT LIEUTENANT PHIL ISLMAN
FLIGHT LIEUTENANT GORDON HANNAM   SQUADRON LEADER TED BALL   FLIGHT LIEUTENANT ROSS BOYENS
SQUADRON LEADER TIM MILLER   FLIGHT LIEUTENANT PETE LEES
FLIGHT LIEUTENANT MIKE RENDER

20

INTO A WIDER WORLD

Over the years boys from Queen Mary's have mostly stayed in the area around their home town. In the past, as a result of their education, many joined the professions in Walsall or more widely in the Midlands area. They became articled clerks and then lawyers and accountants. They joined family businesses. They studied medicine, often in Birmingham, and returned to their home area. They joined the armed forces. A few went further afield to London, and overseas.

Then within the last fifty years, with the growth of higher education, many more stayed into the sixth form instead of leaving at 15, and it became the norm to study for A levels and university. From university, the link with Walsall having been broken, more moved into careers far afield. Some, of course, returned to the Midlands, but most did not. A study of the address list of QMC members shows the 'diaspora' that has taken place.

Many of those who have been QM pupils, including the girls who have passed through the sixth form in the last 25 years, have found their work as lawyers, doctors, accountants, teachers, officers in the forces – as they might have done in the past. Many now are in newer professions linked to marketing, the media, or information technology. Hardly any are in heavy industry or farming. Most do jobs which are honourable but unremarkable, though each has his particular quality, and may look back to Queen Mary's as the source of much they can do. Tony Burton does this in his article, 'Life is like a Bicycle Tyre'.

It is surprising indeed that three Old Marians have in this period risen to become Chief Fire Officers (Eric Whitaker, Sir Bryan Collins and Dennis Davis), that there are three judges from the sixties and seventies (four if you include the present Chairman of Governors, not an Old Marian himself) and of them two are brothers and two are brothers-in-law, this in addition to Neil Denison, Sir Stephen Brown, until 1999 President of the Family Division of the High Court, and Richard Tucker of an earlier generation. David Etherington is a leading QC. There have been at least five international sportsmen in Jan Webster, David Brown, Trevor Homer, and, more recently, Rupert Moon and Colin Charvis (currently Captain of the Welsh Rugby team); many schoolmasters including Brian Bissell – a retired Head, Phil Bull and

Opposite
Top: David Brown with the England Test XI which played Australia at Lords in 1968.

Standing: Colin Milburn, Derek Underwood, John Snow, David Brown, Basil D'Oliviera, Alan Knott.

Seated: John Edrich, Tom Graveney, Colin Cowdrey (Capt.), Ted Dexter, Ray Illingworth.

Middle left: Lloyd S Peck, scientist with the British Antarctic Survey, based in Cambridge

right: Andrew Parrott, conductor and director of the Taverner Choir, Consort and Players which he founded in 1973

lower: Peter Lees with the 1984 Red Arrows Team.

Phil Holmes – retired Deputy Heads, and those still at the blackboard including Chris Blount, Mike Redfern, Steve Gould, Lloyd Allington, Neil Lamb, Jonathan Nunes, Stuart Worrall, Ian Cooksey and Tim Coker, and, teaching at QM, Tim Swain, Steve Law, Richard Johnson, Gary Taylor and David Rushworth. There have been medical men, including a professor of Dentistry (Tony Naylor) and a consultant neurologist (Philip Anslow). There are senior civil servants working in Whitehall (Jonathan Phillips for example), and in Brussels (Roy Dickinson). Paul Walton is a leader in the marketing world. There are at least two professional actors in Frank Windsor and Malcolm Webster. There are serving officers in the Royal Navy, Army and Royal Air Force, several being mentioned in the CCF chapter. And so on. It is most impressive, and news of Old Marians appears annually in the 'From all Quarters ...' section of the school magazine, *The Marian*.

Below is listed a small and randomly chosen group of Old Boys of the school, the variety of whose professional work shows the directions into which these few Queen Mary's boys have moved. I have left out schoolmasters, in that many are well considered in the main text of this book. Each of these owed his education to QM, and many came from quite humble circumstances and have had the Grammar School to thank for much that opened up for them. The examples here are of those whose schooling or work has been largely within the last fifty years.

Lord Harmar-Nicholls of Peterborough (1926–30). Born Harmar Nicholls in 1912, he attended Queen Mary's where he showed his 'forceful character and proper sense of his own importance'(!), and then he soon showed his political interests becoming a Member of Darlaston Urban District Council in 1938, in 1949 being elected its Chairman. His father had been a miner before he was a publican, and Harmar Nicholls incorporated a Davy Lamp into his coat of arms when he became a Life Peer, being always proud of his heritage. He was MP for Peterborough for 24 years (1950 – 74) and then MEP for Greater Manchester South until 1984, holding a number of minor ministerial posts early on, including that of Parliamentary Secretary at the Ministry of Agriculture and then the Ministry of Works. He remained an outspoken and independent-minded Conservative. He became a baronet in 1960 and was raised to a Life Peerage in 1974. He was a called to the Bar in 1941, but never practised, and he was a surveyor. He served in the war as a sapper and was an officer in the Royal Engineers in India and Burma. He had wide business interests, as chairman of insurance companies, Nicholls and Hennessy Hotels, and Radio Luxembourg. He was Chairman of the Malvern Theatre Festival.

Sir Eric J Pountain (1945–50). Born in Cannock, son of a builder, he returned to the family building firm from school before doing National Service in the RAF. He then joined Maitland Selwyn, estate agents, who specialised in marketing new homes. In 1964 the firm ventured into house building, pioneering the fully-furnished show home. They were acquired by McLeans in 1969, and Pountain became Chief Executive. By 1974 they were taken over by Tarmac, and by 1979 Pountain became group Chief Executive of Tarmac, and Chairman by 1983. He decentralised the firm and was so successful in a number of major projects from the Channel Tunnel to the Majes Irrigation scheme in Peru, that he was knighted in 1985. The success was not maintained through the more difficult times of the 1990s, however. He left Tarmac and became for a time Chairman of James Beatties and of IMI. He was Deputy Lord Lieutenant of Staffordshire. He died in 2003.

Archbishop Michael L Fitzgerald (1945–50). For some years based in Rome, Bishop Michael was in 2002 raised to the rank of Archbishop in the Roman Catholic Church. He was born in Walsall in 1937 and lived in Lichfield Street where now are the offices of the Estate Agents, Fraser Wood, and where his father was a doctor. His brother was PJ Fitzgerald (QM 1937–45). Michael was ordained priest in 1961 as a member of the society of White Fathers. He obtained a doctorate at the Pontifical Gregorian University in 1965 and a BA (Hons) in Arabic, London University in 1968. In 1987 he was appointed Secretary of what is now the Pontifical Council for Inter-religious Dialogue. Appointed titular Bishop of Nepte in 1991, he was raised to the rank of Archbishop when he became President of the Pontifical Council for Inter-Religious Dialogue in 2002. The Council's aim is to help Catholic communities around the world in their relations with people of other religions.

Ken Guy (1947–54). Ken died in June 2002. After service in the Royal Corps of Signals where he compiled crosswords to amuse fellow national servicemen, he joined the Midland Bank, and rose to be a Branch Manager. In 1984 he took early retirement after a heart attack. He had already supplied crosswords to the Birmingham Evening Mail, and in 1981 became a regular crossword compiler for the Birmingham Post and Sunday Mercury for 21 years. He used the pseudonym "Mercury" for all his work, except in the Financial Times where he compiled as

"Griffin". He became chief crossword compiler for the Guardian, and more recently he compiled crosswords for the Guardian website. Asked which of his clues pleased him most, he replied: "Tarts or good girls (5,2,6)", producing "maids of honour". He was an enthusiast for old trams, road steam engines and magic. He was a keen organist.

David Brown (1953–60). On leaving QM, he joined Dunlop Rubber to do a sandwich course in industrial research chemistry. Warwickshire CCC offered him a playing contract that winter and he then concentrated on using the sporting qualifications he had honed under Messrs 'Stub' Hopkins, David Fink (in charge of after-school nets) and Sam Crudace ('what a good man'). In 1964, he was picked for England to tour South Africa on the last tour before the apartheid ban. Although he did not play a test match, it was a most wonderful experience. Under a truly fine captain Mike Smith he played alongside schoolboy heroes Ted Dexter and Ken Barrington. He made his test debut in the next series in 1965 against South Africa at Lords, and was then fortunate to be picked for England another 27 times in an era which had a really successful side including many great names, Boycott, Edrich, Cowdrey, Graveney, D'Oliveira, Knott etc, the highlight being back to back series wins, home and away, against the West Indies. During this time his county, Warwickshire, enjoyed a successful period, winning a county championship and two Gillette Cup Finals. When he took over management of the side they actually won the Sunday League in the first season, but unfortunately that was too good a start, and his managerial career was not a huge success! Then David and his wife set up a stud farm, which they still run. Their breeding culminated in having a homebred horse called Bolshoi win the King's Stand Stakes at Royal Ascot in 1998. It was a fantastic day, for them never to be forgotten.

Keith O Butler-Wheelhouse (1957–61). Emigrated to South Africa in 1961 and matriculated from Grey School in 1963. He joined the Ford Motor Company who provided work experience and bursaries for studies in engineering and commerce at Witwatersrand and Cape Town University. He held senior appointments with Ford in manufacturing, product planning, finance and marketing, both in South Africa and America. He moved to General Motors South Africa in 1985, and from 1987 led the management buyout of the renamed Delta Motor Corporation, then becoming Chairman and Chief Executive. In 1992 he moved to Sweden as President and Chief Executive of Saab Automobile. In 1996 he joined Smiths Industries as Chief Executive.

He remains Chief Executive of the enlarged Smiths Group, following the merger with TI in 2000. He is a non-executive director of J Sainsbury plc, the multinational food distributor.

Dennis T Davis OBE, QFSM (1958–63). Dennis Davis has been HM Chief Inspector of Fire Services for Scotland since 1999. Son of a bricklayer, he came to QM from Edgar Stammers School. Starting in Moss Close, he remembers his final year as a 5th former in the new Mayfield buildings. He became a Fireman at the age of 18 with Walsall County Borough Fire Service, where he progressed to Leading Fireman in 1968. Sub Officer in 1970, he became Station Officer with Cheshire Brigade the next year. He then rose through the ranks to be Deputy Chief Fire Officer in 1984, and Chief Fire Officer for Cheshire 1986–99. He is past President of the Institution of Fire Engineers, and is currently Management Committee Chairman. He is widely admired for his innovative approach.

Retired now are ***Eric Whitaker QFSM (1948–50)*** son of a Chief Fire Officer of Walsall, who became Chief Fire Officer of East Sussex; and ***Sir Bryan Collins OBE, QFSM (1944–51)*** who was Chief Fire Officer for Humberside, and then HM Chief Inspector of Fire Services for England and Wales until he retired in 1998. Sir Bryan was an NCO in the RAF Section. He gained a short service commission at No 3 wing RAF Cranwell during the Korean War. He completed flying training in Rhodesia, and then, returning to the UK, converted to jet fighters, piloting Meteor 8s.

Andrew Wright OBE PPRIAS (1958–65). Andrew is one of Scotland's leading architects, and was elected President of his professional institution in 1995-7. He left QM in 1965 and has clear memories of the split site school, returning to Mayfield regularly as it is only a few minutes walk from where his mother lives now. He studies in Liverpool where he gained a First in Architecture, and after two postgraduate years there he moved to Edinburgh where he worked for Sir Basil Spence's office. After six years he moved north to the historic town of Forres, where he still lives, to manage the local office of the Edinburgh architects, Law and Dunbar-Nasmith, becoming a partner in 1981. Latterly he was practice chairman. For many years he was the architect to the Balmoral Estates, where he met on occasions members of the Royal Family. A highlight of his career came in 1997 when he was appointed to lead the major project for the rebuilding of the Liverpool Museum and Walker Art Gallery. In 2001 he pursued his own consultancy career, with much of his time spent as an adviser to the Scottish Parliament on architecture and the historic environment, which includes the new building at Holyrood. A passionate interest in historic buildings and monuments has led to terms as a diocesan architect, a member of the Ancient Monuments Board for Scotland, a Commissioner of the Royal Fine Art Commission for Scotland, and he is presently Vice-Chairman of the Historic Environment Advisory Council for Scotland.

Andrew H Parrott (1959–66). He left Queen Mary's to read music at Merton College, Oxford. He is the conductor and director of the Taverner Choir, Consort and Players which he founded in 1973. Since 2000 he has been Music Director and Principal Conductor, London Mozart Players, and since 2002 Music Director and Principal Conductor, New York Collegium, a Baroque group. He has made festival appearances at Aldeburgh, the BBC Promenade Concerts, and major world venues. He has conducted major symphony and chamber orchestras around the world, and period instrument orchestras. He has conducted opera. He has broadcast for the BBC, and has been involved in many educational symposia and workshops. Contemporary music has played an important part in his work, and he was for some time an assistant to Sir Michael Tippett. At present he is an honorary Senior Research Fellow, University of Birmingham. He has published a wide range of work on early music, is co-editor of the New Oxford Book of Carols (1992), and most recently has written *The Essential Bach Choir* (2000).

David C Etherington (1964–73). After a long career at QM which he explains elsewhere, he studied Law at Keble College, Oxford. He passed his Bar finals in 1978 and was admitted barrister at law in 1979. He was accepted as a tenant at 5 King's Bench Walk in 1980 where his head of Chambers was the then Attorney General, Sir Michael Havers QC MP (later Lord Chancellor), and where Margaret Thatcher had been a pupil. He was appointed Queen's Counsel in 1998 and a Recorder of the Crown Court in 2000. In 2003 he became Chairman of the Professional Conduct Committee of the Bar Council, and Chairman of the Advocacy Standards Board. He has trained many young barristers in advocacy skills and has also travelled a number of times to the Hague to assist in the training of advocates from many countries who are appearing before the International Tribunal for war crimes committed in the former Yugoslavia. He is a leading silk in crime and in fraud appearing both for the prosecution and defence in major police cases and in those brought by the Customs and Excise and Serious Fraud

Office. He has used his acting experience, which began with Geoffrey Paxton, to be legal adviser for major television series, including *Kavanagh QC* and *Judge John Deed*. He presented the prizes at Queen Mary's Speech Day in 1998.

Philip N Green (1964–72). After the University of Wales (Swansea) and the London Business School, he began his period in industry with 3 years in the US. He worked in manufacturing in Lancashire in the eighties, and then in Brussels with DHL, the express distribution business, in the nineties. In 1999 he returned to London with his wife Judy and two daughters, and spent four years with Reuters, the world's leading provider of news and information, as Chief Operating Officer. Since January 2004 he has been Chief Executive Officer of P&O Nedlloyd, one of the largest container shipping businesses in the world, with 11,000 staff, more than 150 ships and £5bn revenue. He has developed a passion for Africa, recently climbing the world's highest free-standing mountain, Kilimanjaro. With his family he spends as much time as he can at their home in the winelands near Cape Town, when they are not in the UK in Berkshire. He is on the Board of SKF, the world's largest manufacturer of ball bearings. He is also on the Board of Mission Aviation Fellowship, a Christian charity which flies medicines, food, etc to parts of the world otherwise inaccessible, often in Africa. He is on the advisory board of the London Business School, and is also a trustee of the London Philharmonia Orchestra.

Michael J Provost (1966–73) left QM in 1973 to read Engineering at Cambridge, before joining Rolls-Royce at Derby in 1976. He spent a year on the graduate training scheme, then 14 years in the Performance Office working on thermodynamic modelling and analysis of the RB211-535 (the engine that powers most of the Boeing 757s produced), and engine health monitoring in service (for which he gained a PhD in 1995, and won the Chairman's Award for Technical Innovation 2000). A seven-year spell in Corporate Development was followed by five years working with Boeing on engines for their Sonic Cruiser and 7E7 Dreamliner projects, and also on more electric engine and aircraft concepts. He currently works as a Senior Technology Consultant for Data Systems & Solutions, a company partly owned by Rolls-Royce that specialises in providing high-integrity software and in-service monitoring of high-value assets, such as aircraft, power stations and railways. Outside work he is currently Treasurer of the Nottingham Astronomical Society.

HH Judge Gary R Hickinbottom (1967–74). He was admitted solicitor in 1981, and Assistant Recorder in 1994. He was appointed a Circuit Judge on the Wales and Chester Circuit from 20th July 2000, one of the new breed of solicitor turned judge. He was appointed a Senior Circuit Judge in 2003. He is Chief Social Security and Child Support Commissioner. Appeals, relating to benefit decisions on points of law only, go through nearly 50 provincial courts and Judge Gary heads this system, which unusually includes jurisdiction in Scotland as well as England and Wales. He still has time to sit as a Deputy High Court Judge in London.

His elder brother, *HH Judge Nigel (1964–71)*, has for some years been a Judge in Lincolnshire, living with his family in Pudsey near Leeds. The brothers share a strong and continuing enthusiasm for Walsall Football Club, meeting only at Bescot, or so they would have me believe. The link between the family and the school has continued for over 100 years.

Professor Lloyd S Peck (1968–75) Scientist with the British Antarctic Survey, based in Cambridge, at the forefront of investigation into animal adaptations in extreme environments. He is leader of a dedicated team of polar biologists evaluating how species live in the coldest, driest, windiest, most isolated place on earth. His interest is in the way environment constrains life on earth. He has completed eight field visits to Antarctica. He is Principal Investigator in the Life at the Edge programme and Head of the BAS Marine Adaptations Project. He is visiting Professor in Ecology, University of Sunderland, and Honorary Lecturer in Zoology, Cambridge University. He gives TV interviews and has done over 30 radio interviews. He has been invited to give the Royal Institution Christmas Lectures in December 2004.

Dr Chris M Florkowski (1968–75). Chris lives in Christchurch, New Zealand and is a consultant in clinical biochemistry to Canterbury Health Laboratories. He is a Clinical Senior Lecturer in the University of Otago, active in diabetes research. This research focuses on the epidemiology of outcomes of diabetes in the NZ population, also cardiac risk factors and mechanisms of complications. He is a leading scientist in this field. He is married with two sons and a daughter.

Dr David R Howarth (1970–77). Fellow of Clare College, Cambridge, college Director of Studies in Land Economy, and university Lecturer. David has been a Fellow and Tutor in Law at Clare for many years. He is a former chairman of the University Board of Scrutiny. He has been Leader of Cambridge City Council, and has been a member of the National Policy Committee of the Liberal Democratic Party. He is now actively campaigning as Lib Dem parliamentary candidate for Cambridge, having fought in several recent elections. He remains an ardent supporter of Aston Villa, whose club history he wrote while in the sixth form at QM.

Melvin Woodhouse (1971–78). Read water engineering and business studies at Aston University followed by two stints as a VSO working on rural water supplies in Kenya. For eight years he worked on a variety of water and environmental health projects in East Africa. In 1994 he began work as a consultant for the UN and various donor governments in East Africa. In 1996 he moved with his Canadian wife and two daughters to Tanzania, being given ten days to conjure up an emergency water supply for Dar es Salaam. Returning to the UK in 2000 he read for a Master of Laws at Dundee, specialising in international water law. In Ghana until mid-2004 with his family, he is involved in a range of water law issues, writing a thesis for his PhD on the Human Right to Water.

Revd Jonathan Ball (1974–81). Ordained 1988, he served as a curate in Walsall and vicar in Rugeley before entering the Army in 1996 as a Chaplain to HM forces, with equivalent rank of major. His recent experience is that, based in Abingdon in 2001/2, he worked with the Royal Logistic Corps with tours in Kosovo and Afghanistan. In 2003/4 he is based in Catterick. Early in 2003, he was posted to Kuwait, and went with the troops into Iraq, returning to the UK in the summer. He is due back in Iraq in the spring of 2004. He is responsible for work with all Christians in his regiment, and is responsible for providing for those of all religions, so that he ensures, for instance, that Muslim troops have places to worship. He has a teaching role, and is a bridge, at home and abroad, with the civilian community around the garrison or camp. He gave the address at the Speech Day service in St Matthew's Walsall in October 2003. Jane, his wife, is ordained and is a curate at Bedale Parish Church, near Catterick and they have two children.

Michael I Hill (1977–84). On leaving school he won an Open Scholarship to read Engineering Science at St Edmund Hall, Oxford. Post-university he moved to London to work for PA consulting Group 1988/90, evaluating the financing of selected new technologies, including the combination of BSB and Sky to create BSkyB. After three years of Consulting he then studied in Spain and France including a full Scholarship to complete an MBA at Insead Business School. Between 1993 and 2000 he worked for Goldman Sachs & Co in New York and London, as a Vice President focused on US and European mergers and acquisitions. After a two year stint as a Managing Director in Frankfurt, Germany he returned to Goldman Sachs, London, to run the Pharma and Biotech practices. Married to American wife with three children.

David M Riley (1978–85). He writes from Washington DC. He gained a First in Electronic Engineering at Southampton University, developing growing interests in business, finance and international affairs. He joined the LEK partnership, working three years in Munich, and then was accepted with full scholarship to do a two year MBA program at Harvard (1992–94). Developing his interests in macro economics in what he describes as the 'flexibility, breadth, and dynamic nature' of Harvard, he was offered a position with Capital Group, one of the world's largest privately owned investment groups. He moved to Washington in 1999, and is likely to remain there. He is a Vice President of their mutual fund company, Capital Research Company. He gardens and collects furniture.

Mark Purcell (1982–89) read Modern History at Oriel College, Oxford, where – so far as anyone knows – he was the first Marian Oxford Organ Scholar. He subsequently spent a year out as Organ Scholar at Chichester Cathedral, before returning to Oxford to work at the Bodleian Library. After a year's postgraduate work in London, he worked as an early printed book specialist at various Oxford libraries until 1999 when, following a major fund-raising appeal in the United States, he was appointed to the new post of Libraries Curator to the National Trust. He is responsible for specialist work in a collection of 250,000 books in over 150 locations, the books themselves ranging from medieval manuscripts to the personal library of George Bernard Shaw.

Some who have been educated at Queen Mary's have become famous men. The seventeenth century Lord Chancellor, Lord Somers, was probably a Queen Mary's boy. Those listed above are a group, marked by the variety of their careers rather than their fame, though some have been, or are, clearly successful.

However I feel that one might do worse than conclude with the following, often read at the Speech Day service:

Let us now praise famous men, and our fathers that begat us.
The Lord hath wrought great glory by them, through his great power from the beginning.
Such as did bear rule in their kingdoms, men renowned for their power,
> *Giving counsel by their understanding, and declaring prophecies:*
Leaders of the people by their counsels, and by their knowledge of learning meet for the
> *People, wise and eloquent in their instructions:*
Such as found out musical tunes, and recited verses in writing:
Rich men furnished with ability, living peaceably in their habitations:
All these were honoured in their generations, and were the glory of their times.
There be of them that have left a name behind them, that their praises might be reported.

And some there be which have no memorial; who are perished as though they had never been;
and are become as though they had never been born; and their children after them.
But these were merciful men, whose righteousness hath not been forgotten.
Their bodies are buried in peace, but their name liveth for evermore.

Ecclesiasticus Chapter 44

Memories
& Reflections

MEMORIES FROM THE SIXTIES
By Mike Redfern

Sport at QM

Sport was a big part of my life. I looked forward to playing my first game for the school at under 13, but my collarbone was broken by Alan Kempson, and Hoppy told me that 'you can't call yourself a rugby player till you've broken your collarbone'. I progressed through the years at stand-off, but while in the 5th year I was asked to step into the shoes of Jan Webster and play scrum half for the 1st XV. Never having played scrum half, I was told by John Burgess to take a rugby ball home and practise feeding the scrum by throwing it against a wall. I remember being made 1st XV captain, and sustaining a catalogue of injuries, and playing games too numerous to mention, but returning to school, just before going to Univ, to watch the new 1st XV, 7 of whom played County rugby.

We started to play soccer as a team when Eric Taylor arrived to teach economics. It was all done a little clandestinely at first, but then we progressed to play local schools. Eric took three of us, Scott Orchard, Johnnie Walker and myself, for a trial to WBA. We were introduced to basketball by the American teacher Dr Nunes who taught English and Drama. I enjoyed the game and went on to play at college and afterwards.

Cricket was dominated by the shadows of David Brown and his contemporaries. Our side did not reach that standard, but we enjoyed the games and learned to play the game in the correct way. A large group of us, including the Dutton twins, formed the basis of a strong junior side at Blakenhall CC, and we played much of our club cricket there.

Athletics was something I rather fell into. By doing well in a 400m race at school, I found myself on the coach to Blackburn to run in a triangular match. I was a complete novice as a 400m runner and it showed, but I stuck at it and won some races at that distance. Cross Country was something most of us detested as youngsters, but by the 5th year I improved my running ability, and enjoyed the run around the Arboretum extension. Much later, I continued to run, using Cannock Chase as a training ground, and recording respectable times in 10K races, before injury finally ended my running.

Gaining my school colours for Rugby, Cricket and Athletics was a source of great pride for me. I wore my cricket colours on a sweater for many years afterwards until shrinkage and an expanding figure made it impossible to wear.

I eventually went to Loughborough to do PE and Geography. My first teaching post was at Walton School, Stafford, and I built up the 1st XV there sufficiently to return with them to play QM. John Burgess left at the same time as me, and I met Dick Cooper often in the years after through our involvement with Staffs schools rugby.

Academic Life

I can clearly remember my first homework for Geography. I spent ages on enlarging one square of an ordnance survey to scale. I still have all my exercise books, including that first piece of Geog. work. I was inspired by Brian Edwards: an artist at the blackboard, his maps being always works of art as well as Geography.

My first science lessons with Bill Kitchen were not so inspiring. We spent a long time learning how to write correctly. Woe betide anyone who started a line without touching the margin! I never did enjoy science after that. Having started Physics O level, a group of us went to see Sam Darby to ask if we could drop Physics and do extra English. He said no, but we could study Greek Lit in translation which he would teach. So for two years we had the benefit of his enthusiastic teaching of Thucydides' Peloponnesian Wars, and Homer's Odyssey and Iliad. It could never happen like that nowadays.

I enjoyed most of my lessons. I was never a high flyer. I remember being spanked by Daddy Symes, putting people in cupboards while waiting for lessons, and having my sideburns tweaked by Mr Birkby for not speaking clearly in French. I remember wondering how John Burgess could play Rugby in pumps on the muddiest pitches and never fall over. I remember the kindness shown to me and my parents by Eric Boothroyd who recognised what it meant to them, from a working class background, to have a son at QM. I remember language classes with Mr Wilf Taylor and Mr Bull, both of whom were inclined to nod off. Then being asked to write a General Studies essay on 'The Intractability of Circumstance', which surprisingly started my interest in Thomas Hardy, and Machiavelli.

And the Rest ...

I enjoyed my 4 years in the CCF. I remember rushing back from the 1966 Sennybridge Camp through the town in full kit to get home to watch the World Cup Final on TV. We had been sent up the mountain behind the range at Brecon in thick fog to recover the danger flag, and finding everyone had left by the time we got down. At that camp, Col Bull had walked through our section as we engaged in trying to attack a position, claiming he was just observing, and then lobbing several thunderflashes into our midst. I remember weekends at Farchynys, when we seemed to be taken somewhere into the countryside, given a map reference, and told to report there two days later.

I spent many assemblies reading the memorial boards, and feeling disappointed that more of the company did not turn out for Remembrance Sunday parade to honour them.

Back in school, we bought doughnuts at break from the section of the school which adjoined the High School. We watched High School prefects being escorted into the old Prefects' Room and wondered what went on! With the High School sixth form, later on, we organised events, trips, dances and a joint leavers' party. I remember organising the Rugby Club dinner with guest Micky Steele-Bodger, and having to propose a vote of thanks. That was my first act of public speaking.

I so much enjoyed my seven years at QM in a way that my students today seem unable to do. They have more commitments and interests away from school, and spend more time in paid employment.

Mike Redfern is Head of Geography and Head of Humanities, Sir Graham Balfour School, Stafford and County Secretary, Staffordshire Schools Rugby. (QM 1961–68)

THE SCHOOL 1964–73
By David Etherington, QC

I arrived at the school in 1964 and so was part of the last generation to enjoy the dubious splendours of Lichfield Street. We moved up to Mayfield the very next term. The contrast could hardly have been greater. Light had been substituted for dark. Change is never that simple of course. It was the next few years which brought the true development. A generation of older masters were replaced by new, younger men who breathed a different life into the school in its fresh buildings. The best of these new masters were simply reinterpreting traditional schoolmastering in a new era, and many stayed to become in turn the old generation to the school of the late 1990s. Some blazed a trail much shorter in duration but with great effect on our impressionable minds: Bob Bradshaw in a pink shirt sending us off to Sam with a note written in ancient Greek, and Will Chipchase who brought the swinging sixties to Walsall are but two examples.

The Sixth Form was for us a supremely happy time. Everything in the late sixties and early seventies combined to give us confidence and ambition. We truly believed we could fly. The culture was challenging every form of authority and established idea, and QM was not immune. It was the era of 'If …', the film about the public schoolboys who turned to armed revolt against the system. Luke Rhinehart's novel *'The Dice Men'* had cult status: basing every action on choices dictated by the roll of the dice. We spent two hours discussing the implications with Jack Jones, instead of planning an essay on the importance of class in Jane Austen's Persuasion. It was the Vietnam War and Woodstock. It was a time for youth.

In my last year we sat in Clive Westlake's periods as though we were in the French National Assembly with the monarchists on the right and the revolutionaries on the left. Clive took us countless times to hear the increasingly respected CBSO in Birmingham. Bob Fletcher had his home occupied by us as we debated the great issues late into the night. Geoffrey Paxton, who came to QM from the world of the BBC and Cambridge theatre and revue, brought a standard of directing never equalled for me by any professional or amateur directors I worked under at Oxford. Geoffrey was for us a taste of that world we knew was waiting out there.

There was a price to be paid for the good times. It could not be all joint dramatic productions with the High School (of which *Oh! What a Lovely War* was the best), endless hours of private study in the Prefects' Room drinking coffee, playing Bridge and listening to Radio 1. I had been accepted at Oxford to read Law. I needed Maths or a Science 'O' level to matriculate. I opted for Human Biology O level: 24 periods of Human Biology with 'Drac' Wiggin. Drac seemed to take a great pleasure in making me dissect rabbits in front of the first year. Still, Andrew Elliott (now a surgeon) dragged me through, and the knowledge now proves useful when reading the pathologists' reports in murder trials.

So my last term at school dawned. I was in the fourth year sixth by myself, and was Captain of School. I sat on the stage at assembly. What was Sam saying? 'This day in 1965, the school assembled here for the first time. None of you is old enough to remember that day'. A ripple of laughter. A look of synthetic puzzlement on Sam's face. 'Were you here then, David?' Full circle.

David C Etherington, Captain of School 1972-73

CAPTAIN OF SCHOOL & A WATER ENGINEER
By Melvin Woodhouse

Snowballing at School
On a particularly cold winter morning in December 1977 the attention of the school strayed from the notices during assembly to observe the beginnings of a heavy snowstorm. From the vantage point of the Captain of School's lectern it was immediately obvious that the minds of the scholars were occupied in forming up hit squads to seek revenge upon their prefects. This was not going to be a good day to be a prefect, especially when turning a blind corner.

And so it was that by the close of morning break the future of the Amazon rainforest was already in doubt. The quality of the literary impositions given had lost all penal and academic merit, and the senior prefects were pushing for the introduction of a summary snowball firing squad. From somewhere came the suggestion that the only way of curbing sniping attacks was to organise a serious snowball fight for the whole school.

Sam Darby's genial smile did not falter, silence fell in his study, and he approved the scheme – on condition that I returned at the end of morning school with rules to prevent the operation getting out of hand.

By lunchtime two ranks of 300 boys stood facing each other on the field. It was entirely my oversight not to have told the Duty Master what was going on, and he appeared just one minute before the start of the festivities, and began to walk down the middle of the opposing lines. It was very unfortunate that such a mild avuncular member of the English department had let his curiosity get the better of him. There was no signal to postpone the start time. Not all the 600 projectiles found their mark, and the only word I heard him say after the first volley was 'Passchendaele'. Following his retreat the school let rip for 15 minutes. It was well ordered, and as a result of settling all outstanding scores, the school remained in good humour to the end of term.

* * * * * * * * *

QM in Kenya

For most of the time since university I have lived in Africa and worked as a water engineer. I was lucky enough in the mid 1980s to work in the Chyulu Hills in Kenya. They present an interesting problem because they are of recent volcanic origin, and so whilst it rains, the rain soaks straight into the rock and seeps away. The only effective way to harvest this water was to make some sort of impermeable surface. Coupled with the local people's desperate desire to have a school resulted in some creative accounting to build a school with a very large roof. The project took a year to complete because we had to wait for it to rain before we could mix the concrete. However it all worked out. The temptation was to leave a mark of QM at this fledgling school, and the end result was to line the sides of the first half mile of track leading from the school with flowering trees alternating red and yellow. The place is called Mukungula, in Kibwezi District. Six years later I flew over the area, and it has to be said that the colour scheme stands out very well.

Melvin Woodhouse (1971-78)

4
FIRST IMPRESSIONS OF QUEEN MARY'S 1979
by Keith G Howard

When I went through the interviews for the Headship of Queen Mary's in January 1979, I had been made aware that the school's future could lie in one of four directions: to continue as a selective grammar school for boys; to become an area 6-form entry comprehensive school; to become a sixth-form college; or to opt out and become independent. In May 1979, four months after my appointment, the conservative government came to power, and as a consequence the school was able to continue as a selective grammar school. Virtually all my previous teaching experience had been in grammar schools, so the atmosphere of Queen Mary's was familiar and congenial.

Inevitably, my first contact was with the governors at the two interviews, and in a slightly more informal context outside the interviews. What struck me was the pride the governors felt in the successful fight they had fought to maintain the selective status of the school serving the whole of Walsall and offering an academic and broad educational grounding to Walsall boys on the basis of academic ability alone, irrespective of social background. The governors and the Headmaster, Mr Darby, were clearly determined to continue the struggle should that prove to be unavoidable. Their commitment, clear ability, strength and pride in the school were impressive.

The Headmaster was a man of great quality and stature, and he was very helpful; and in those early days before taking up my duties, I was also greatly helped by the two deputies, Phil Bull and John Anderson. I made one serious mistake early on by asking Phil Bull to hum or sing to me the tune of the School Song in preparation for Speech Day: unwittingly, I had chosen arguably the most tone-deaf person in the community of Queen Mary's, and I was no wiser at the end of his rendering than I had been before.

The next contact was with the teaching staff, who gave every impression of being very supportive both in and out of the classroom, and this was reflected in any case in the school's achievements. The first impressions of the pupils were very favourable, but I did feel that a vigorous and rather uncompromising approach to matters of school discipline would be helpful in those early stages. Despite this approach, I very quickly became aware of the cheerful ability and goodwill of the boys, not only in the quality of their academic work, but across the whole range of activities outside the classroom.

Finally, one factor which struck me from the outset was the immense pride and commitment of the parents working through the numerous committees of the Queen Mary's Association for the good of the school, raising much-needed extra money and helping with all sorts of school activities. Many parents had themselves been educated at the school or at Queen Mary's High School, and the local pride in the school was a strong feature of the school's spirit which pervaded the whole community.

I count myself very fortunate and privileged to have been able to serve such a fine school and community as Headmaster for 16 years. I feel confident that, under Mr Holtam, and I hope, thereafter, the school will continue to thrive as it has done for the past 450 years.

Headmaster, 1979–1995, Keith Howard now lives in retirement in Leominster, with his wife, Elsbeth.

THE EIGHTIES
By Ian Cooksey

When asked to describe my impressions of QMGS in the late 80s, to my surprise, I found myself reflecting upon a 1950s vision of schooling. A school in which the power of the prefect loomed large and younger pupils would be set essays or lines for standing up in classrooms during break, or walking down the third year corridor – imagine that! The height of rebellion: to sneak down a corridor when no-one was looking instead of going down the stairs in to the quad and back up at the other end. The rules were arcane, but could, no doubt, be justified in some way. The prefect could be a wily beast. I remember once being required to write an essay on 18th century politics as a second year pupil still languishing in Moss Close. He almost certainly passed off this treatise on Pitt the younger (or older – which was it?) as his own.

We would sit at desks with ink wells and lifting lids with storage space for our books – eminently sensible but terribly old-fashioned, and from these desks we would learn a body of knowledge from an eccentric staff ascribed all manner of zoomorphic nicknames. This was a traditional school with very traditional values and a Head with a principled vision of education.

In 1987, after laying a wreath at Bloody Mary's tomb, all of the 'fusties' were led down Downing Street to meet Maggie before she set off to the House of Commons to slay another socialist. To everyone's delight she emerged from Number 10, strutted over, greeted the expectant crowd and shook hands with the staff. She was smaller than me (I was standing on a kerb) and I was less than impressed by this diminutive bouffant on legs, but the staff declared that they would not be washing their hands for weeks!

It is understandable I suppose. After decades of threat, Conservatism in the 80s offered the only hope of survival for QM, and it was a school worth fighting for. The traditions and constraints presented a framework for everyone to flourish. The more cerebral students had the freedom to discuss issues of real worth, like the existence of God, perpetual motion machines and the true colours of the Tudor rose; whilst the rogues could be embraced by the cadet force and the disciplines inherent to a militaristic organisation. Most importantly, the staff, by and large, loved teaching in that environment and fostered a very real sense of community. When league tables were first published in 1992 QMGS was the top state school in the country. A small group of us were invited to appear on the Kilroy chat show. Unfortunately we were sufficiently uncontroversial to make a mark and the bronzed and oily fellow Brummie failed to explore our argument. League tables are limited. QMGS was top of the academic pile in that year and whilst it may not be in the next it would always be great school because it was not a simple exam factory. It was an exciting and vibrant community and I embraced everything on offer: drama, singing, orchestral playing, the Duke of Edinburgh's Award Scheme, rugby and the cadet force. Whilst failing to excel at any of these, I had a fantastic time and I am forever grateful to the staff who dedicated their lives to these extra-curricular activities in a decade when they were disappearing elsewhere.

In particular, I am indebted to the QM staff that introduced me to Farchynys and the Mawddach estuary (technically a fjord of course – the useful trivia one learns at school). After travelling extensively, the Cadair Idris range and the estuary below continue to represent one of my favourite vistas in the World! This is not hyperbole. How fantastic that a school could have its own residential centre/hut of its own in such a fabulous setting. I was hooked from the outset despite being hung upside-down from the fire escape by a particularly vindictive prefect (the precocious, cheeky fustie probably deserved it!). I was back at Farchynys on thirty more occasions during my time at QM and it really did become home from home. Most of the visits were with the cadet force where we would engage in extraordinary ventures like attempting to climb Cadair Idris from sea level to summit and back in 5 hours, scrambling up Tryfan on a crisp icy Autumnal morning after waking at 4am or losing numerous cadets, every year, in the bog on the way to Freddy Brown's campsite (Ffridd-bryn-côch).

Being left in the Mawddach estuary up to my knees in mud on the Biology field course will always form an enduring memory. As I measured various cockles and mussels a storm gathered and lightning began to strike in the surrounding hills. I was easily the tallest figure for miles around the mud flats and presented a fine target for the next bolt. Luckily it never did come, for neither did my rescue. Only after an hour in the storm did my biology teacher finally rack up in the minibus – a delay for which he will never be forgiven; but he will also be remembered for taking me to study biology in the hills where Darwin himself would hunt for beetles with clergymen as a boy. He enthused, as did so many others.

QM was not a perfect school. I am not prepared to fall into the trap of believing that all things past are by definition 'great and glorious.' There are elements of that experience that I hope no longer exist, but there is so much that continues to impress. My experiences at school affected me so deeply that after graduating I went straight into a job that would enable me to live that life for longer. I now teach in a school with a similar ethos and approach and I make a pilgrimage, with my own students, to Afon Mawddach every year.

Ian A Cooksey (1986–93) is now teaching at Tiffin School, Kingston upon Thames

AN INDIAN AT QUEEN MARY'S
By Jude Daniel

I have been asked, time and again, by parents of potential QM students, as well as those from other schools, what it is like to study in such a traditionally English school. In particular, there are questions about what it is like for people from the Indian sub-continent. The mention of grammar schools conjures up for many an unpleasant monochromatic image of grim schoolmasters and grey students, with strange rituals such as the reciting of Latin verbs, daily prayers, caning and cross-country. So is it possible for someone from an Asian background to fit in well into such an atmosphere?

To be totally honest, I had the same reservations before I joined, but they were proven to be unfounded. But in order to make sure that I was not an anomalous case, I asked some of my classmates on their experiences too. They seem to be unanimous in the view that they totally enjoyed their years in Queen Mary's, albeit considering it with hindsight.

Fitting in with the teachers is no problem at all. Asian parents (especially from the first and second generation, mine included) are usually very strict with their children. Also, I was brought up (and I know most Asian children are too) with the teaching that the most important virtue is to respect your elders. So although there are not many of the traditionally authoritarian teachers around in QM, those that are there don't compare to Asian parents. Making friends in class is no different to any other school. People often think that just because someone comes from a grammar school, they are completely different to 'normal' people. But when it comes to relations with classmates, the same rules hold true as in any other school, and there is no formality to it. Our year group was extremely unusual, in that there was some racial friction that suddenly appeared, but did not last long, in one of the years between some of the students, at the same time as a widespread appearance of acne, spots and facial hair (largely to do with teenage hormones, I suppose).

Replacing the Christian school assemblies (or at least the 'Christian-ness' of it) seemed to be an issue. There was even an article about it in *The Marian* a couple of years ago. Personally, I have no problem with it, as I am a Christian. I thought some of my friends from non-Christian backgrounds might disagree with me. But I found that most of them were indifferent towards it too, as long as they did not have to say any prayers or sing any Christian songs. The feeling was that the assemblies were part of what the school was, one of the traditions like Speech Day, and could not be changed. However, the common view was that there could be some leeway to allow for special assemblies for Diwali, Eid and so on, not as religious rituals, but at least to inform others about the significance of these festivals. To Asian parents who ask me about the advantages of sending their sons to QM, one of the answers that I often give them in jest is that it is a boys' school. The opportunities in QM are available to all, and although the idea of a grammar school may seem foreign to a lot of people, I can guarantee that all reservations will be dispelled within the first week.

Jude W Daniel was Vice Captain of School, 2002 – 2003

MEMORIES OF THREE SISTERS: SIXTH FORM GIRLS AT QUEEN MARY'S
By Sheba, Priya and Josie Jose

The following account is based on the memories of three sisters who attended QM 1988, 1991, and 1997. We all came from a small private school in Walsall and were used to wearing a uniform and quite strict discipline.

Sheba
'My memories of QM are happy ones. I obviously enjoyed myself as I came back for a 6^3! As one of six girls to start in 6^1 (with 2 girls in 6^2) we were a rare species within the school and met with differing reactions. Everyone was polite – opening doors, carrying books etc. – at least to start with. Some played it cool, others obviously thought we were aliens from the planet Zog and avoided us as much as possible. Then there were the would-be 'Casanovas'! Sadly for them, teenage girls brought such grand aspirations quite firmly back to earth! Not to say there wasn't romance – it would be impossible to avoid that, but such liaisons were either clandestine or else the talk of the school!

'My favourite boys were the First Years (now Yr 7s). As a 1st Form Prefect, I had great fun along with another girl, herding our 'little lambs' to assembly or sitting with sick boys at break or lunchtimes when we weren't chasing them out of classrooms. There was a rumour that a certain cat food was named after me – I was thrilled when they relayed the story to the new intake the following year! So this is how myths begin!

'I was involved with Joint Orchestra and with many of Mr Paxton's excellent productions (*As You Like It*, *Café Chat*, etc.). I had great fun and made some good friends along the way.

'There were obvious practical difficulties of having girls in a boys' school. Games would be one example. We could get out of the PE block by the back entrance (thus avoiding the boys' changing rooms) but there was only one way in if we wanted to get to the gym to play badminton! Still we survived. We even coped with having to make tea for the visiting rugby teams – some staff still had gender roles very specifically laid out! It never bothered me personally, though it riled some of the girls at the time! As for the purpose of being at school – to study – there was plenty of that! Only two girls did science in our year, I was one of them! I am slightly biased, but the science department was excellent when I was at QM – the staff encouraging and helpful. The biology field trip was great fun and being a girl I got a bedroom and bathroom to myself! I remember Mr Yates and Mr Brudenell took good care of me but made sure I did my share of the chores! All the girls in my year passed their A-levels with grades A-C, so we did OK!'

Priya

'I remember we used to get lots of attention – more than if we'd been at a normal 6th form, which was quite nice most of the time. Little things seemed to get noticed. Someone always commented if you had a ladder in your tights or were wearing a different hair clip! Being the only girl doing English, I was always called upon to give the 'Female point of view'!

'I enjoyed doing drama and especially remember the *A to Z of Women* as I had multiple roles to play! I always thought it was an odd choice of drama for a boys' school. I was involved in the Christian Union and found this encouraging. From an educational point of view QM cannot be faulted. I was taught well and successfully managed to get into medicine. All in all, it was an interesting if somewhat challenging 2 years.'

Josie

'I remember thinking I had entered an institution with a long tradition that I would never be one with. I found the school quite regimented and felt very new and different especially as the boys were used to being together and were used to the system. Saying that, I made some really good friends with boys in the upper sixth who were already accustomed to having girls in their classes. My year, however, took time to warm up to me and my quirky girly way of hiding in the female toilets on every available occasion.

'I'd moved from a small school where everyone knew me very well to a school where I knew only a few people. Music and drama made up a large part of life at my previous school and I missed that when I moved to QM – a downside of moving to a bigger school. However one of the highlights of my time at QM was the performance of "the Gloria's" at St. Matthews. Rehearsals were always a drag – but the hard work paid off and it was if I remember correctly a wonderful choral performance! What's more we were not accompanied by the girls' school – brilliant! I thoroughly enjoyed the pseudo rivalry with the girls' High School. I was on the wrong side for all the wrong reasons!

'The girls tended to be treated well by the staff and pupils, holding open doors, etc. It was nice to think that a small pocket of men in the future may hold a door open for me. Academically I had a mixed time of it. I struggled to adjust to the pace and style of the teaching. Chemistry was the bane of my life (despite Mr Metcalfe being a very patient teacher and form tutor) However I found English lessons to be very rewarding and animated. English was my forte. I enjoyed the challenges presented by staff and the course material – I even got the School Prize for English. The biology field course was great fun and I learnt so much from the late Mr. Yates and his fantastic moth and butterfly collection that was so beautifully preserved and labelled. I thoroughly enjoyed the practical aspects of the course (collecting sea slaters in our wellies) and sometimes but not always hiding my beach combing finds in the boys dormitory ... who says the girls were the squeamish ones! Inspired by Farchynys I went on to complete a Psychology degree at the University of Wales, Bangor.

'Although we are from an Asian family, race was never an issue, as we were never the targets for abuse. Perhaps this was because the school's ethos would not tolerate bullying in any form – or maybe it's because we were girls!'

With thanks to Sheba Sergeant (née Jose) for writing this memory with her sisters. Sheba was at QM 1988–91, Priya from 1991–93, and Josie 1996–98.

A WOMAN'S INSIGHT
By Janet Martin

At the point when I joined Queen Mary's in the Autumn of 1999, newcomers to the staff were something of a rarity. Information for newcomers was at a premium as everyone knew how things worked, and it was assumed that a new member of staff would pick things up by osmosis. And by and large that is what happened, osmosis, and experience.

Assembly was something new. I had never taught in a school which could fit in its entirety in the Hall, nor one with such a strong tradition of assembly presentations of such quirky excellence. In the spirit of nervous enjoyment, and a desire to make a contribution on my first morning, I found the hymn in my hymn book and soared into the first verse. It was a pleasure not many others opted to share with me, and it took me but a few lines to realise that what in fact was required was a discreet murmur which nodded in the direction of the tune. Trying to fit in with the unexpected kept me on my toes.

The greatest shock was reserved for Fridays when the school seemed transformed into a military academy. I was surprised to see how quickly I became accustomed to the sight, almost as quickly as boys tired of my 'who said that?' camouflage joke.

A single-sex school invites debate. It's a topic everyone has an opinion about, and having attended an all-girls school myself, an experience I recall as being rather miserable,

I was prepared to be critical. What in fact I found was quite surprising. In the all male environment of Queen Mary's there was a far wider spectrum of character options open to everyone than I had found within my co-educational experience. Gentle and eccentric personalities thrive, not least in the Staff Common Room, who would probably have been crushed anywhere else. I am honoured to include myself among them.

Mrs Janet Martin arrived at QM in 1999 to be Head of Religious Education when David Hart retired. There have been ladies on the staff since Miss Emma Flint arrived as a 'master' in 1915. In 1995 there were four women teachers, in 2003 there were eight.

l to r: Andy Hawkins, Michael Sones, John Taylor, MJ Cockayne, Raymond Marsh,
Paul Bullock, Phillip Taylor, Roger Tranter, Roger Boak, Peter Talbot
taken during a coach trip to London

Appendix 1

MASTER PETYPHER'S VIRGIL

The book known as 'Master Petypher Virgil' was printed in Lyon by Jacques Sacon in 1499. It contains the text of the complete works of the Latin poet Virgil, along with commentaries by various authorities, ancient and modern. These include the fifth-century commentary of Marius Servius Donatus, which was specifically intended for use in schools, and concentrates particularly on grammatical and stylistic points in the text. As fifteenth-century books go, it is not especially uncommon: another 21 copies are known, though the only other examples in Britain are in the British Library and the Bodleian Library at Oxford. It closely resembles other editions printed in Venice in 1493, 1494 and 1495 – it is in fact an almost exact copy of the 1493 edition. It seems clear that Jacques Sacon, a rather minor figure in the Lyon book trade, set out to copy the prestigious Venetian editions. There is no mention of Lyon in the colophon – the paragraph at the end of an early book giving details of its place and date of production – and instead contains the phrase 'Venetiis Caractere' ('in the Venetian style'), which was pretty obviously intended to mislead the unwary purchaser into believing that the book was printed in Venice.

We know nothing about the whereabouts of the Virgil before it came to Walsall in the 1550s, but it could easily have been in the country for some time, since most Latin books used in England were imported from the Continent. But the back flyleaf is inscribed:

Thys boke Mr Petypher hath gyven to the School of Wallsoll who in the 2 and 3 yere of the rayne of Phillippe and Marye kynge and quene of England was chosen schollm[aste]r of the sayd town the use whereof he wyllithe the schollm[aste]r for the tyme beying allwais to have.

A different hand (perhaps that of John Clarke, Master of the School in 1584) has then added:

This booke was given for the use of the poore scholers of Walsall by that reverend father mr petypher.

The identity of Master Petypher has been hotly debated for many years. Petypher (or Petifer) is certainly a Midland name, and our Master Petypher seems to have been a priest, was probably reasonably well-off, and is likely to have been a university graduate. Only one man comes near to fitting the bill: a Protestant scholar called William Petifer who was associated with Magdalen College, Oxford, was Vicar of Standlake in Oxfordshire from 1562, and died in 1581. He would have been an impressive candidate to be the first Master of Queen Mary's new grammar school, since Magdalen's own school was famous, and trained up men who introduced the teaching of good Renaissance Latin into schools right the way across the country. But unfortunately the college records suggest that he was acting as Bursar of Magdalen in 1556 ('the 2 and 3 yere of the rayne of Phillippe and Marye kynge and quene of England'). However, there is evidence that there may have been some sort of cover-up: other records imply that William Petifer was not necessarily where he should have been, and is possible that he quietly absented himself during the dangerous 1550s, when Archbishop Cranmer was burned at the stake in Oxford. Another possibility is that we should read the inscription literally, and that Petifer was indeed chosen to take charge of the school, but never took up the post. This is less implausible than it sounds, for the simple reason that Queen Mary ordered in 1556 that all schoolmasters should be approved by the local bishop, which might just have been enough to convince a Protestant scholar that Walsall was no safer than Oxford. Ultimately we may never know, and it is quite possible that the School's first Master was another man entirely; but if so there is no sign of him in any of the places where there should be, and there is no mention in the town records that anyone called Petypher was living in Walsall during the reign of Mary Tudor. This is very surprising, as a schoolmaster and priest would have been an important man in what was then a small market town.

Much of this is speculation, but Master Petypher's Virgil provides a very tantalising glimpse into the Tudor classroom. The book is no longer in its original binding, but the position of the donation inscription on the back flyleaf suggests that it was originally kept chained to a lectern, perhaps something like the one which still survives in the church at Wootton Wawen in Warwickshire (upside down to our way of thinking, but we know that this is how books were kept in several Oxford colleges of the period). This is not surprising, and we know that other Midland grammar schools had libraries. The boys seem to have been allowed to write all over the book, and there are many manuscript notes, often explaining difficult words or concepts, so evidently it was well used. Some of the notes are rather basic, and since Virgil would have been an advanced text, this may indicate that even some of the older boys were not terribly good at Latin. There are also a number several examples of 'vulgaria' – English sentences set by the Master for translation into Latin. And finally there are many notes in a fine Italic script. These are much more learned than the schoolboy scribblings, and appear to have been written by a young man called Peter Langton. He was a native of Staffordshire, and studied at St Mary Hall in Oxford; afterwards he became Rector of Maveysn Ridware, near Rugeley, where he died in 1604, aged about 30. He may well have been educated in Walsall, and certainly seems to have owned the book, though we do not know whether he stole it from the school, bought it, or was given it.

The Virgil is next sighted in 1770, when a clergyman called Samuel du Gard presented it to the library of Chichester Cathedral. It remained there until the late 1940s, when it was sold by the Dean and Chapter, only to be bought by John W. Whiston, an old boy, book collector and local history enthusiast. He presented it to the school as a 400th birthday present in 1954.

From The Book Collector *Winter 2001 by Mark Purcell (QM 1982–89), Librarian to the National Trust.*

Appendix 2

MARSHALL'S MARTIAL – THE SCHOOL MOTTO
By SL Darby (Headmaster), 1973

Thanks to the imaginative generosity of an Old Boy – Professor AS Whitfield – the school has a very valuable text of Martial (a Latin poet who died in 104 AD) printed in Paris in 1617. It contains all the poems, together with elegant Greek translations of many of them. Why did Archie Whitfield give us this book? Because in the last line of Book 5, 43, we recognise our School Motto, and can see it in its original setting as the last pentameter of four elegiac couplets on the theme of generosity to friends.

Martial is addressing a rich man who (like all rich men) has a problem. How can he stay rich, or increase his riches? The poet has a simple answer. Give your money away to your friends! Riches are at the mercy of fortune and can soon disappear – because of a cunning thief, a household fire, a defaulting debtor ... , but

> *Extra fortunam est, quicquid donatur amicis:*
> *Quas dederis solas, semper habebis opes.*
>
> But beyond fortune's reach is any gift to friends:
> Only the wealth you give away, will you keep for always.

It is to be feared that Martial's sentiment was probably mercenary. He was a poor poet and to be a poor Roman citizen in his days was a sombre destiny; he could not work (only slaves did that); he could only live on the privileges of citizenship and his association (*clientela*) with some wealthy household of which he could claim to be a friend.

Headmaster Marshall knew all this and the motto he chose sums up in one respect his own constant search for money to buttress the fortunes of QMS. But on a deeper level, a school can hardly have a nobler motto for all its manifold activities – intellectual, moral and spiritual. It is a community of friends spread over the centuries. To give what riches we can to this community of friends is to stay rich for always.

Why should this be? The Greek translation interprets our motto further 'Only of what you *share*, will you remain the owner'. We must share our riches (of intellect or character as well as much else) with our friends; only in sharing them will we truly possess them. Martial and Marshall remind us of this lasting truth.

SLD

Appendix 3

Believe it or not!
"NOTES ON PRONUNCIATION"

In his 'Memoirs of a Maverick', Maurice Wiggin referred to his experience as a Bloxwich lad being taught to pronounce his vowels correctly in the early 1920s, when he arrived at Queen Mary's with his strong local dialect.

It is noteworthy that as late as 1960 Phil Bull should have produced notes for use which are in the same tradition. The following is an extract:

NOTES ON SPEECH

Faults of speech may be divided into faulty vowels, Walsall intonation, mispronunciation, and bad grammar.

The first two require early special treatment (JWLS *); the others are the concern of the whole staff.

Correction of Vowel Sounds

The first essential is co-operation from the boys and understanding of what we are trying to do.

Suggestion that first one or two lessons be spent in round the form reading – to enable the worst offenders to be spotted and to let the boys hear various pronunciations. Point out that some boys are bi-lingual. Let them try reading (a) in Walsall, (b) in good, but not 'posh' English (PMA* has some passages tape-recorded in 'Liverpool' which might be useful for contrast).

From the third day onwards, some time might be spent (say 10 mins per lesson) on individual vowels.

Below is an analysis of vowel sounds and their common mis-pronunciations and practice drills, also a few hints.

A	Acceptable	as in – fall, ball
		as in – father
		as in – fat, glass, bath (it is assumed that standard Midland and N Country 'bath' is aimed at)
	Unacceptable	as in – fate, date
		This a is a diphthong ei (vowels from beg, beat) but one or constituent is often changed to a sound like u in 'fur'.

	Practice	If you are late, wait by the gate
O	Acceptable	as in – hot, tom
	Unacceptable	as in – roast, no, road, spoon, cool etc
		These are all diphthongs and the tendency is to split them into two separate parts.
		Splitting produces "ro (w) ad", "spoo (wu) n" etc.
	Practice	He alone knows the code She will soon use a spoon We hear the sound of the cows on the downs The toys were spoilt by the oil.

Other vowels were all listed with similar details and suggested practice sentences.

Analysis of vowel sounds, particularly of diphthongs, should help boys to recognise their own errors. That, and practice, should be enough except for the lazy or obstinate.

Hard cases could be made to stand up and say the practice sentences aloud every lesson until they get them right.

* REFERS TO Messrs JWL Symes, and PM Alexander.

Appendix 4

QUEEN MARY'S GRAMMAR SCHOOL   SUTTON ROAD,
                                                     WALSALL.

To all parents:

   After a meeting of the Governing body yesterday the 11th of May the
following announcement was authorised for circulation by the Chairman of
the Governors:

   "Consequent upon the publication of the Section 13 notice the
Governors have appointed Mr. S.L Darby M.A. as Head Teacher Designate of
the proposed enlarged Queen Mary's Grammar School. Mrs. B.E. Richardson B.A.
The Headmistress of Queen Mary's High School had indicated that she did not
wish to be considered for the post but fully supported the appointment of
Mr. Darby".

   No doubt this will appear in the press and I am most anxious that
all parents shall learn of it and of its proper implications from the
School, not just from outside sources.

   It does not affect in any way my present position as Headmaster of
the Grammar School and my responsibilities to the Governors and to you
for the welfare of the boys. It is a preparatory move which will not be
implemented unless Section 13 proposals are accepted by the Secretary of
State and Government approval given for the proposed enlargement of the
Grammar School. Much preparatory work has to be done in readiness for
such an eventuality, for example in dealing with staffing and plans for
possible building extensions.

   The Governors have now appointed me to be responsible to them for
such preparatory work and have indicated that if the proposals were
implemented I should then continue as Head of the enlarged school. May
I assure you that if, in any plans concerned with the future, matters
arise which are of immediate consequence to parents you will be consulted.
I should also like to assure you that the Headmistress of the High School
is fully in the picture and indeed is giving and will give invaluable help.

                                          S W Darby
                                          Headmaster.

12th May, 1976.

QUEEN MARY'S SCHOOLS VALSALL

To all parents and staff.

Reorganisation of Secondary Education

At a meeting on Monday 17th April the Town Council directed that a draft plan for the completion of comprehensive education in Walsall be submitted to the Secretary of State, after consultation with Voluntary Aided Schools affected, the chief one being ourselves.

The plan envisages the eventual establishment of a mixed comprehensive school by the Queen Mary's Foundation at Mayfield, taking in about 180 children each year, and with expanded provision for the 16 - 19 age group.

Since the plan differs in some respects from the one previously agreed, the Governors will need to seek detailed clarification, particularly about arrangements for admission at the ages of 11 and 16, and to consider how practicable it would be from their own point of view. They will ensure that staff, parents and old pupils are consulted before any view is officially expressed by the Governors.

18th April, 1978.   J. Aspinall.

                                                        Chairman of the Governors.

Appendix 5

THE STAFF OF 1953 is listed in
David Fink's *Queen Mary's Grammar School* page 462.

STAFF 1979

Headmaster:
KG Howard MA

Second Master:
PA Bull TD BA

Second Deputy Head:
JS Anderson MA

Assistant Masters:
JA Akroyd MA
GM Austin BSc
   (Head of Physics)
GG Brudenell BSc
   (Year Master)
GM Chesterman BSoc Sci
N Cooper DLC
   (Head of Handicraft)
RC Cooper BSc
   (Director of Physical Education)
PGK Davies BA
IR Davison MA
   (Head of German)
JA Dickson MA
BJ Edwards BA
   (Head of Geography)
   (Head of Resources)
JRR Emery MA
   (Head of History)
JF Farrington BSc
   (Head of Applied Mathematics)
RF Fletcher BA MPhil
   (Head of Economics)
   (Master i/c Sixth Form)
DS Hart BD
   (Head of Religious Education)
   (Year Master)
KG Henderson BSc

SG Holtam BA
JL Hutchinson BA
MG Jackson MA
   (Senior Mathematics Master)
G Jameson MA PhD
   (Head of Classics)
   (Head of Careers)
J Jones BA
   (Head of English)
GA Larkin BSc PhD
SJ Law BSc
T Lawrence MA
R Metcalfe BSc
FG Nash BSc
   (Head of Chemistry)
   (Senior Science Master)
GG Paxton BA
   (Head of Drama)
   (Year Master)
TF Perrett BA
DE Pomeroy BSc
T Siddiqui MSc
MC Stainforth BA
RG Stokes NDD RBSA
JK Warburton MA
   (Senior Modern Languages Master)
AJA Wiggin MA MSc MIBiol
   (Head of Biology)
JG Worth BSc
B Wragg BMus LGSM ARCM
   (Director of Music)
KI Yates BSc

Part-time Staff:
Mrs KE Sturt MA
Mrs D Milo-Turner ALCM LLCM

STAFF 2004

Headmaster:
SG Holtam BA

Second Master:
TJ Swain BA

Senior Master:
R Metcalfe MSc
(Head of Chemistry)

Assistant Head Teachers:
M Donnan MA
(Director of Language College)
(Head of MFL)
(General Studies Co-ordinator)
T Lawrence MA
(Senior Year Tutor)
(Head of History)
(Head of Sixth Form)
B Wragg BMus LGSM ARCM
(Director of Music)

Teachers:
JP Blackshaw BA
(Head of Classics)
(School Librarian and Archivist)
(Primary School Liaison)
MR Borcherds BA
NS Canning BA
(Head of ICT)
DJ Clough BSc
(Year Tutor)
(KS3 Science Co-ordinator)
RD Davies BSc MSc
PAE Elsden BSc
Miss HC Field-Mears BA
(Head of English)
RA Francis BSc
MJ Holden BSc ACA
Miss L Horden BSc
(Co-ordinator for French)
R Johnson BA
RG Jones BSc
(Careers Co-ordinator)
(Work Experience Co-ordinator)
SJ Law BSc
(Head of Geograpy)

MH Lawson MA
(Co-ordinator for German)
MA Lax BA
Mrs J Martin BA
(Head of Religious Studies)
Miss B Miranda-González BA MA
(Co-ordinator for Spanish)
DL Pennington BEd
(Head of Design)
RS Preese BSc
(Head of Biology)
JM Rockett BSc
SG Rout BSc
(Head of Mathematics)
D Rushworth BA MA
R Saran BSc
(Year Tutor)
(Year 7 Science Co-ordinator)
MD Shepherd BA PhD
Mrs P Smith BA
(Head of Drama)
G Taylor BA
(Head of Physical Education)
(Year Tutor)
LJ Taylor BEd
AJ Thomas BSc
TM Walton BSc
(Head of Economics)
JP Wilkinson BSc MSc ARCS
(Head of Science)
(Head of Physics)
Mrs D Wood BPhil
(Head of Art)
(Year Tutor)
(PSHE Co-ordinator)
JG Worth BSc

Part-time and visiting Staff:
Mrs A Powell BEd
Mrs J Cooper
(Careers Advisor)
(Connexions Careers Service)
Mrs NJ Roderick BA
Frau R Sturtzkopf
Mme C Swain MA DEA
Mrs VJ Waits
B H Wootton BA

Appendix 6

THE GOVERNORS 1953
are listed in David Fink's *Queen Mary's Grammar School* page 463.

GOVERNORS 1979 *

J Aspinall (Chairman)
GA Caddick OBE MA LLB
J Cheesewright MA
RJB Christie MBE FRIBA
FD Jeffries FCA
Mrs M Kitchin SRN ARD

Mrs DA Carter (Old Girls' Club)
Dr Jennifer Milne
WA Stephens MA JP
PW Evans LLB (Queen Mary's Club)
Dr B Jones (Birmingham Univ)
Dr WA Reid (Birmingham Univ)

T Burnside (Walsall LEA)
Cllr W Clarke (Walsall LEA)
Cllr PH Musgrove (Walsall LEA)
Cllr JA Withnall (Walsall LEA)
Mrs J Ralphs (Staffordshire LEA)
Mrs S Middlebrook (Staffordshire LEA)

Clerk: BGW Rogers LLB

* One Board of Governors for the
Grammar School, High School and
Mayfield Preparatory School.

GOVERNORS 2004 †

His Hon Judge PJ Stretton (Chairman)
RC Nowell (Vice Chairman)
JS Anderson MBE MA
Mrs M Causer
NJ Chomyk BA
Dr AR Cunnington BSc MD FRCP
Mrs J Kirby-Tibbits
TJ Luckin FCA
Mrs VM Fairbank BA MSc
TF Perrett BA
JN Punch FRICS

JA Vallance B Phil Ed (Queen Mary's
Club)

Cllr BJ Sanders (Walsall LEA)
Mrs AC Wilson BSc (Walsall LEA)

Mrs S Coleman (Parent Govr)
Mrs YP Calogirou (Parent Govr)
TJ Griffin (Parent Govr)

SJ Law BSc (Teacher Govr)
T Lawrence MA (Teacher Govr)

MS Haig (Staff Govr)
SG Holtam (Headmaster)
Responsible Officer: A Phillips FCA
Clerk: GC Underwood LLB

† The Board of Governors for the
Grammar School only. There is a
separate Board for the High School, and
Committee for Mayfield Preparatory
School.

Appendix 7

CAPTAINS OF SCHOOL

1953	TJ Fox (1953-July 1954)	1978	IS Felix
1954	AV Hughes (till Dec)	1979	PM Taylor
	M Fuller (From Jan 55)	1980	MJ Schorah
1955	DGW Edwards	1981	SJ Tromans
1956	CP Fulford	1982	RH Summers
1957	EG Jarvis	1983	JM Waters
1958	DE Jones (till Dec)	1984	RC Snow
	LE Smith (from Jan)	1985	SJ Harper
1959	D Wildman	1986	AJ Williams
1960	DR Wiggin	1987	NE Kirk
1961	CC Dodd	1988	DM Swinnerton
1962	GD Evans	1989	PN McCleverty
1963	CE Nicholls	1990	MJ Holden
1964	GH Evans	1991	PG Hughes
1965	PJ Sturrock	1992	AJ Pountney
1966	MG Heeley	1993	AJ Cunnington
1967	MJ Benton	1994	SW Marshall
1968	HJ Lindon-Morris	1995	JM Punch
1969	HJ Lindon-Morris	1996	AJ Smith
1970	WR Holmes	1997	ND Manchester
1971	M Baynham	1998	RJ Bowen
1972	DC Etherington	1999	AC Cork
1973	PP Tredwell	2000	DJ Sutton
1974	SD Parsons	2001	AV Ingram
1975	SE Ball	2002	DWA Preece
1976	NL Hunt	2003	SD Smith
1977	M Woodhouse		

Appendix 8

QUEEN MARY'S CLUB CHAIRMEN

1956	FD Jeffries FCA		1981	MF White MA
1957	DC Jackson MPS		1982	J Vallance
1958	PW Evans LLB		1983	RJ Meller BA
1959	NE Parkes		1984	DW Judson MPCA
1960	GF Philpot		1985	TJ Luckin FCA
1961	RJ Bull JP		1986	DW Yarnall
1962	J Aspinall		1987	Dr BW Davis
1963	AD Ballinger JP		1988	JS Anderson MA
1964	J Cheesewright MA		1989	AP Corbet
1965	KJ Stockley		1990	BJ Perry
1966	VF Penn		1991	JN Punch FRICS
1967	RA Burton OBE JP		1992	ANM Mitchinson LLB
1968	PA Bull TD BA		1993	ANM Mitchinson LLB
1969	M Cheesewright		1994	GJ Padmore FCIB
1970	J Woodward		1995	A Porter
1971	J Hubble JP BA		1996	SG Watkins
1972	BW Bibb FCA		1997	SP Fletcher BSc
1973	DW Judson MPCA		1998	DS Breeden BDS
1974	DW Gilbert FSVA		1999	AJ Dickson GI FireE
1975	GR Belding		2000	AJ Dickson GI FireE
1976	KE Wilson		2001	PW Lawrenson MSc
1977	AR Wootton		2002	DW Yarnall
1978	Dr BW Davis		2003	DW Yarnall
1979	WA Stephens JP MA		2004	JS Anderson MBE MA
1980	JN Barratt JP RIBA			

Appendix 9

UNIVERSITY & OTHER DESTINATIONS 2003

DP Bagbee	Sheffield University (Geography)
JF Baker	Loughborough University (Industrial Design & Technology)
AE Banks	Kingston University (Motorcycle Engineering Studies)
H Beckett	Abbey College (A-levels)
DP Binks	Sheffield University (History)
E Blake	Manchester University (Law)
RJ Bond	Loughborough University (Industrial Design & Technology)
JA Bourgeois	Birmingham University (Music & Mathematics)
AJ Bridges	Birmingham University (Physics with Biomedical Physics)
JW Bridgman	Manchester University (History)
NP Brookes	Lancaster University (Biological Sciences)
M Brown	Birmingham University (Physics)
MA Cannan	Sheffield University (International/European & Comparative Law)
HE Carroll	Nottingham University (French and History)
GS Cheema	Leicester University (Medical Biochemistry)
SG Coleman	2004: Escape Studios (3D Graphic Animation)
SG Coley	Loughborough University (Mechanical Engineering)
RI Collins	Birmingham University (Music)
SJ Corns	Exeter College, Oxford (Chemistry)
PD Cottrell	Aston University (Optometry)
JW Daniel	2004: London School of Economics (Economics)
LA Degville	Warwick University (Mathematics and Physics)
G Dhami	Queen Mary, London University (History and Politics)
IS Dhariwal	Birmingham University (Mathematical Economics and Statistics)
AS Dhillon	2004: Birmingham University (Law)
D Draper	Liverpool University (History)
AC Evans	Liverpool University (Social and Economic History)
JS Foster	Hull University (Business Studies)
NS Ghatoura	Year out
JC Giles	Manchester University (Mathematics)
PS Goray	Leicester University (Economics and Law)
AR Grinsted	Manchester University (French Studies)
DM Hackett	Aberystwyth University (History)
RGJ Hawkins	Sheffield University (Geography)
KS Hayer	Birmingham University (Medicine)
CM Hemmings	Sussex University (Computer Science and Artificial Intelligence)

MT Hird	Leeds University (Mechanical Engineering)
WJ Hiscock	Edinburgh University (Geography)
RJ Horton	Birmingham University (Geology)
PK Jeavons	Hull University (Psychology with Philosophy)
DP Jevon	Exeter University (Ancient History)
S Johal	Loughborough University (Industrial Design and Technology)
B Johnson	Abbey College (A-levels)
CJ Jones	Nottingham University (French and German)
G Jones	Birmingham University (Medical Science)
GV Jose	Leeds University (Medical Sciences)
TA Kapadi	Birmingham University (Medicine)
RJ Karadia	Liverpool University (Zoology with Evolutionary Psychology)
BA Kilhams	Durham University (Geological Sciences)
A Knight	Birmingham University (Law and Business Studies)
D Krishnareddigari	Warwick University (Accounting and Finance)
DJ Lautman	Liverpool University (European Studies)
J Law	Sheffield University (History)
PD Madeley	Hull University (History)
GS Malhi	Birmingham University (Medicine)
HPS Matharu	Nottingham University (History)
JAS McKail	Loughborough University (Commercial Management and Quantity Surveying)
TG McLean	Year out
DJ Mears	Loughborough University (Automotive Engineering)
BJ Millington	MLIB (Mountain Leaders Award)
DC Moxey	Warwick University (Mathematics)
RW Munn	Aberystwyth University (Physics with Planetary and Space Physics)
A Natawala	Birmingham University (Medicine)
AP O'Donohue	Year out
LM O'Mahoney	Lancaster University (Marketing)
L Pacheco	Wolverhampton University (Media and Communication Studies)
P Parekh	London School of Economics (Mathematics and Economics)
K Patel	2004: Robinson College, Cambridge (Engineering)
RG Patel	Aberystwyth University (Law)
HJ Phipps	2004: World Expeditions
MK Phull	Year out
MJ Poulton	Hatfield College, Durham University (Mathematics)
DWA Preece	Sheffield University (Law)
P Reynolds	Hatfield College, Durham University (Theoretical Physics)
RJ Riley	Exeter University (Computer Science)
M Sahev	Leicester University (Psychology and French)

JS Saini	West Midlands Police (Police Officer)
RPS Samra	Leicester University (Economics)
MS Sehmi	Birmingham University (History)
V Sharma	Cardiff University (Accounting and Economics)
P Sharpe	Warwick University (Computer Systems Engineering)
PD Shipp	Edinburgh University (Geography)
SS Sidhu	Leeds University (Computer Science and Economics)
SS Sihota	Leicester University (Management Studies)
M Singh	Birmingham University (Computer Science and Mathematics)
AM Smith	Air Crew, Royal Navy (Observer)
JR Snowden	Sheffield University (International History and International Politics)
HS Sohal	Aston University (Pharmacy)
B Sperring	Manchester University (Drama with English)
Z Tabani	Leicester University (Medical Biochemistry)
BL Tippins	Aston University (Optometry)
DJ Twells	Liverpool Hope University (American Studies and Sociology)
N Uppal	Year out
KS Virk	Loughborough University (Aeronautical Engineering)
IW Westley	Cardiff University (E.U. Studies with French)
A Williams	Warwick University (Engineering)
AK Younes	Leicester University (Medical Biochemistry)

Appendix 10

DEVELOPMENT CAMPAIGN FUND
APRIL 1996 TO DECEMBER 2003

Fund Raising	£	Expenditure	£
Direct	345,105	Computer Room 1	144,370
Transfers from School non Public funds arising from QMA etc	137,392	Subsequent computer Expenditure	107,166
Interest	43,213	Design Technology DT and C Room 2	75,687
Tax rebates	58,675	School contribution to Language Coll Wing	50,000
Income Total	**584,385**	Lab refurbishment Rooms S3, S6 and S8	14,391
		School Hall lighting	13,688
		School contribution to 1st floor library devt	7,680
		Conservatory for Sixth form In Sutton Rd Houses	7,497
		Campaign costs	3,121
Expenditure Total	423,600	Expenditure Total	**423,600**
Balance Held 31/12/03	**160,785***		

*£150,000 of this balance is committed to the Sports Hall Project

Appendix 11

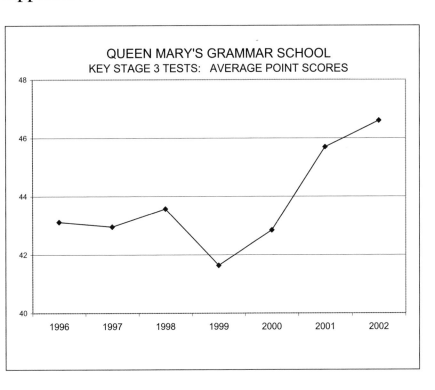

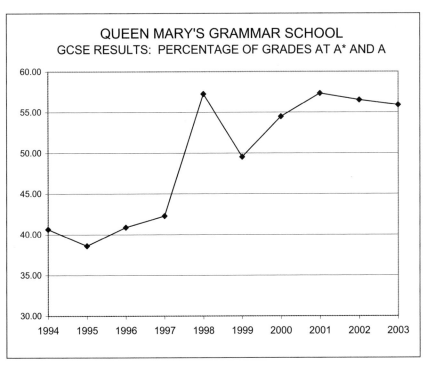

Appendix 12

From a termly newsletter of 2003. A snapshot of much that takes place in a term at QM.

- Over the summer, Cdt Cpl Sean Linney and Cdt Cpl Ben Ko were selected to take part in the prestigious Whitehorse Cadet Summer Training Camp in Canada. We received their reports in September. Sean 'put to good effect all the principles of leadership and showed himself a very competent instructor both in the classroom and on the drill square. He is to be congratulated on winning the Public Speaking Award for an amusing and informative talk that greatly impressed the judging panel. He also achieved a Gold Level Award in the Army Cadet Fitness Test.' Ben 'worked hard from the start of the course, helping others less able or confident than himself, proving an excellent team member. He gained a reputation for reliability and exuded an air of calm confidence; he was a pleasure to work with and a credit to his unit ...'

September
- Geraint Davies attended a Cadet Leadership Course at Frimley Park and was selected for Officer training at Sandhurst. The course report described Geraint as a 'hardworking young man with a very professional approach. His obvious confidence resulted in him being selected to be platoon commander on the first evening...'
- The Biedenkopf exchange: details of this and other Language College activities are found in the Language College newsletter.
- 8 cadets took part in Air Experience Gliding at Cosford.
- Well over a thousand visitors came through the School doors for our annual Open Evenings. They saw an impressive range of displays and demonstrations and, for the first time, could *watch* as well as listen to the Headmaster's speech on PowerPoint!
- Most Year 11 pupils took the opportunity to develop the ability to sell themselves at interview in practice sessions organised with local businessmen under the auspices of the Education Business Partnership.
- At the end of the month, Queen Mary's emerged winners in the British Army Staffordshire 7s U16s rugby competition.

October
- Queen Mary's joined 350 schools and 10,000 pupils nationally to take part in the Shakespeare Schools' Festival. A team of Y10s performed a condensed version of Julius Caesar at the Prince of Wales Theatre in Cannock and, by popular demand, gave a special performance to Y8 and Y9 back in Sutton Road. They chose to bring the play bang up to date with a staging set in Caesar's Palace, Las Vegas!
- Jonathan Choi proved his prowess with racquet sports when he was selected to play badminton for the Warwickshire County U17 squad.
- Grey cotton and polyester were superseded by denim as the School raised a few hundred pounds for research into genetic disorders under the auspices of the Jeans for Genes Day.
- Over 200 Y7 parents and pupils made the trip to Barmouth to visit Farchynys for the first time at the annual QMA Open Day. The rain stopped in time for everyone to enjoy a walk round the headland.
- Under the leadership of CSM Geraint Davies, 10 cadets took part in the 143 Brigade Military Skills Competition at Nesscliff. Queen Mary's won the Speed March and Assault Course phase and was placed 3rd overall in this prestigious event.

November
- Nine schools participated in the annual Queen Mary's Cross Country Relay. Around a hundred runners competed for the team trophy that for the last three years had been won by RGS Worcester. The QM team battled hard to secure a respectable fifth place, but the cup ended up a little nearer home: it was won by old rivals Bishop Vesey's.
- During the month, there was a string of excellent rugby results in the Staffordshire Cup and Daily Mail Vase competitions.
- The QMA Fireworks Event attracted 1300 visitors to Mayfield. They witnessed one of the most spectacular displays in living memory. It was also one of the loudest: the Library windows only just survived the decibel onslaught.
- The PE department did its bit to improve the fitness of Walsall by staging the inter-form cross-country competition. In Y10, 10H emerged the winners, followed by 10L, 10T and 10J. In the individual competition, Peter Mellar took the gold medal, Andrew Reid the silver and Edward Jagger the bronze. In Y9: 9F were the winners, followed by 9R and 9S. Ben Butterfield took gold, Mandeep Johal silver and Jordan Marsh bronze. In Y8: 8B were winners, with 8E closing out 8P for second place. Manveer Dhanda was the U13 gold medallist, Damon Harrison silver and James Lavery bronze. In Y7, Mr Pennington's form stole the march on Mr Taylor's 7T; Miss Horden's boys came in third. In the individual competition for the Fusties, Liam Hardy struck gold; Daniel Threlfall took silver and Joseph Philpott bronze.
- While the PE department struggled to get the weight off, Mr Jones saw that it was put straight back on by recruiting a number of budding chefs to take part in the Rotary International Young Chef of the Year Competition. The winner of the School heat in the Y10 and Y11 competition, Nimesh Mistry was unfortunately ill and unable to take his place in the Walsall final. *There is no truth in the rumour that he had food poisoning, Ed.* Our Y7-9 winner, Philip Wigfield grilled some more salmon and his mouth-watering white wine sauce earned him a runner-up prize of £25, a book and a handsome trophy.
- In the UK Senior Mathematical Challenge, nineteen pupils took part, earning 5 gold certificates, 10 silver and 2 bronze. Their prowess at hard sums was recognised when three of the competitors were invited to take part in the British Mathematical Olympiad (even harder sums!). That took place in early December; we await the results.

December
- The Beggar's Opera looked and sounded stunning in three performances in early December.
- The Stage Crew struck an eighteenth century London set and immediately got to work on scenery for the traditional Sixth Form pantomime: an end of term treat!
- Peter Rawlinson and Daniel Lindsay were invited to attend trials for the *Midlands* U18 rugby squad.
- The Chamber Choir and a proclamation of readers prepared us for Christmas in the annual Carol Service at St Matthew's.

Subscribers

The following have subscribed to this volume by purchasing copies prior to publication. The Queen Mary's Club and the author are very grateful for this indication of support.

Geoff Allman
Nick J Archer
Thomas Ashley
Gavinder Atwal
Parminderjit Atwal
JD Baker
MD Baldwin
Stuart K Baldwin
Alexander Bartlett
Steve Bateman
Ian M Beardall
Timothy J Beech
Manpreet Beghal
Aaron Bhakta
Curtis Bhatoe
Brian Bissell
J Philip Blackshaw
MJ Blakeway
Dean Blower
TH Bolshaw
AG Bolton
Ian Boneham
Brian Boothroyd
Neil Boynton
Paul Brayford
Roger D Brayford
Alan Breese
Robert Bridgman
Ian Brooks
Simon Broom
JC Bruce
Gordon Brudenell
Tim Bryars
S Buller
David Burton
Desmond Burton
Noel Burton
Paul Burton
Andrew Calogirou
Mark Calogirou
Mrs Dawn Carter
Robert C Champ
J Cheesewright
Mark Chester
Jeevan Cholia
Mrs Barbara Church
Thaddeus Clifton
Daniel Clough
Sir Bryan Collins

Mrs G Columbine
Peter J Cook
Rod Cooper
Arthur Corbet
Phillip Corbett
S Dallaway
James Davies
Bill Dean-Myatt
Charles C Dodd
MJ Dolan
John Drake
Nicholas Duggins
Sterling Dutton
Tony Eccleston
Peter H Edge
John Essex
David Etherington
David Evans
Jonathan Farrow
MV Fereday
James Ferris
Garrick Field
Dr Robert Fisher
MTH Francis
Stuart Freeman
David Gelder
Ben Gray
CP Gray
Philip N Green
AC Gregory
M Gregory
DC Groom
Philip G Hadley
MV Hale
AJ Halfpenny
Mrs LM Harding
Will Harrington
GN Hawkes
Donald Heitzman
Gary Hickinbottom
Nigel Hickinbottom
Callum Higgins
C Holcroft
Roy Holden
KS Holloway
Phillip H Holmes
Richard Holmes
Stuart G Holtam
Peter J Hopkins

Keith G Howard
John E Humphries
Paul Ingram
WJ Jackson
Adam Jeffrey
Ken Jeffrey
Paul Jeffrey
F David Jeffries
PW Jeffries
JE Jones
David W Judson
Ben Kilhams
Matthew Killian
John L King
Daniel Labran
Mark A Latham
Paul D Latham
Jonathan Law
RJ Law
Stephen J Law
Tim Lawrence
Peter Lawrenson
MH Lawson
Ewart Lee
Keith Lester
Matthew Lewis
David Loh
Mina Louka
Tim Lowe
Mrs Mary Matthews
Philip Mayling
PJ Mayling
Peter Mellar
Roy Meller
J Messenger
Henry J Moon
SGS Nicholls
Nick Paddock
RS Panesar
John Parkes
WF Perkins
Andrew Phillips
Jonathan Phillips
Ben Pipkin
JR Plant
Alan Porter
REM Powell
David Preece
Gareth Preece
RCT Prior
MJ Provost
Glenn Pugh
John Punch

Mark Purcell
Garen Ranji
Alistair Reader
MJ Redfern
Thomas Richmond
Graham Rockett
Derek Rogers
Chris Rolinson
Matthew Rounds
Gagandeep Sandhar
Christopher Sargeant
Edward Sargeant
Ricky Shamji
TK Shutt
Narinder Singh
Andrew Smith
GW Snowden
Neil Stanley
Bill Stephens
Leo T Stokes
John Sutton
David Swinnerton
Peter Szanocki
Viren Tewani
David Thomas
PJ Thompson
Timothy Tolley
MJ Tonks
Howard Toussaint
Paul P Tredwell
Andrew Turner
Miss Carole Turner
WJ Turner
Michael Twining
Prakash Vaducul
John Valance
John Wait
Robert L Walker
Robert M Walker
Robert Wallis
Keith Walton
Paul C Walton
JK Warburton
Stephen Watkins
Malcolm J Webster
P Wells
Darren Wheeler
Philip Wigfield
John Wilcox
MAF Williams
Malcolm R Wootton
Dr Andrew Worthington
Andrew PK Wright

Names Index

NB: page numbers in italic indicate illustrations and photographs

Index

NB: page numbers in italic indicate illustrations and photographs

Picture Acknowledgements

We are grateful to many individuals for providing images for the book. The portrait of Queen Mary Tudor is by Antonio Moro, 1554 and was originally used in the 1954 School History by kind permission of the Marquess of Northampton. We are grateful to St John's College, Cambridge for permission to reproduce the portrait of Sir Harry Hinsley by Michael Noakes. The maps for end-papers and a photograph including the Duke of York are reproduced by permission of Crown Copyright. Works by Adam Draper, Seamus Moran and RG Stokes are reproduced by permission of the artists. Portraits of SL Darby and SG Holtam are reproduced by kind permission of HF Blewitt & Co, Photographers; David F Vodden gave much assistance especially providing new photographs and various others from his collection including photographs of Walsall town centre by RA Brevitt. We are grateful for permission to reproduce photographs from Robert Champ's book *Patriotic Scholars*. Numerous other pictures appear by permission of the *Express and Star* and the *Walsall Observer*. We apologise for any omissions.

The end-papers are taken from the O.S. 6" map of 1955.

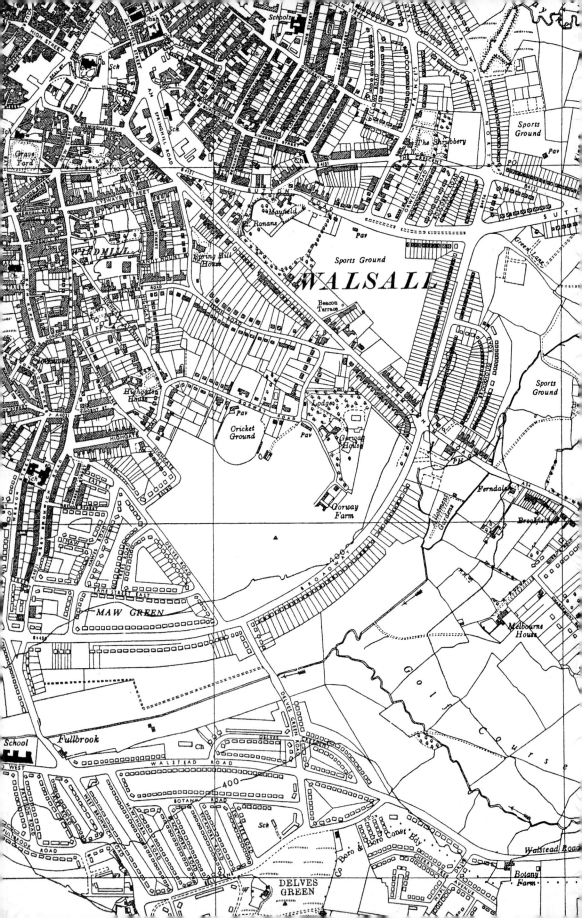